# LAST TIME OUT

# LAST TIME OUT

*Big-League Farewells of Baseball's Greats*

## JOHN NOGOWSKI

**TAYLOR TRADE PUBLISHING**

*Lanham · New York · Dallas · Boulder · Toronto · Oxford*

Published by Taylor Trade Publishing
An imprint of The Rowman & Littlefield Publishing Group, Inc.
4501 Forbes Boulevard, Suite 200
Lanham, Maryland 20706

Distributed by National Book Network

Library of Congress Cataloging-in-Publication Data

Nogowski, John, 1953-
  Last time out : big-league farewells of baseball's greats / John Nogowski.—1st Taylor Trade Pub. ed.
      p. cm.
  Includes bibliographical references.
  ISBN 1-58979-080-4 (cloth : alk. paper)
  1. Baseball—United States—History—20th century. 2. Baseball players—Retirement—United States. I. Title.
  GV863.A1N64 2005
  796.357'092'2—dc22                                                    2004014637

♾™ The paper used in this publication meets the minimum requirements of American National Standard for Information Sciences—Permanence of Paper for Printed Library Materials, ANSI/NISO Z39.48–1992.
Manufactured in the United States of America.

To John Jr.:

I will always see you, running across the lawn, arms wide open after your very first catch of a fly ball. On Father's Day. For me, getting a chance to grow up again in the game, through your eyes, has been magical. Sort of like that first catch. You've always understood—better than anyone I've ever known—to play this game right, you have to love it.

Like a father loves a son.

Love,

Dad
Summer 2004

# Contents

# Preface

"That last game has gotten so much more important as the years go by. I wish I could remember every minute of it, but I can't."—Ted Williams, *My Turn at Bat*

On a cold and damp Wednesday afternoon in late September 1960, novelist John Updike took a seat behind third base in the shadow of Fenway Park's Green Monster.

He was there to watch the final home game of Boston Red Sox star Ted Williams. He didn't know he would be a witness to history.

After enduring eight drab innings of end of the season baseball between the Baltimore Orioles and Red Sox, Williams batted one final time in the eighth. To Updike's delight, Williams delivered an exquisite parting shot—a dramatic, majestic home run into the center-field bullpen.

"The ball climbed on a diagonal line into the vast volume of air over center field," Updike wrote. "From my angle, behind third base, the ball seemed less an object in flight than the tip of a towering, motionless construct, like the Eiffel Tower or the Tappan Zee Bridge. It was in the books while it was still in the sky."

"Hub Fans Bid Kid Adieu," Updike's extraordinary account of Williams's final game, was a triumph. Looking back, it seemed to be a turning point in the way America saw the difficult Red Sox star.

Nobody remembers it now, but in 1960, Williams was not a universally beloved figure upon leaving the game. Fenway wasn't close to a sellout for his final home game. No major columnist attended the contest. National TV paid no attention to his departure. Even the Red Sox's own pregame ceremony was brief and uncomfortable. Williams was seen as difficult to deal with as Barry Bonds is now or as Albert Belle was a few years ago.

Yet Updike's penetrating portrait of Williams, the cranky, ever-distant star, and his complicated relationship with the Boston fans, made us reconsider someone we thought we knew.

Updike wrote so convincingly, one Boston sportswriter sensed what it might do for Williams. He then sat down and wrote Updike an explicit, angry note.

In many ways, Williams's farewell home run was one of the last truly "pure" events in modern-day sports history. It became historic by the action on the field, not a fluke of the calendar or by TV coverage or media hype or anyone on the team's promotional staff. It was a blow for the ages. And maybe for the last time, we had to have somebody else tell us about it.

Having Updike there as our eyes, our ears, as superfan—he made no attempt to interview Williams or talk with any of his teammates or his opponents—helped us see a baseball game and assess a career with a poet's sensibility.

It was written from afar and the distance helped him cast Williams and his brilliant career in a new light. Unlike many of the players in this volume, Williams gave some thought to his parting shot and what it would mean someday.

———

The idea for *Last Time Out* came after a brief meeting with Updike himself, who was speaking at a workshop at Florida State University in the fall of 2000.

"Williams was the biggest sports star in the history of New England," he said, recalling that long-ago September afternoon. "It was his last game and . . ." he paused, still amazed, "nobody was there."

On the way home, remembering Updike's wonderful essay, I wondered if there were other moments that baseball history had somehow passed over?

How did Babe Ruth bow out? Hadn't he had a three-home run game? And Ty Cobb? Willie Mays? Bob Feller? How did they leave the game that was their life? How did some of the game's greatest players decide to say goodbye? Did any of them do it as dramatically as Williams?

To my surprise, there wasn't a lot of documentation on that kind of thing. There was no easy way to find out. Even if you knew what year a player retired, baseball season runs from April through October. Not everybody got off on the last stop. Particularly if that last season wasn't very impressive.

There were many afternoons spent on the microfilm machine at Florida State's Strozier Library. There were searches through 50-, 60-, and 70-year-old box scores, game stories, and notes columns.

Having been in the sportswriting business for a while, at least I had some idea where to look. Either on the day after the game itself or on a day when that individual was honored (Hall of Fame induction) or maybe, in some cases, an obituary.

Gradually, through newspaper accounts of the day, biographies, out-of-print baseball books, magazine pieces, and, in one case, memory—(everybody who grew up in New England watched every second of Carl Yastrzemski's farewell Fenway weekend)—the stories of the final games of 25 of the game's greatest players came together. That's what *Last Time Out* is all about.

Some of their farewells are sad. Some are triumphant. Some are shocking. Some are perfect.

From Christy Mathewson to Cal Ripken Jr.—the latest entry in the book—all of these men ranked among the game's giants.

In telling their stories and recounting the circumstances surrounding their final games, I've tried to find a way to put you in the stands or on the mound or at the plate, listening to what they might have been thinking as the final moments of their careers passed by. I've tried to find a way to put you there, in a box seat, as their world and their games came to an end. Since I didn't have a time machine, I had to find other eyes and ears to bring those moments alive for us. I'm grateful for all the hard work and diligence of those men on the beat and those biographers and baseball historians. Many of them were a witness to history, even if they hadn't exactly planned on it.

Mark Twain once suggested the famous last words of some of history's greatest figures should be as memorable as the careers that preceded them.

"A distinguished man should be as particular about his last words as he is about his last breath," Twain wrote. "He should never leave such a thing to the last hour of his life, and trust to an intellectual spirit at the last moment to enable him to say something smart with his latest gasp and launch into eternity with grandeur."

Our memories of these baseball giants endure with grandeur, long after the last swing or final pitch. In looking back at these 25 moments in time, maybe each one of them will help us understand why.

———

Consider the case of Ted Williams. When, after his dramatic farewell home run, Williams disappeared into the dugout without a response to Fenway's sea of noise, it put the retiring star in a most unflattering light.

Petulant star ignores wild adoring fans—sounds like Barry Bonds, circa 2002.

Updike showed us something else. He explained how Williams, even in this magnificent moment, could not bring himself to say one final, meaningless "thank you." Not after two decades at the mercy of the merciless Boston press.

Only the man who says "No" is truly free. He could not, finally, tip his cap. And he didn't. Updike was the first to understand that Williams's gesture wasn't as much a snub of the fans as it was him listening closely, honestly, to his own heart.

Reflecting back on all that's changed in our view of Williams today, it does seem as if Updike's story did, in fact, contribute heavily to the reconsidered, revisionist version of the Williams's legend.

There's no mistaking, it truly did seem to take off from that day. And there's a delicious irony in that.

As a player, Williams's rocky relationships with writers cost him at least one and maybe two Most Valuable Player awards. He was not a man people spoke kindly of. Yet once he'd retired, world-renown writers seemed to go out of their way to catch up and reconsider Williams's extraordinary career as a baseball player, as a war hero, as a controversial figure.

Maybe they went after Joe DiMaggio, too, and he wanted no part of them. Williams seemed to welcome the reconsideration.

Gradually, we all came to see that what had always seemed a flaw—his single-mindedness—was really a virtue. Updike pointed us in that direction. "The papers said that the other players, and even the umpires on the field," Updike wrote, "begged (Williams) to come out and acknowledge us in some way but he refused. Gods do not answer letters."

Oh, that some novelist or sportswriter would dare wrap up a piece in this day and age with such mighty words.

Oh, that some latter-day hero would give him reason to.


John Nogowski
Tallahassee, Florida
February 14, 2004

# Acknowledgments

For *Last Time Out* to get its turn at bat, a number of people had to juggle their lineup card, so to speak.

The author would like to thank those wonderful unsung heroines—newspaper librarians (like Fannie Witherspoon at the *Kansas City Star*) at the *Boston Globe* and the *Cleveland Plain Dealer* for their help and cooperation. Similarly, the librarians at Florida State's Strozier Library were friendly, patient, and helpful, usually in that order, wondering why an aging sportswriter was spending so much of his summer vacation in the stacks.

The author would also like to send a special note of thanks for Gerry and Mary Janet Dube, for their help in gathering Ted Williams's material on very short notice. Thanks also go out to Jimmy Salisbury for his help some years ago, to all those men and women in the sportswriting profession then and now for their contribution to the record of their time.

I'd also like to thank Liz Nogowski for her unwavering support, her passion for baseball, and her willingness to endure yet another story about some dusty old ballplayer. Thanks, too, to my first audience for most of these chapters, John Jr., who laughed at all the right places and (correctly) booed intermittently throughout the DiMaggio/Mantle chapters.

The cleanup hitter in all this, of course, was Jill Langford, my first contact at Taylor Trade, The Rowman & Littlefield Publishing Group, and the driving force behind getting this book into print. She could show both Ted and Babe a little about how to hit with two strikes on you. Special thanks and blessings to her.

Finally, I suppose I ought to thank baseball, too. Like most of us who've played it, coached it, lived it, the game has come to mean so much more than just scores and stats and pennants.

In fact, I've got a game to go to tonight.

Lucky me!


John Nogowski

Tallahassee, Florida

May 12, 2004

# LAST TIME OUT

Babe Ruth looks sad-eyed and beefy in a Boston Braves uniform.
Photo courtesy of National Baseball Hall of Fame Library, Cooperstown, New York.

# BABE RUTH

## *Missing the Proper Exit*

| | |
|---|---|
| **DATE:** May 30, 1935 (first game of Memorial Day doubleheader) | |
| **SITE:** Shibe Park, Philadelphia, Pennsylvania | |
| **PITCHER:** Jim Bivin of Philadelphia A's | |
| **RESULT:** Ground out to first baseman Dolph Camilli | |

**May 30, 1935, Philadelphia**—The final swing of the game's greatest player did not result in a long, soaring home run. There was none of the mincing majesty of a Ruthian trot around the bases or even the extraordinary drama of a mighty whiff from the Sultan of Swat.

"No home run that Babe Ruth ever hit managed to hint at the energy, power, effort, and sincerity of purpose that went into a swing as much as one strikeout," Paul Gallico once wrote. "Just as when he connected the result was the most perfect thing of its kind, a ball whacked so high, wide, and handsome that no stadium in the entire country could contain it, so was his strikeout the absolute acme of frustration. He would swing himself twice around until his legs were braided. Often he would twist himself clear off his feet. If he had ever connected with that one. . . ."

There was none of that here. When Babe Ruth came to bat for the 8,399th and final time of his magnificent career, he was, finally, harmless. The Braves' aging slugger had an aching knee, the result of an embarrassing fall on the left-field incline at Cincinnati's Crosley Field a few days earlier.

What hurt just as much, perhaps, was Ruth's unsightly .183 batting average with just six home runs in the team's first 27 games. It was a sad way for the game's greatest home run king to wind up. Everyone around the game knew he was done.

Ruth's teammate on the Braves, 19-year-old rookie Albie Fletcher, watched with sadness.

"He couldn't run, he couldn't bend down for a ball," Fletcher told Donald Honig in his book *Baseball America*. "And of course, he couldn't hit the way he used to. It

*"Bum knee sends Babe Ruth packing"*

was sad watching those great skills fading away. To see it happening to Babe Ruth, to see Babe Ruth struggling on a ballfield, well, you realize that we're mortal and nothing lasts forever."

A contemporary of Ruth's, Hall of Fame third baseman Fred Lindstrom put it even more plainly: "It was like watching a monument beginning to shake and crack," he said. "You know, when I think back on it, it was an awful thing to see."

So here he was, stepping into the batter's box in the first game of a Memorial Day doubleheader at Philadelphia's Baker Bowl, the stands barely half-full. Ruth looked out at the guy on the mound, a guy about as nondescript as it gets. He saw a 26-year-old rookie right-hander named Jim Bivin, who finished 2-9 in this, his only big-league season, allowing 220 hits in 162 innings of work.

When Ruth came up with two outs and nobody on in the first, a roar, of course, went up from the crowd. It was Babe Ruth, after all. Ruth swung mightily and topped a slow roller to first baseman Dolph Camilli.

Running down to first, he felt the pain in his knee from his fall the other day. But he trotted out to left field, to try to make a go of it. The doubleheader had just started. There might be some kid who hadn't gotten there yet.

As he trotted to left, he had to be thinking about when he should have quit, when he really wanted to, about a week earlier.

He knew how he should have gone out. Nobody ever had a greater sense of the dramatic than Babe Ruth.

Who hit the first All-Star Game home run? Who hit the first home run in Yankee Stadium? Who hit a home run the first time he walked up to the plate wearing his famous No. 3?

What about his called shot in the 1932 World Series, whether he did it or not? Was there another player in baseball history who might even have dared do such a thing?

And, Ruth thought, he had the perfect finish. He blew it.

Just five days earlier, Ruth had one of the finest games of his remarkable 22-year romp through the big leagues, swatting three home runs against the Pittsburgh Pirates. That included an extraordinary parting shot—the 714th of his career—a belt that cleared the entire stadium, the first fair ball ever hit over the right-field roof at Forbes Field.

Ruth left that game to a thunderous ovation. Why the hell didn't he keep on walking?

Former Red Sox outfielder Duffy Lewis, now the Braves' traveling secretary, told the Babe right after that home run that he should quit and go out on top. Ruth's wife, Claire, told him the same thing.

But Braves' president Emil Fuchs, dangling the possibility of a managerial position over Ruth's head, lured him back.

"There are people who want to see you, Babe," he'd tell him. He knew how badly Ruth wanted to be a big-league manager. And he knew his Braves, the worst team in baseball history, were an even worse draw without a fading Babe Ruth.

Ruth had already threatened retirement two weeks before that magnificent day in Pittsburgh.

On May 12, with his average at a sickly .154 with only three home runs in 21 games, Ruth told Braves' president Emil Fuchs what he already knew—that he was washed up and wanted out right then and there.

Fuchs insisted that Ruth go on the team's upcoming road trips to Pittsburgh, Cincinnati, and Philadelphia, all National League cities that were planning Babe Ruth Days for the former American League star.

According to Fuchs, they'd already sold a lot of tickets. Since Ruth, a career American Leaguer, had never played in National League cities Pittsburgh or Cincinnati during the regular season, reluctantly, he agreed to make the trip.

But now, his knee aching, his batting average below .200, he knew it was a bad idea. Just like leaving New York.

When, in 1935, the New York Yankees dealt the aging Ruth to the worst team in baseball, the Boston Braves, just a few days after his 40th birthday, it seemed like the end was near.

Ruth wanted to manage but all the Yankees would offer him was a spot managing their Newark farm club. Ruth wasn't interested in that.

So when Fuchs hinted that Ruth might be in consideration for a managerial role—if he earned it with a season of good behavior—that was all the Babe needed to hear.

Ruth opened the 1935 season with a long home run off future Hall of Famer Carl Hubbell of the New York Giants in his first National League game—incidentally,

Ruth's first at-bat against Hubbell since Ruth was part of Hubbell's memorable All-Star Game whiff streak—Braves fans may have thought the old boy could turn back the clock.

Though Ruth had slid to a .288 average with 22 home runs and 84 RBI in his final year with the Yankees, maybe there was some kick left.

The Braves—and Ruth—found out quickly that there wasn't. He was old, out of shape, and couldn't hit anymore.

His teammates wanted no part of him. Had it been put to a vote, there's no question that Ruth's teammates on the Braves would have told him to leave.

He reported to Spring Training in St. Petersburg, Florida, at least 25 pounds overweight. He'd been wining and dining in Europe in the off-season. And at 40, he couldn't move or field his position. As the season continued, two Braves' pitchers even planned to mutiny over his poor defensive play.

*"Ruth leaves Braves in huff over party"*

But as warm weather hit the Northeast in mid-May, Ruth's final week showed a bit of an upturn. The Babe rolled into Pittsburgh on May 23, a day that the Pirates chose to honor longtime Ruth pal Rabbit Maranville.

Ruth went hitless in three trips in a 7-1 loss, but once sent Paul Waner to the fence where he made a leaping catch of Ruth's bid for a home run.

As Waner trotted in, Ruth passed the 5-foot 8-inch "Big Poison" on the way out to his position and shook his head.

"Say, you're a mighty little fellow to be such a big thief," Ruth told Waner.

The next afternoon, the Braves fell again, 7-6, and Ruth managed a single, his ninth hit of the season, but Waner again robbed him with a one-handed catch of a 400-foot Ruth drive.

But on that last great Saturday, Ruth had the last laugh for the last time.

He homered off Pirates' starter Red Lucas in the first, then singled off reliever Guy Bush, then homered again and in the seventh, hit one of the longest home runs of his career, a true grand finale—No. 714—that cleared the right-field pavilion.

"He still had that swing," Bush remarked years later. "You could hear it go 'swish.'"

Newspapers were ecstatic.

"A prodigious clout that carried clean over the right-field grandstand that bounced into the street and rolled to Schenley Park," one account said.

Even the staid *New York Times* was gushing: "Rising to the glorious heights of his heyday, Babe Ruth, the Sultan of Swat, crashed out three home runs against the Pittsburgh Pirates Saturday afternoon but it was not enough."

Ruth was so excited by his third home run of the afternoon, he swung by the Pittsburgh dugout after rounding the bases.

"Fellas," he told the stunned Pirate players, "that one felt good."

It was only the second time in Babe's career that he had homered three times in a regular-season game—he also did it twice in the World Series.

The only other time Babe hit three during the season was in Philadelphia's Shibe Park in 1930. On that day, in his fourth at-bat, Ruth waggishly took the first two strikes batting right-handed, before switching back to lefty and whiffing.

But the moment didn't linger. The following Sunday, the Braves played in Cincinnati and Ruth showed that Saturday's game was truly his last hurrah. He whiffed three times in a 6-3 loss on Babe Ruth Day before 24,300 fans.

The next day, Ruth pinch hit in the ninth inning of a 9-5 loss and walked. On that Tuesday, he went 0-2 in a 13-4 loss but scored a run, the 2,174th of his career, just 71 fewer than Ty Cobb, then the all-time leader.

But it was in that game that Ruth also stumbled, trying to go back and field a ball on the strange Crosley Field incline in left field.

He fell flat on his face and left the game in a huff. The knee continued to bother him.

After an off-day, the Braves came into Philadelphia on Wednesday for Babe Ruth Day and Ruth went 0-1 in a rare 8-6 Braves' win.

But here he was the next afternoon, out in left field, his knee sore, and his game gone.

He looked up and here was a shot off the bat of Philadelphia's Lou Chiozza in the gap. He tried to lunge after it but missed it and fell.

The ball squirted to the wall and Chiozza got to third. And suddenly, here was Ruth, walking in with a limp, calling for a replacement. The Babe never came back.

With Ruth trying to mend his knee, the Braves headed back to New York for a weekend series with the Giants. And in the meantime, Ruth got an invitation to go to a grand party for the new ocean liner *Normandie*. He wanted to go. The Braves said no. And the fight resulted in Ruth getting his unconditional release from the Braves on Sunday night in Boston.

It was headline stuff in Monday's *New York Times*.

"Babe Ruth 'Quits' Braves and Is Dropped by Club."

"The blow-off came today when Judge Fuchs refused my request that I be allowed to go to New York Tuesday night for the *Normandie* celebration," Ruth told the *New York Times* Sunday night in Boston.

"Here's my argument. I've got a bad leg, threatened with water on the knee unless I keep off it and can't play ball. We have an exhibition game [in Haverhill, Massachusetts] scheduled for tomorrow.

"I'm willing to go and hobble around in that to please the crowd. The game and my appearance have been advertised for a long time—and the Braves need the money.

"But I am not fit to play in a league game. . . . So when I received this special invitation . . . I thought it would be a great honor and that it would mean a great deal to the Braves if I attended. . . . When I put it up to the Judge, he said, 'Nothing doing!'

"Yes, I have just received my unconditional release from the Braves and I am mighty glad of it. . . . Now I'll go to the *Normandie* celebration on Tuesday night, and represent baseball—but not the Braves."

Braves' president Fuchs sounded happy to get rid of him.

"The matter came to a head today when Ruth requested permission to go to New York," Fuchs told the *Times*. "[Braves manager Bill] McKechnie felt, and I agreed with him, that Ruth's place was here, as we have games with the Dodgers on Tuesday and Wednesday.

"When permission was refused, Ruth did not take the refusal in a sportsmanlike way at all," Fuchs concluded. "For the sake of discipline, we could not give him the extra privileges he asked for."

At the same time Fuchs was announcing he was releasing Ruth, he also took advantage of the front-page publicity to announce that the struggling team was for sale.

"I am willing to sacrifice the large equity I have in the Braves if some sportsman (who will get his reward, in my opinion, both financially and otherwise), or group of sportsmen, will come along and retain the outstanding players on our club, promise me they will not sell them to other cities, and that they will protect our small stockholders."

The newspapers were not kind to Babe, regarding the matter.

Gallico, generally a Ruth supporter, mocked the Babe in a nasty farewell column that ran in the *Chicago Tribune*.

"There are two minor notes of appealing pathos in the quitting of Babe Ruth," he wrote. "The matter that brought this long-brewing retirement from the Boston

Braves to a head was a little boy's fit of pique and disappointment because Judge Fuchs wouldn't let him go to what looks like a pretty swell party, the welcome to the S.S. *Normandie.*

"And in the Boston clubhouse, Ruth was quoted as saying, 'The team and [Manager Bill] McKechnie are swell. They are giving me a ball autographed by all the members of the team.' There is laughter in the first and tears in the second."

If that's all the Braves had for one of the greatest players in the game's history, an autographed ball, Gallico hinted, shame on them.

"They call him Babe, and Babe he is," Gallico concluded. "Life to him is very often the life of a child and bosses are not bosses at all but grownups who interfere with his fun the way grownups always do. The greatest masters of men are those who treat them like well loved children. Poor Babe. He wanted to go to a party where all the other kids were going."

"*Babe says he's done with Braves*"

Even crusty old John Kieran of the *New York Times* took a shot at both parties.

"It seems that they won't stop swinging in baseball's Boston team party until everyone around the place has had a chance to come to bat and hit a loud foul," he wrote.

"Let it go. Too much has been said on all sides. The Babe should have smiled and walked away. Judge Fuchs should have sent him off with a bouquet of flowers. Bill

McKechnie should have gone on quietly without popping off. Each one had been doing his best with a plan that didn't pan out. The mistake they all made was to fill the parting of ways with the sound and sight of battle."

With Babe or not, Fuchs's Braves finished the 1935 season with a record of 38-115, the worst record in the history of baseball until 1962's Amazin' Mets lost 120 games.

The next night, The Babe went to the *Normandie* party.

# Leaving with a Limp

| BOSTON (N.) | ab. | r. | h. | po. | s. | e. |
|---|---|---|---|---|---|---|
| Urbanski, ss | 4 | 0 | 2 | 2 | 3 | 1 |
| Thompson, rf | 4 | 1 | 0 | 2 | 0 | 0 |
| Ruth, lf | 1 | 0 | 0 | 0 | 1 | 0 |
| Lee, lf | 4 | 1 | 3 | 0 | 0 | 0 |
| Berger, cf | 5 | 1 | 1 | 2 | 0 | 1 |
| R. Moore, 1b | 4 | 2 | 2 | 14 | 1 | 0 |
| Mallon, 2b | 3 | 1 | 2 | 2 | 4 | 1 |
| a Mowrey | 1 | 0 | 0 | 0 | 0 | 0 |
| Whitney, 3b | 5 | 0 | 3 | 0 | 3 | 0 |
| Spohrer, c | 5 | 0 | 0 | 2 | 0 | 0 |
| Frankhouse, p | 4 | 0 | 1 | 0 | 5 | 0 |
| Cantwell, p | 0 | 0 | 0 | 0 | 0 | 0 |
| **TOTALS:** | **40** | **6** | **14** | **24** | **17** | **8** |

| PHILADELPHIA (N.) | ab. | r. | h. | po. | s. | e. |
|---|---|---|---|---|---|---|
| Allen, cf | 4 | 1 | 0 | 4 | 1 | 0 |
| Watkins, lf | 5 | 1 | 1 | 3 | 1 | 0 |
| J. Moore, rf | 3 | 2 | 1 | 0 | 0 | 0 |
| Camilli, 1b | 3 | 3 | 2 | 7 | 1 | 0 |
| Haslin, ss | 4 | 2 | 3 | 1 | 0 | 0 |
| Chiozza, 2b | 4 | 0 | 3 | 5 | 2 | 1 |
| Todd, c | 5 | 1 | 1 | 4 | 1 | 1 |
| Verges, 3b | 3 | 1 | 0 | 2 | 2 | 0 |
| Bivin, p | 2 | 0 | 0 | 1 | 1 | 0 |
| b Boland | 1 | 0 | 0 | 0 | 0 | 0 |
| Jorgens, p | 0 | 0 | 0 | 0 | 0 | 0 |
| c Wilson | 1 | 0 | 1 | 0 | 0 | 0 |
| C. Davis, p | 0 | 0 | 0 | 0 | 0 | 0 |
| **TOTALS:** | **35** | **11** | **12** | **27** | **9** | **2** |

a Batted for Mallon in ninth.   b Batted for Bivin in sixth.   c Batted for Jorgens in eighth.

| Boston | 0 1 1 | 0 2 1 | 1 0 0 | 6 |
|---|---|---|---|---|
| Philadelphia | 3 0 0 | 1 0 0 | 0 7 x | 11 |

## GEORGE HERMAN (BABE) RUTH

Born February 6, 1895, at Baltimore, Md.
Died August 16, 1948, at New York, N.Y.
Height 6-2  Weight 215
Threw and batted left-handed
Named to Hall of Fame, 1936

| YEAR | CLUB | LEAGUE | POS. | G. | AB. | R. | H. | 2B. | 3B. | HR. | RBI. | B.A. | PO. | A. | E. | F.A. |
|------|------|--------|------|----|-----|----|----|-----|-----|-----|------|------|-----|----|----|------|
| 1914 | Balt.-Prov. | Int. | P-OF | 46 | 121 | 22 | 28 | 2 | 10 | 1 | — | .231 | 20 | 87 | 4 | .964 |
| 1914 | Boston | Amer. | P | 5 | 10 | 1 | 2 | 1 | 0 | 0 | 0 | .200 | 0 | 8 | 0 | 1.000 |
| 1915 | Boston | Amer. | P-OF | 42 | 92 | 16 | 29 | 10 | 1 | 4 | 20 | .315 | 17 | 63 | 2 | .976 |
| 1916 | Boston | Amer. | P-OF | 67 | 136 | 18 | 37 | 5 | 3 | 3 | 16 | .272 | 24 | 83 | 3 | .973 |
| 1917 | Boston | Amer. | P-OF | 52 | 123 | 14 | 40 | 6 | 3 | 2 | 10 | .325 | 19 | 101 | 2 | .984 |
| 1918 | Boston | Amer. | OF-P-1 | 95 | 317 | 50 | 95 | 26 | 11 | 11 | 64 | .300 | 270 | 72 | 18 | .950 |
| 1919 | Boston (a) | Amer. | OF-P | 130 | 432 | 103 | 139 | 34 | 12 | 29 | 112 | .322 | 270 | 53 | 4 | .988 |
| 1920 | New York | Amer. | OF-1-P | 142 | 458 | 158 | 172 | 36 | 9 | 54 | 137 | .376 | 259 | 21 | 19 | .936 |
| 1921 | New York | Amer. | OF-1-P | 152 | 540 | 177 | 204 | 44 | 16 | 59 | 170 | .378 | 348 | 17 | 13 | .966 |
| 1922 | New York | Amer. | OF | 110 | 406 | 94 | 128 | 24 | 8 | 35 | 96 | .315 | 226 | 14 | 9 | .964 |
| 1923 | New York | Amer. | OF-1B | 152 | 522 | 151 | 205 | 45 | 13 | 41 | 130 | .393 | 378 | 20 | 11 | .973 |
| 1924 | New York | Amer. | OF | 153 | 529 | 143 | 200 | 39 | 7 | 46 | 121 | .378 | 340 | 18 | 14 | .962 |
| 1925 | New York | Amer. | OF | 98 | 359 | 61 | 104 | 12 | 2 | 25 | 66 | .290 | 207 | 15 | 6 | .974 |
| 1926 | New York | Amer. | OF | 152 | 495 | 139 | 184 | 30 | 5 | 47 | 155 | .372 | 308 | 11 | 7 | .979 |
| 1927 | New York | Amer. | OF | 151 | 540 | 158 | 192 | 29 | 8 | 60 | 164 | .356 | 328 | 14 | 13 | .963 |
| 1928 | New York | Amer. | OF | 154 | 536 | 163 | 173 | 29 | 8 | 54 | 142 | .323 | 304 | 9 | 8 | .975 |
| 1929 | New York | Amer. | OF | 135 | 499 | 121 | 172 | 26 | 6 | 46 | 154 | .345 | 240 | 5 | 4 | .984 |
| 1930 | New York | Amer. | OF-P | 145 | 518 | 150 | 186 | 28 | 9 | 49 | 153 | .359 | 266 | 10 | 10 | .965 |
| 1931 | New York | Amer. | OF-1B | 145 | 534 | 149 | 199 | 31 | 3 | 46 | 163 | .373 | 237 | 5 | 7 | .972 |
| 1932 | New York | Amer. | OF-1B | 133 | 457 | 120 | 156 | 13 | 5 | 41 | 137 | .341 | 212 | 10 | 9 | .961 |
| 1933 | New York | Amer. | OF-P | 137 | 459 | 97 | 138 | 21 | 3 | 34 | 103 | .301 | 215 | 9 | 7 | .970 |
| 1934 | New York (b) | Amer. | OF | 125 | 365 | 78 | 105 | 17 | 4 | 22 | 84 | .288 | 197 | 3 | 8 | .962 |
| 1935 | Boston | Nat. | OF | 28 | 72 | 13 | 13 | 0 | 0 | 6 | 12 | .181 | 39 | 1 | 2 | .952 |
| American League Totals—16 Years | | | | 2475 | 8327 | 2161 | 2860 | 506 | 136 | 708 | 2197 | .343 | 4665 | 561 | 174 | .968 |
| National League Totals—2 Years | | | | 28 | 72 | 13 | 13 | 0 | 0 | 6 | 12 | .181 | 39 | 1 | 2 | .952 |
| Major League Totals—17 Years | | | | 2503 | 8399 | 2174 | 2873 | 506 | 136 | 714 | 2209 | .342 | 4704 | 562 | 176 | .968 |

a Sold to New York Yankees for $125,000, January 3, 1920.
b Released to Boston Braves, February 26, 1935.

## WORLD SERIES RECORD

| YEAR | CLUB | LEAGUE | POS. | G. | AB. | R. | H. | 2B. | 3B. | HR. | RBI. | B.A. | PO. | A. | E. | F.A. |
|---|---|---|---|---|---|---|---|---|---|---|---|---|---|---|---|---|
| 1915 | Boston | Amer. | PH | 1 | 1 | 0 | 0 | 0 | 0 | 0 | 0 | .000 | 0 | 0 | 0 | .000 |
| 1916 | Boston | Amer. | P | 1 | 5 | 0 | 0 | 0 | 0 | 0 | 1 | .000 | 2 | 4 | 0 | 1.000 |
| 1918 | Boston | Amer. | P-OF | 3 | 5 | 0 | 1 | 0 | 1 | 0 | 2 | .200 | 1 | 5 | 0 | 1.000 |
| 1921 | New York | Amer. | OF | 6 | 16 | 3 | 5 | 0 | 0 | 1 | 4 | .313 | 9 | 0 | 0 | 1.000 |
| 1922 | New York | Amer. | OF | 5 | 17 | 1 | 2 | 1 | 0 | 0 | 1 | .118 | 9 | 0 | 0 | 1.000 |
| 1923 | New York | Amer. | O-1B | 6 | 19 | 8 | 7 | 1 | 1 | 3 | 3 | .368 | 17 | 0 | 1 | .944 |
| 1926 | New York | Amer. | OF | 7 | 20 | 6 | 6 | 0 | 0 | 4 | 5 | .300 | 8 | 2 | 0 | 1.000 |
| 1927 | New York | Amer. | OF | 4 | 15 | 4 | 6 | 0 | 0 | 2 | 7 | .400 | 10 | 0 | 0 | 1.000 |
| 1928 | New York | Amer. | OF | 4 | 16 | 9 | 10 | 3 | 0 | 3 | 4 | .625 | 9 | 1 | 0 | 1.000 |
| 1932 | New York | Amer. | OF | 4 | 15 | 6 | 5 | 0 | 0 | 2 | 6 | .333 | 8 | 0 | 1 | .889 |
| World Series Totals | | | | 41 | 129 | 37 | 42 | 5 | 2 | 15 | 33 | .326 | 73 | 12 | 2 | .977 |

## PITCHING RECORD

| YEAR | CLUB | LEAGUE | G. | IP. | W. | L. | Pct. | H. | R. | ER. | SO. | BB. | ERA. |
|---|---|---|---|---|---|---|---|---|---|---|---|---|---|
| 1914 | Balt.-Prov. | Int. | 35 | 245 | 22 | 9 | .710 | 219 | 88 | — | 139 | 101 | — |
| 1914 | Boston | Amer. | 4 | 23 | 2 | 1 | .667 | 21 | 12 | 10 | 3 | 7 | 3.91 |
| 1915 | Boston | Amer. | 32 | 218 | 18 | 8 | .692 | 166 | 80 | 59 | 112 | 85 | 2.44 |
| 1916 | Boston | Amer. | 44 | 324 | 23 | 12 | .657 | 230 | 83 | 63 | 170 | 118 | 1.75 |
| 1917 | Boston | Amer. | 41 | 326 | 24 | 13 | .649 | 244 | 93 | 73 | 128 | 108 | 2.02 |
| 1918 | Boston | Amer. | 20 | 166 | 13 | 7 | .650 | 125 | 51 | 41 | 40 | 49 | 2.22 |
| 1919 | Boston | Amer. | 17 | 133 | 9 | 5 | .643 | 148 | 59 | 44 | 30 | 58 | 2.97 |
| 1920 | New York | Amer. | 1 | 4 | 1 | 0 | 1.000 | 3 | 4 | 2 | 0 | 2 | 4.50 |
| 1921 | New York | Amer. | 2 | 9 | 2 | 0 | 1.000 | 14 | 10 | 9 | 2 | 9 | 9.00 |
| 1930 | New York | Amer. | 1 | 9 | 1 | 0 | 1.000 | 11 | 3 | 3 | 3 | 2 | 3.00 |
| 1933 | New York | Amer. | 1 | 9 | 1 | 0 | 1.000 | 12 | 5 | 5 | 0 | 3 | 5.00 |
| Major League Totals | | | 163 | 1221 | 94 | 46 | .671 | 974 | 400 | 309 | 488 | 441 | 2.28 |

## WORLD SERIES RECORD

| YEAR | CLUB | LEAGUE | G. | IP. | W. | L. | Pct. | H. | R. | ER. | SO. | BB. | ERA. |
|---|---|---|---|---|---|---|---|---|---|---|---|---|---|
| 1916 | Boston | Amer. | 1 | 14 | 1 | 0 | 1.000 | 6 | 1 | 1 | 4 | 3 | 0.64 |
| 1918 | Boston | Amer. | 2 | 17 | 2 | 0 | 1.000 | 13 | 2 | 2 | 4 | 7 | 1.06 |
| World Series Totals | | | 3 | 31 | 3 | 0 | 1.000 | 19 | 3 | 3 | 8 | 10 | 0.87 |

Cincinnati player-manager Christy Mathewson pitched just once for his new
National League team and it was enough.

Photo courtesy of National Baseball Hall of Fame Library, Cooperstown, New York.

# CHRISTY MATHEWSON

## *"Big Six" Makes a Great Escape*

**DATE:** September 4, 1916 (second game of Labor Day doubleheader)

**SITE:** Weegman Park, Chicago, Illinois

**OPPONENT:** Mordecai "Three-Finger" Brown of the Chicago Cubs

**RESULT:** Complete game 10-8 victory

**September 4, 1916, Chicago**—Christy Mathewson stood on the mound quietly at Weegman Park, watching Vic Saier trot around the bases. It was a helpless feeling, a feeling the great Mathewson rarely experienced on the hill. It was now 10-8, Cincinnati. But he still needed an out.

The home run was the seventh Sauer had hit—more than any other player of Mathewson's time—off the fading ace right-hander. Though the game was winding down, Mathewson could hear 17,000 Cub fans let him know exactly how far his fadeaway had faded. What a way to wind up.

Barely two months into his new job as player-manager of the lowly Cincinnati Reds, the season nearly done, Mathewson hadn't really figured on pitching at all. He was trying to learn what it took to be a successful manager, like his old boss John McGraw.

With the team out of the pennant race, he considered the gate for his Labor Day doubleheader with the Chicago Cubs. Both teams were well out of pennant contention, so somebody—history doesn't record exactly who it was—had the wise idea to match up Mathewson one last time with his old Cubs' rival, Mordecai "Three-Finger" Brown, then also playing out the string with the Cubs.

It was a stunt, sure. But the Mathewson-Brown matchup was the Ali-Frazier duel of their time. The two future Hall of Famers had faced off against each other 23 times through the years and Brown had won 11 of them, including the famous playoff duel of 1908, the one caused by the infamous (Fred) Merkle boner, when he failed to touch second base on what appeared to be a game-winning hit during a key regular-season game.

So with a win, Brown would finally square the account with Mathewson, who was a fine pitcher and gentleman but also the darling of the New York media. They wrote about "Big Six" like he was a living legend and their glowing words only served as fuel for Brown's competitive furnace.

You didn't have to be a psychiatrist to read the envy in Brown's words as he talked about dueling the Giants' great.

"I can still see Christy Mathewson making his lordly entrance," Brown wrote in his autobiography. "He'd always wait until about 10 minutes before game time, then he'd come in from the clubhouse across the field in a long linen duster like auto drivers wore in those days. At every step the crowd would yell louder and louder."

Brown never heard that kind of cheering, even though his 1908 season, the year he beat Mathewson in that playoff, was one of the finest in baseball history. He was 29-9, appeared in a league-leading 50 games, 32 complete games with nine shutouts, a league-leading five saves, working 312 innings, allowing just 214 hits and a glittering 1.31 ERA.

*"Christy edges 'Three-Finger' Brown in slugger's duel"*

He earned his money that year. With the end of the season approaching, Brown had pitched both ends of a doubleheader the day before the Giants' Fred Merkle failed to touch second base on a potential game-winning hit, a mistake that ended up propelling the Cubs into a neck-and-neck race with the slumping Giants.

In order to win the pennant for the Cubs, Brown had to pitch (and win) in 11 of the team's final 14 games to tie McGraw's Giants. He did.

It was Brown, too, that saved the Cubs in that 1908 playoff game and beat Matty. It was a loss after which, some said, Mathewson wept.

With the game set at New York's Polo Grounds, Cubs' manager Frank Chance had the lame-brained idea to start little-known Jack Pfiester in that game. After the Giants pounced on him for one run and had the bases loaded with no outs, Chance had to frantically wave in Brown from the bench.

Without so much as a warm-up, Brown shut the Giants out the rest of the way to get the Cubs into the World Series.

He would never forget what it was like at the finish of that game.

"As the ninth ended with the Giants going out one-two-three, we all ran for our lives, straight for the clubhouse with the pack at our heels," Brown wrote in his autobiography.

"Some of our boys got caught by the mob and beaten up some. Pfiester got slashed on the shoulder by a knife. We made it to the dressing room and barricaded the door.

"Outside wild men were yelling for our blood—really. As the mob got bigger, the police came up and formed a line across the door. We read the next day that the cops had to pull their revolvers to hold them back.

"When it was safe we rode to our hotel in a patrol wagon, with two cops on the inside and four riding the running boards and the rear step.

"That night when we left for Detroit and the World Series, we slipped out the back door and were escorted down the alley in back of our hotel by a swarm of policemen."

Mathewson, a pitcher of such personal integrity that baseball legend has it that umpires sometimes would consult with him on a close play, seemed above that sort of thing. But he wasn't that September afternoon, standing on the hill as hits rained all over Weegman Park.

He looked around him, seeing a game that he once had at his fingertips turning on him, he remembered the words he'd written for *Baseball Magazine* just a couple years earlier. "Strange impulses can grip a man as he stands on the pitcher's mound," Mathewson wrote. "There may be thousands of people in the stadium but for all practicable purposes the pitcher is alone. I mention this in relation to another subject that has been more or less a sore point with me. It has to do with those occasions when a pitcher, who has been working well all afternoon, will suddenly surrender a series of hits in a late inning."

This was a particularly sensitive spot with Mathewson, who was famous for "coasting" in one-sided games, much to the consternation of Giants' manager John McGraw.

"Often, at this point, the fans will start demanding that the manager take him out," he continued in the *Baseball Magazine* article. "I have heard more than one manager severely criticized by the fans for going along with a pitcher under these circumstances. It is my theory that the fans in instances such as this are too severe on both the pitcher and the manager.

"They are, in fact, ignoring the rules of chance that dominate the game. It is a mathematical certainty that over the course of any given season, batsmen including pitchers and weak hitters, will compile an over-all average of .250 against pitchers (take or give a few points). I am a great believer in these averages.

"Sooner or later they catch up with all of us."

They had caught up with him now. And he knew it. With old Mordecai over in the other dugout, itching for a chance to have the last laugh, Mathewson had to find a way to get out of this. Had to. He just needed one more out.

It might have been Mordecai who pushed for the matchup. Maybe he figured he had one more game in him. A right-hander with a once-wicked curveball—he lost part of the index finger and thumb of his right hand in a farm accident as a child—he was a single game shy of breaking even with the great right-hander.

Nobody, it seemed, ever realized that. If he won this game, even with both of them washed up, they'd each have 12 wins against the other. Now, wouldn't that be a nice stat for Mathewson's adoring New York media.

Brown had a point. He had beaten Mathewson 11 times in head-to-head meetings, including that memorable Cubs-Giants playoff game of 1908, a game played right in the Polo Grounds, Mathewson's home turf. But all you ever heard was Matty, Matty, Matty.

Tall, handsome, and college educated, Mathewson was always above the fray. But a win would not only deadlock their head-to-head matchups, it would also send Matty into retirement on a loss.

Weegman Park was roaring. Mathewson looked around him. After Sauer's home run, two more men were on. A home run would win it. Would this game ever end? He thought about what he read in the Chicago paper that day. There was an almost morbid fascination in watching how time had dealt with these two once-great hurlers.

"Gone are the days when Matty and Brownie could give the greatest batsmen in the game a winning argument nine times out of ten and when shutout scores were frequent when they performed," wrote I. E. Sanborn in the *Chicago Tribune*. "Gone was the fearsome and deadly hook with which the veteran of the Cub slab used to mow down his antagonists in the pinches; gone was the effectiveness of Matty's far famed fadeaway.

"Still, a great group of baseball rooters stood in the rain for an hour before time to start the games and, soon after it was decided to play, filled the plant. The dollar sign has not driven all the sentiment out of the nation's pastime."

He thought back over the game, one of the ugliest he was ever involved in. While the Reds were pounding Brown for 19 hits, with Mathewson (a career .215 hitter) collecting three of them, including a double, the Cubs responded by ripping 14 hits off Mathewson. Brown (a career .206 hitter) had two of them. Though the Cubs jumped on Mathewson, pitching his first and only game for the Reds, for a pair of runs in the first, the Reds scored eight runs in the next six innings off Brown, sending Mathewson into the ninth with a 10-6 lead. One out away from a career-ending win, he faltered. It must have been a humbling feeling for a pitcher who had been so masterful for so many years.

How far he seemed from the pitcher Ring Lardner wrote about this way: "There's a flock o' pitchers that knows a batter's weakness and works accordin'. But they ain't nobody else in the world that can stick a ball as near where they want to stick it as he can. I bet he could shave you if he wanted to and if he had a razor blade to throw instead of a ball. If you can't hit a fast one inch and a quarter inside, and he knows it, you'll get three fast ones an inch and a quarter inside, and then, if you swang at 'em, you can go get a drink o' water.

"Take him in a common, ordinary ballgame, agin' an average club, and everyday pitchin' and what he's tryin' to do is stick the first one over so's he won't have to waste no more'n one ball on one batter. He don't stick it over right in the groove, but he puts it just about so's you'll get a piece of it and give the Giants a little easy fieldin' practice. If the Giants get a flock o' runs and goes way out in front, he'll go right on sticking that first one over, an' maybe he'll allow a little scorin'."

Well, there was plenty of scoring here. What would Ring Lardner have written about it? Mathewson, maybe for one of the few times in his career, was frightened. This was no way to end a career.

A few years earlier, former Pittsburgh star Max Carey had written a piece about Mathewson that talked about his passion for the game.

"Mathewson has the ability and all that," Carey said. "But I believe the main factor that has held him up so long has been his love of the game. Thirteen years is a long time to be under fire. . . . But I've watched Mathewson closely and I've never seen him pitch a ballgame in which he didn't look as if he were having a lot of fun. He always looks as if he had rather be

*"Reds' player-manager wins in career finale"*

out there pitching than doing anything else. It doesn't look to be work with him, but only pure sport—an afternoon's romp as a businessman might go out to play golf or tennis. He either likes it immensely or is the greatest actor I ever saw."

He wondered what ol' Max would say now. Mathewson could already imagine the headlines in the next day's paper. "Washed-up Matty Collapses at Finish." "'Three-Finger' Gets Last Laugh." "Even Matty Can't Rescue Last-Place Reds."

But the Cubs weren't in the strong part of their batting order. He looked over at the dugout to see a pinch-hitter, Fritz Mollwitz, coming up for light-hitting Charlie Pechous (.145). Earlier, Pechous had hit his only double of the 1916 season off the once-great Mathewson. But Cubs' manager Joe Tinker had a hunch and wanted to try Mollwitz, who was dealt from the Cincinnati club 65 games into the season.

He was a light hitter (.241) with only one home run in a seven-year career as a part-time first baseman. But maybe he could keep the rally alive.

He wasn't on the Cincy club in July when Mathewson, outfielder Edd Roush, and infielder Bill McKechnie were dealt from the Giants for outfielder Red Killefer and former manager Buck Herzog.

But Mathewson knew him. He had no power. He just wanted to make him hit it at somebody and get this endless game over with.

The big right-hander wound and threw the final pitch of his career. Mollwitz swung and lifted a harmless fly ball to the outfield. The duel—and Mathewson's career—was over.

Christy Mathewson never pitched again. He managed the Reds until midway through the 1918 season, then left to fight in World War I. While in France, he inhaled some mustard gas and never fully recovered his health.

Mathewson died at New York's Saranac Lake on October 7, 1925, just as the World Series between the Pittsburgh Pirates and Washington Senators was getting under way.

A nation mourned the loss of the man who was probably baseball's first true superstar.

"While the captains and the kings of baseball were gathered here last night after the first game of a World Series, there died at Saranac the best loved of all the baseball players and the most popular of all American athletes of all time—Christy Mathewson," wrote W. O. McGeehan, sports editor of the *New York Tribune*.

"Let none of us insult the memory of Christy Mathewson by making of him one of those sanctimonious and insufferably perfect heroes. He was a real man and essentially, a man's man. . . . He was the exalted man from whom every man wants to play the game straight and to carry his head high as a man who could learn something.

"He played for all that was in him, he fought the good fight and the clean fight. He was the incarnation of all those virtues with which we endow the ideal American."

Mathewson's death, coming as it did at the start of the World Series, seemed to jolt baseball fans far and wide. In the game stories of the World Series, there was more attention to Matty's death than to the game itself.

"John McGraw's gray head was tilted back as his eyes, wrinkled with the years, tried in vain to blink back the tears that came up with a rush. Billy Evans, who started his career soon after Matty started as a pitcher, bowed his head to the memory of a man who never had questioned a decision.

"Hughey Jennings, who was a grass-eating, fiery-haired manager of the Detroit Tigers when Matty was in his prime, made no pretense of hiding his handkerchief.

"Other thrills came later, as the innings went by and the crisis came and was passed. Through the innings the multitude's mind was on the action before them, but in the hearts of the throng was a deep, dull, dormant ache was that the still and silent Matty gone home."

Twenty years later, Mathewson was an original—and posthumous—inductee in the very first election for the new Baseball Hall of Fame in Cooperstown, New York.

The perennially overlooked Mordecai "Three-Finger" Brown made the Hall, too.

He was elected 10 years later, in 1949, just about exactly a year after he died in Terre Haute, Indiana, on Valentine's Day, 1948, at the age of 72.

# A Narrow Escape

|  | ab. | r. | h. | po. | a. |
|---|---|---|---|---|---|
| **CINCINNATI** | | | | | |
| Neale, lf . . . . . . | 6 | 2 | 2 | 3 | 0 |
| Groh, 3b . . . . . . | 3 | 1 | 1 | 0 | 5 |
| Roush, cf . . . . . | 2 | 1 | 2 | 2 | 0 |
| Chase, 2b . . . . . | 5 | 1 | 1 | 3 | 4 |
| Griffith, rf . . . . . | 6 | 1 | 2 | 4 | 0 |
| Wingo, c . . . . . . | 4 | 3 | 4 | 4 | 2 |
| Louden, ss . . . . | 5 | 0 | 2 | 3 | 0 |
| Chase, 1b . . . . . | 5 | 0 | 2 | 7 | 2 |
| Mathewson, p . . | 5 | 1 | 3 | 1 | 3 |
| **TOTALS:** | **41** | **10** | **19** | **27** | **14** |

|  | ab. | r. | h. | po. | a. |
|---|---|---|---|---|---|
| **CHICAGO** | | | | | |
| Flack, rf . . . . . | 4 | 2 | 1 | 1 | 0 |
| Doyle, 2b . . . . | 5 | 1 | 3 | 2 | 5 |
| Kelly, lf . . . . . | 5 | 2 | 1 | 4 | 0 |
| Saler, 1b . . . . . | 4 | 1 | 2 | 10 | 0 |
| Williams, cf . . | 5 | 0 | 4 | 2 | 0 |
| Wilson, c . . . . | 5 | 0 | 1 | 3 | 0 |
| Pechous, 3b . . | 4 | 0 | 1 | 2 | 2 |
| Wortman, ss . . | 4 | 0 | 0 | 3 | 5 |
| Brown, p . . . . | 4 | 2 | 2 | 0 | 2 |
| **a** Mollwitz . . . | 1 | 0 | 0 | 0 | 0 |
| **TOTALS:** | **41** | **8** | **15** | **27** | **14** |

**a** Batted for Pechous in ninth.

Cincinnati . . . .  0 1 2  1 2 2  0 1 1—10
Chicago . . . . . .  2 0 1  0 2 0  0 0 3—8

E: Chase, Wilson, Wortman. 2B: Griffith, Doyle, Groh, Saler, Mathewson, Neale, Pechous. 3B: Kelly, Roush, Flack. HR: Saler. SB: Neale, Groh, Roush. S: Groh. SF: Saler, Wingo, Roush. DP: Wortman, Doyle, Saler (2). LOB: Cincinnati 7, Chicago 8. First base on errors: Cincinnati 1, Chicago 1. BB: Off Mathewson 1, off Brown 1. ER: Off Brown 9, off Mathewson 8. HBP: By Brown (Roush). SO: By Mathewson 3, by Brown 2. WP: Mathewson. U: Rigler, Eason. T: 2:10.

## CHRISTOPHER (BIG SIX) MATHEWSON
Born August 12, 1880, at Factoryville, Pa.
Died October 7, 1925, at Saranac Lake, N.Y.
Height 6-1 1/2  Weight 195
Threw and batted right-handed.
Named to Hall of Fame, 1936.

| YEAR | CLUB | LEAGUE | G. | IP. | W. | L. | Pct. | ShO. | H. | R. | ER. | SO. | BB. | ERA. |
|------|------|--------|----|-----|----|----|------|------|----|----|-----|-----|-----|------|
| 1899 | Taunton | N. Eng. | 17 | — | 5 | 2 | .714 | — | — | — | — | — | — | — |
| 1900 | Norfolk | Va. | 22 | 187 | 20 | 2 | .909 | 4 | 119 | 59 | — | 128 | 27 | — |
| 1900 | New York (a) | Nat. | 6 | 34 | 0 | 3 | .000 | 0 | 34 | 32 | — | 15 | 20 | — |
| 1901 | New York | Nat. | 40 | 336 | 20 | 17 | .541 | 5 | 281 | 131 | — | 215 | 92 | — |
| 1902 | New York | Nat. | 34 | 276 | 14 | 17 | .452 | 8 | 241 | 114 | — | 162 | 74 | — |
| 1903 | New York | Nat. | 45 | 367 | 30 | 13 | .698 | 3 | 321 | 136 | — | 267 | 100 | — |
| 1904 | New York | Nat. | 48 | 368 | 33 | 12 | .733 | 4 | 306 | 120 | — | 212 | 78 | — |
| 1905 | New York | Nat. | 43 | 339 | 31 | 9 | .775 | 9 | 252 | 85 | — | 206 | 64 | — |
| 1906 | New York | Nat. | 38 | 267 | 22 | 12 | .647 | 7 | 262 | 100 | — | 128 | 77 | — |
| 1907 | New York | Nat. | 41 | 315 | 24 | 12 | .667 | 9 | 250 | 88 | — | 178 | 53 | — |
| 1908 | New York | Nat. | 56 | 391 | 37 | 11 | .771 | 12 | 281 | 85 | — | 259 | 42 | — |
| 1909 | New York | Nat. | 37 | 274 | 25 | 6 | .806 | 8 | 192 | 57 | — | 149 | 36 | — |
| 1910 | New York | Nat. | 38 | 319 | 27 | 9 | .750 | 2 | 291 | 98 | — | 190 | 57 | — |
| 1911 | New York | Nat. | 45 | 307 | 26 | 13 | .667 | 5 | 303 | 102 | — | 141 | 38 | — |
| 1912 | New York | Nat. | 43 | 310 | 23 | 12 | .657 | 0 | 311 | 107 | 73 | 134 | 34 | 2.12 |
| 1913 | New York | Nat. | 40 | 306 | 25 | 11 | .694 | 5 | 291 | 93 | 70 | 93 | 21 | 2.06 |
| 1914 | New York | Nat. | 41 | 312 | 24 | 13 | .648 | 5 | 314 | 133 | 104 | 80 | 23 | 3.00 |
| 1915 | New York | Nat. | 27 | 186 | 8 | 14 | .364 | 1 | 199 | 97 | 74 | 57 | 20 | 3.58 |
| 1916 | N.Y. (b) Cinn. | Nat. | 13 | 74 | 4 | 4 | .500 | 1 | 74 | 35 | 25 | 19 | 8 | 3.04 |
| Major League Totals | | | 635 | 4781 | 373 | 188 | .665 | 83 | 4203 | 1613 | — | 2505 | 837 | — |

a Joined Giants midseason, 1900. Turned back to Norfolk at end of campaign, but drafted by Cincinnati and traded to Giants for pitcher Amos Rusie.
b Traded with outfielder Edd Roush and infielder Bill McKechnie to Cincinnati for infielder Charles Herzog and outfielder Wade Killefer, July 20, 1916.

### WORLD SERIES RECORD

| YEAR | CLUB | LEAGUE | G. | IP. | W. | L. | Pct. | ShO. | H. | R. | ER. | SO. | BB. | ERA. |
|------|------|--------|----|-----|----|----|------|------|----|----|-----|-----|-----|------|
| 1905 | New York | Nat. | 3 | 27 | 3 | 0 | 1.000 | 3 | 14 | 0 | 0 | 18 | 1 | 0.00 |
| 1911 | New York | Nat. | 3 | 27 | 1 | 2 | .333 | 0 | 25 | 8 | 6 | 13 | 2 | 2.00 |
| 1912 | New York | Nat. | 3 | 28 2/3 | 0 | 2 | .000 | 0 | 23 | 11 | 5 | 10 | 5 | 1.57 |
| 1913 | New York | Nat. | 2 | 19 | 1 | 1 | .500 | 1 | 14 | 3 | 2 | 7 | 2 | 0.95 |
| World Series Totals | | | 11 | 101 2/3 | 5 | 5 | .500 | 4 | 76 | 22 | 13 | 48 | 10 | 1.15 |

Ty Cobb still had the glint in his eye as an outfielder for Connie Mack's Philadelphia Athletics, but by the end of his career, he and teammate Tris Speaker were on the bench.

# TY COBB

## *The Last Angry Man Leaves Quietly*

| | |
|---|---|
| **DATE:** September 12, 1928 | |
| **SITE:** Yankee Stadium, New York, New York | |
| **PITCHER:** Henry Johnson of New York Yankees | |
| **RESULT:** Pop out to shortstop Mark Koenig | |

**September 12, 1928, New York City**—Connie Mack, the gentlemanly manager of the Philadelphia Athletics, sitting ramrod stiff in his high celluloid collar and immaculate suit, motioned with his ever-present scorecard to the older man, sitting on the bench at the other end of the dugout.

"Ty, go up and hit for Jimmy," he said. Heads turned in the Philadelphia A's dugout.

For one thing, Mack almost always called everyone "Son." For another, here was arguably baseball's greatest hitter, now being sent up as an afterthought pinch-hitter in a game, and now a season, lost.

Ty Cobb nodded and went up to pick out his bat. Dykes was supposed to lead off the ninth inning of a game the A's already trailed, 5-3.

Cobb couldn't think about that now. His long and difficult career was finally at the end. The flame that had burned so hot and so brilliantly for so long was nearly out. He wasn't going to get back to a World Series.

"Cobb pinch-hits in A's loss to Yanks"

He stepped out of the dugout on a Friday afternoon at Yankee Stadium and the crowd of 50,000 erupted. Once the greatest player in baseball, he strode to the plate with the catcalls, the insults, the boos burning in his always sensitive ears.

There was a time when their hatred fueled him and drove him to colossal, monomaniacal heights of baseball excellence. Not now.

There was a bitterness in his mouth as he waited for a pitch. Denied again.

Maybe New York had had an extraordinary start to the 1928 season, winning 39 of its first 49 games—those 1927 Murderers' Row Yankees were still mostly intact. But once Mack's A's began to find themselves, they took over.

A clever blend of youth and experience, Mack's club put on a magnificent run, catching fire in July. Sparked by Lefty Grove's league-leading 24-win season and the combination of promising youngsters like Mickey Cochrane, Jimmy Foxx, and Al Simmons—all Hall of Famers—and old pros (and eventual Hall of Famers) like Cobb, Tris Speaker, and Eddie Collins, the A's came roaring back. By early September, they had taken over first place from Ruth and Gehrig and the mighty Yanks.

For Cobb, who came to Philadelphia only because he felt as though Mack could get him in one last World Series, this was what he'd hoped for.

But when the A's couldn't hold their ground and the Yankees climbed back into first place, it all changed. Heading into this make-or-break series in New York, the A's, a game and a half out and a tough road schedule ahead, needed a sweep to have a chance to catch the Yankees. And in the morning, on paper, it looked good. The A's started 24-game winner Grove, the best pitcher in baseball, while the Yanks' started Henry Johnson, a marginal right-hander who, in the old phrase, had left no footprints on the sands of time. Johnson, in fact, had missed the entire 1927 season with arm trouble and had just four big-league starts prior to this season.

But when the most important series of the season began in the Big Apple on a sunny September afternoon, Cobb and Speaker found themselves where Mack had put them since the middle of summer. On the bench. It made them sick.

Cobb had wanted to hang it up two seasons ago, after a difficult finish in Detroit as a player-manager and a betting controversy with the commissioner. Cobb and

Speaker had been accused of betting (and fixing) games in 1919 in a letter written by former pitcher Dutch Leonard.

The way the story went, Leonard told American League president Ban Johnson in the spring of 1926 that Cobb and Speaker had allegedly fixed a game late in the 1919 season.

Perhaps fearing a Cobb outburst, Johnson, waited until the season was over before he told Commissioner Kenesaw Mountain Landis of Leonard's charges. Landis suspended Cobb and Speaker for a while, then let them back on their respective rosters. Neither player was ever a manager again.

As a result, Cobb was ready to sue Landis. But when Mack came and visited him, the old man was able to convince Cobb that he had a team that could make a real run at the pennant. He also told him that he'd pay him a dollar more than Babe Ruth. Cobb couldn't say no.

Cobb and Mack got along surprisingly well. But the early moments had all the elements of a sparring session between two wary champions.

Former Philadelphia sportswriter Al Horwits recalled in Jerome Holtzman's fine *No Cheering in the Press Box* that "Cobb hated to be told what to do. At first, when he was playing right field and Connie (Mack) waved his scorecard at him, Cobb acted as though he didn't see it.

"But finally Connie got him over there, and the very next batter hit the ball right at Cobb. He didn't have to move to catch it. He said afterwards he would never challenge the old man again."

That was just how Mack remembered it, too.

"When Ty Cobb played his first game for the A's, I felt somewhat embarrassed," Mack wrote in his memoir, *My 66 Years in the Big Leagues*.

"Here was the greatest player of his time, twenty-two years as the star fielder with Detroit and six years its able manager. He was noted as an expert on the strong and weak points of all the batters of all the other teams. I hesitated in giving orders to this great of the greats.

"However, I realized that I was responsible for the strategy of the game. A rival batter came to the plate. I felt that Ty knew where to play him, but it seemed to me that he was playing too far to the right of the batter. I was about to signal my pitcher to put the ball where, if hit, it would go far to the left of where Ty was standing.

"Standing up in the dugout, I waved to Ty with my scorecard to move over to the left. Everybody saw the signal. Even the pitcher turned and looked. What would the great Cobb do? Would he follow his judgment or would he accept my decision? He saluted me as a soldier salutes a general and followed orders.

"Now I was on the spot. If the batter hit the ball to where Ty had been standing, I'd certainly look silly. Ty had barely reached the position I had designated when the batter walloped the ball. Where did it go? Right into the hands of Ty Cobb! Did I feel relieved? I'll say I did."

To Horwits, bringing Cobb and Speaker together for that 1928 season was a wise move—for business.

"Bringing Cobb and Speaker together in 1928 for their last year was a great piece of showmanship. They didn't win the pennant for Connie. In fact, they didn't even finish the season as regulars. But they did a lot of business and were a great draw on the road, too."

Cobb had himself a fine 1927 season, playing in 134 games, hitting .357, fifth in the league. He drove in 93 runs, not bad for a 41-year-old.

He tried for an encore in 1928 and hit decently. But the A's, like the rest of baseball, were no match for the Yankees. This series, at Yankee Stadium, was their last chance.

As expected, Mack's surging A's reached Yankees' no-name starter Johnson for two runs in the first, then added an unearned run in the fifth to stake the great Grove a commanding 3-0 lead.

But after the Yanks got to Grove for one run in the seventh, Cobb suspected what would happen next. He'd seen it too many times before.

While the two old war eagles, he and Speaker, had to sit and squirm, the A's just collapsed behind the tempestuous Grove in the bottom of the eighth. There was a Grove walk, a ground ball that bounced off Dykes's shins, then a wild throw past Jimmy Foxx at first to put a runner on third. The knot was tightening.

Groves wild-pitched the second run in, making a 3-2 game. When Lou Gehrig tried to duck out of the way of a Grove inside pitch, it clicked off his bat into left field for a lucky single.

The crowd was electric. After Gehrig went to second on a bad throw, up stepped Ruth with a chance to break it open.

Nobody hated Ruth more than Cobb, who hollered at him from the bench. This was it right here.

First, Ruth tried to cross up Grove by dropping down a surprise sacrifice bunt. It rolled foul by inches. On Grove's next pitch, Ruth drove the ball high and deep into the right-field seats for his 49th home run—he went on to whack 54 that season—and the race was all but over. The Yankee Stadium crowd burst into cheers for the Babe. Cobb sat and sizzled.

"A's pennant chances die, Cobb pops out in final at-bat"

Ruth had always gotten the better of Cobb. Once, in 1921, when Cobb was really giving it to Ruth from the Tiger dugout, Ruth clubbed seven home runs in a five-game series. To top it off, The Babe volunteered to come in and pitch in the last game of the series. He struck Cobb out.

Cobb had always hated the way Ruth's long-distance hits changed the game he had mastered. What bothered him more was the way Ruth was loved everywhere he went, by fans, newspapermen, everybody.

One year, Cobb, fed up with all the attention going to Ruth, told the newspapermen that he could play that game if he wanted to. With his Tigers stuck in last place having lost 14 of its first 19 games and Ruth grabbing headlines every day, the Tigers' star pulled Detroit News writer H. G. Salsinger and a few others aside before a May 5 game at Sportsman's Park in St. Louis. He told them to watch. He was going deep.

"Gentlemen," Cobb said, "I would like you to pay particular attention today because for the first time in my career, I will be deliberately going for home runs."

He got them, too. Cobb whacked three home runs and went 6-for-6 in a Tiger win. The next day, he hit two other balls out of the ballpark, giving him five in two games and a major-league record for total bases (16) that stood for years.

His point illustrated, Cobb then went back to his usual slashing style and hit just 17 more home runs over the remaining three and a half seasons of his career.

He could hear the bench jockeys as he approached the plate. Cobb took a long look around Yankee Stadium, the House Ruth Built. Why didn't anybody build a house for him? Cobb had more hits, more batting titles, more steals, more runs.

As he stepped in, Cobb knew he was hitting .324 in 95 games, which wasn't bad. But he and Speaker had barely played down the stretch as Mack went with the younger men. It was somebody else's team now. And he was starting to realize there would be no World Series.

It had been nearly 20 years since his last one in 1909, the last of three straight Series losses for Cobb's Tigers. He was just a kid then. He'd have lots of World Series ahead of him, he figured. Wrong.

Over his shoulder, he could see Mack had sent another veteran, future Hall of Famer Eddie Collins, out to the on-deck circle to hit next. Must be Old Home Week, he thought.

Cobb looked out at Henry Johnson and waited for the next pitch. He stood there, flexing his strange hands-apart grip on the bat, staring out at the young right-hander who was born in 1906, the year Cobb really hit the big time with Detroit.

With the pitch on him, Cobb swung for the final time, chasing a high pitch, lifting a popup into foul territory over and behind third base. Yankee shortstop Mark Koenig drifted over and made the catch.

When Collins also fouled out to Koenig, a carbon copy of Cobb's final out, pinch-hitter Walt French followed with a fly ball to Bob Meusel and the game—and the race—was over.

The Yanks' lead went to two and a half games and stayed there for the rest of the season.

After 3,034 games, 11,437 at bats, and 4,192 hits, Cobb never played in the majors again. Though there were two weeks left in the season, Cobb had vowed that once the A's were out of the race he would leave the team.

Once the team sadly left New York, their World Series hopes gone for good, that's just what he did.

# One Last Pop

| PHILADELPHIA | ab. | r. | h. | po. | a. | e. |
|---|---|---|---|---|---|---|
| Bishop, 2b ... | 4 | 0 | 1 | 2 | 3 | 0 |
| Haas, cf ..... | 3 | 1 | 0 | 2 | 0 | 0 |
| Cochrane, c .. | 4 | 1 | 3 | 6 | 0 | 0 |
| Simmons, lf . | 3 | 0 | 0 | 1 | 0 | 0 |
| Foxx, 1b .... | 4 | 1 | 1 | 9 | 0 | 0 |
| Miller, rf .... | 4 | 0 | 1 | 1 | 0 | 0 |
| Dykes, 3b ... | 2 | 0 | 0 | 1 | 1 | 1 |
| **a** Cobb ..... | 1 | 0 | 0 | 0 | 0 | 0 |
| Boley, ss .... | 2 | 0 | 1 | 2 | 4 | 0 |
| **b** E. Collins .. | 1 | 0 | 0 | 0 | 0 | 0 |
| Grove, p .... | 2 | 0 | 0 | 0 | 1 | 0 |
| **c** French .... | 1 | 0 | 0 | 0 | 0 | 0 |
| **TOTALS:** | 31 | 3 | 7 | 24 | 9 | 1 |

| NEW YORK | ab. | r. | h. | po. | a. | e. |
|---|---|---|---|---|---|---|
| Combs, cf ... | 3 | 1 | 1 | 5 | 0 | 0 |
| Koenig, ss ... | 4 | 1 | 2 | 3 | 2 | 0 |
| Gehrig, 1b ... | 4 | 1 | 1 | 6 | 0 | 0 |
| Ruth, rf ..... | 3 | 1 | 1 | 3 | 0 | 0 |
| Meusel, lf ... | 4 | 0 | 1 | 2 | 0 | 0 |
| Lazzeri, 2b .. | 4 | 1 | 0 | 2 | 0 | 0 |
| Gazella, 3b .. | 2 | 0 | 1 | 1 | 2 | 1 |
| Bengough, c . | 2 | 0 | 0 | 5 | 0 | 0 |
| **d** Paschal .... | 1 | 0 | 0 | 0 | 0 | 0 |
| P. Collins, c .. | 1 | 0 | 0 | 0 | 1 | 0 |
| Johnson, p ... | 3 | 0 | 0 | 0 | 2 | 0 |
| **TOTALS:** | 31 | 5 | 7 | 27 | 7 | 1 |

**a** Batted for Dykes in ninth.    **b** Batted for Boley in ninth.    **c** Batted for Grove in ninth.
**d** Batted for Bengough in seventh.

```
Philadelphia .  2 0 0   1 0 0   0 0 0—3
New York  ..  0 0 0   0 0 0   1 4 x—5
```

RBI: Cochrane 1, Simmons 1, Boley 1, Gehrig 1, Ruth 2, Paschal 1. 2B: Gazella. 3B: Cochrane.
HR: Ruth. SB: Gazella. S: Simmons, Boley, Grove. LOB: Philadelphia 6, New York 6. BB: Off
Johnson 1, Grove 4. SO: By Johnson 3, Grove 5. HBP: By Johnson (Haas). WP: Grove. U: Nallin,
Dineen, McGowan, Owens. T: 1:55.

## TYRUS RAYMOND (GEORGIA PEACH) COBB
Born December 18, 1886, at Narrows, Banks County, Ga.
Died July 17, 1961, at Atlanta, Ga.
Height 6-03/4  Weight 175
Threw right and batted left-handed.
Named to Hall of Fame, 1936.

| YEAR | CLUB | LEAGUE | POS. | G. | AB. | R. | H. | 2B. | 3B. | HR. | RBI. | B.A. | PO. | A. | E. | F.A. |
|---|---|---|---|---|---|---|---|---|---|---|---|---|---|---|---|---|
| 1904 | Augusta | Sally | OF | 37 | 135 | 14 | 32 | 6 | 0 | 1 | — | .237 | 62 | 9 | 4 | .946 |
| 1904 | Anniston (a) | S.E. | OF | 22 | — | — | — | — | — | — | — | .370 | — | — | — | — |
| 1905 | Augusta | Sally | OF | 104 | 411 | 60 | 134 | — | — | — | — | .326 | 149 | 15 | 13 | .927 |
| 1905 | Detroit | Amer. | OF | 41 | 150 | 19 | 36 | 6 | 0 | 1 | 12 | .240 | 85 | 6 | 4 | .958 |
| 1906 | Detroit | Amer. | OF | 97 | 350 | 44 | 112 | 13 | 7 | 1 | 41 | .320 | 107 | 14 | 9 | .931 |
| 1907 | Detroit | Amer. | OF | 150 | 605 | 97 | 212 | 29 | 15 | 5 | 116 | .350 | 238 | 30 | 11 | .961 |
| 1908 | Detroit | Amer. | OF | 150 | 581 | 88 | 188 | 36 | 20 | 4 | 101 | .324 | 212 | 23 | 14 | .944 |
| 1909 | Detroit | Amer. | OF | 156 | 573 | 116 | 216 | 33 | 10 | 9 | 115 | .377 | 222 | 24 | 14 | .946 |
| 1910 | Detroit | Amer. | OF | 140 | 509 | 106 | 196 | 36 | 13 | 8 | 88 | .385 | 305 | 18 | 14 | .958 |
| 1911 | Detroit | Amer. | OF | 146 | 591 | 147 | 248 | 47 | 24 | 8 | 144 | .420 | 376 | 24 | 18 | .957 |
| 1912 | Detroit | Amer. | OF | 140 | 553 | 119 | 227 | 30 | 23 | 7 | 90 | .410 | 324 | 21 | 22 | .940 |
| 1913 | Detroit | Amer. | OF | 122 | 428 | 70 | 167 | 18 | 16 | 4 | 65 | .390 | 262 | 22 | 16 | .947 |
| 1914 | Detroit | Amer. | OF | 97 | 345 | 69 | 127 | 22 | 11 | 2 | 57 | .368 | 117 | 8 | 10 | .949 |
| 1915 | Detroit | Amer. | OF | 156 | 563 | 144 | 208 | 31 | 13 | 3 | 95 | .369 | 328 | 22 | 18 | .951 |
| 1916 | Detroit | Amer. | OF | 145 | 542 | 113 | 201 | 31 | 10 | 5 | 67 | .371 | 325 | 18 | 17 | .953 |
| 1917 | Detroit | Amer. | OF | 152 | 588 | 107 | 225 | 44 | 23 | 7 | 108 | .383 | 373 | 27 | 11 | .973 |
| 1918 | Detroit | Amer. | OF-1B | 111 | 421 | 83 | 161 | 19 | 14 | 3 | 64 | .382 | 359 | 26 | 9 | .977 |
| 1919 | Detroit | Amer. | OF | 124 | 497 | 92 | 191 | 36 | 13 | 1 | 69 | .384 | 272 | 19 | 8 | .973 |
| 1920 | Detroit | Amer. | OF | 112 | 428 | 86 | 143 | 28 | 8 | 2 | 63 | .334 | 246 | 8 | 9 | .966 |
| 1921 | Detroit | Amer. | OF | 128 | 507 | 124 | 197 | 37 | 16 | 12 | 101 | .389 | 301 | 27 | 10 | .970 |
| 1922 | Detroit | Amer. | OF | 137 | 526 | 99 | 211 | 42 | 16 | 4 | 99 | .401 | 330 | 14 | 7 | .980 |
| 1923 | Detroit | Amer. | OF | 145 | 556 | 103 | 189 | 40 | 7 | 6 | 88 | .340 | 362 | 14 | 12 | .969 |
| 1924 | Detroit | Amer. | OF | 155 | 625 | 115 | 211 | 38 | 10 | 4 | 74 | .338 | 417 | 12 | 6 | .986 |
| 1925 | Detroit | Amer. | OF | 121 | 415 | 97 | 157 | 31 | 12 | 12 | 102 | .378 | 267 | 9 | 15 | .948 |
| 1926 | Detroit (b) | Amer. | OF | 79 | 233 | 48 | 79 | 18 | 5 | 4 | 62 | .339 | 109 | 4 | 6 | .950 |
| 1927 | Philadelphia | Amer. | OF | 134 | 490 | 104 | 175 | 32 | 7 | 5 | 93 | .357 | 243 | 9 | 8 | .969 |
| 1928 | Philadelphia | Amer. | OF | 95 | 353 | 54 | 114 | 27 | 4 | 1 | 40 | .323 | 154 | 7 | 6 | .964 |
| Major League Totals | | | | 3033 | 11429 | 2244 | 4191 | 724 | 297 | 118 | 1954 | .367 | 6394 | 406 | 274 | .961 |

a League not in Organized Ball.
b Released by Detroit Tigers November 2, 1926, and signed with Philadelphia Athletics, February, 1927.

### WORLD SERIES RECORD

| YEAR | CLUB | LEAGUE | POS. | G. | AB. | R. | H. | 2B. | 3B. | HR. | RBI. | B.A. | PO. | A. | E. | F.A. |
|---|---|---|---|---|---|---|---|---|---|---|---|---|---|---|---|---|
| 1907 | Detroit | Amer. | OF | 5 | 20 | 1 | 4 | 0 | 1 | 0 | 0 | .200 | 9 | 0 | 0 | 1.000 |
| 1908 | Detroit | Amer. | OF | 5 | 19 | 3 | 7 | 1 | 0 | 0 | 4 | .368 | 3 | 0 | 2 | .600 |
| 1909 | Detroit | Amer. | OF | 7 | 26 | 3 | 6 | 3 | 0 | 0 | 6 | .231 | 8 | 0 | 1 | .889 |
| World Series Totals | | | | 17 | 65 | 7 | 17 | 4 | 1 | 0 | 10 | .262 | 20 | 0 | 3 | .870 |

Jackie Robinson looks happy—and relaxed—after another win for the Brooklyn Dodgers.

# JACKIE ROBINSON

## *Fire's Out for Trailblazer Robinson*

| | |
|---|---|
| **DATE:** October 10, 1956 (Game Seven of the 1956 World Series) | |
| **SITE:** Ebbets Field, Brooklyn, New York | |
| **PITCHER:** Johnny Kucks of New York Yankees | |
| **RESULT:** Strikeout to end game, series, season | |

**October 10, 1956, Brooklyn, New York**—When he stepped out of the Ebbets Field dugout, the stadium was emptying and it seemed like he could hear most of the city crying.

Broken-hearted Dodger fans were again cursing their World Series luck, heading home sadly to a lousy dinner and another lousy off-season. As it turned out, Brooklyn's very last World Series game in cozy Ebbets Field was just about to come to close.

Jackie Robinson, due up third, couldn't have known what lay ahead for him or his franchise. Not just the last at-bat of the World Series and the last at-bat of the 1956 season. It would also be his final at-bat in the big leagues. The journey that had begun with so much drama so long ago was finally over. What a rotten ending. To think that the night before, early Tuesday evening, his dramatic 10th-inning hit against the New York Yankees—repaying them for an earlier insult—had forced a Game Seven here in Brooklyn, lifting the hearts of Dodger Nation. That title last year wasn't a fluke; they were going to win it again. After all those losses to the Yankees, Brooklyn was going to start a dynasty of its own.

There was going to be one more game for the baseball championship. Yeah, Dem Bums were coming back, starting 27-game winner Don Newcombe in ol' Ebbets Field against whomever the Bronx Bombers would trot out. Didn't matter. Brooklyn was going to do it again and send that stuck-up, pinstriped mob back across town to stew on a Game Seven loss all winter.

Except it didn't quite work that way. Not at all.

Robinson knelt down in the on-deck circle and could hear how quiet the park was. Ebbets Field wasn't usually like that. Even in a loss. The hurt was palpable.

In Game Five, New York's Don Larsen had thrown a perfect game, stilling the near-dead Dodger bats and moving the Yankees within a victory of the title. But in Game Six, the Dodgers fought back with one of the most stirring triumphs in franchise history to set the stage for this.

On Tuesday, Dodgers' manager Walt Alston had sent reliever Clem Labine to the mound to face New York fireballer Bob Turley and the two of them put on a pitching display to nearly rival Larsen's brilliance. Labine hadn't started a game since the second game of the 1951 playoffs vs. the Giants and Turley was razor sharp. And neither team was hitting.

Through nine pressure-packed scoreless innings, the tension rose over Ebbets Field like a magnetic field. In the bottom of the eighth, Labine himself clouted a double, the only extra-base hit of the day for the weak-hitting Dodgers.

After two outs, Yankees' manager Casey Stengel ordered Duke Snider walked to put it all on Jackie Robinson's shoulders, to see if the proudest Dodger could force a Game Seven with a clutch hit. The Brooklyn fans were aghast. True, it hadn't been that great a season at the plate for Robinson—he hit only .275 and in the Series, he was just 6-for-24 (.250.) And this time, the Yankee fireballer won the battle, getting Robinson to pop out, preserving the scoreless tie.

The situation repeated itself in the 10th, the game still scoreless. Again, Stengel ordered Snider walked to face Robinson with the game on the line. Triumphantly, Robinson came through, lashing a rocket over the head of Yankees' left fielder Enos Slaughter—his final big-league hit—and Junior Gilliam came all the way around to give the Dodgers a 1-0 10-inning thriller.

After a victory like that, how could the Dodgers *not* win? Robinson quietly shook his head. He looked up at the scoreboard and saw all zeroes on the Brooklyn side. The Yankees had a run for every inning, leading 9-0. It all seemed a cruel joke.

He took one last long look around the ballpark, the signs along the left-field wall, "Brass Rail," and "Luckies Taste Better," and "Stadlers" and, of course, the "Van Heusen Shirts" sign out in right-center field.

He could see the two-tiered stands, the World Series banners ruffling emptily in the cool October breeze, all nearly deserted now. There had been so much optimism in the place just a couple hours ago. Where did it all go wrong? In his very first big-league season—1947—Jackie Robinson had led the Dodgers into the World Series and they lost to New York in seven games. Here he was, leaving the same way. Well, almost the same.

In that 1947 World Series, the Yankees broke it open at the finish of that Game Seven to take a 5-2 win and take the title. At least, it was close for a while. Wednesday's box score wouldn't be as kind.

At first, it looked so good for the Dodgers. They were going to start 27-game winner Don Newcombe while New York manager Casey Stengel decided to bypass veteran ace Whitey Ford to go with skinny right-hander Johnny Kucks, an 18-game winner during the regular season. Kucks wasn't bad but he hadn't been able to win a game in over a month.

Though Newcombe bore the tag of a man who couldn't win the big one, surely he'd shake that 0-3 World Series mark here. This was a different Dodger team, wasn't it?

Maybe not. There were indications that Newcombe might not have been the Dodgers' best choice. When he had been shelled earlier in the Series, he was so upset about it that he got into a brawl with a parking lot attendant on the way home. His final World Series start wasn't much better.

Hank Bauer opened the game with a single and stole second. Newcombe fanned Billy Martin and then Mickey Mantle. He got an 0-2 count on Yogi Berra, just one strike away from getting out of the inning unscathed. But his third pitch to the little catcher was one he'd always regret. He fired a high fastball, a fat one, and Berra lined it over the right-field fence. 2-0, New York.

In the third, Berra did it to him again, ripping another two-run homer to make it 4-0, Yankees. The Brooklyn fans were crestfallen.

When Elston Howard blasted a Newcombe pitch into the seats in the fourth to make it 5-0, Alston had seen enough and gave him the hook.

And so, from the sound of it, had Brooklyn's faithless. As Newcombe slowly walked off the mound, the Dodger fans cut loose with such a chorus of boos, even the Yankees were appalled.

"I feel great that we won," Whitey Ford said afterwards, "but it was awful the way the fans booed him. Why should they boo a guy who did so much for them this year?"

But Newcombe was a good symbol for the Dodgers on this day, Robinson could see that. He was one of the best pitchers in baseball, everybody knew that. And the Dodgers were one of baseball's best teams. But they weren't quite as good as the Yankees. And never would be. This final Yankee-Dodger World Series win—this 1956 title—assured that.

Writing for the *New York Herald Tribune*, the famed columnist Red Smith began his column with the departure of Newcombe, too.

"This is a game for boys, and Don Newcombe is no kid. He is large and grumpy and not necessarily the most cuddly character in baseball. He is mean to hitters and a soft touch for gossips who have made him the victim of a cruel slander. Because the Dodgers' big pitcher can win 27 games in the National League but has never won one in a World Series, they call him a coward, a choke-up guy.

"It isn't true, but now he may never have a chance to prove it false. . . . They booed Newcombe out of the park."

"'Calling all parking lot attendants,' the funnymen in the press box were shouting as the big guy shambled off. 'All parking lot attendants—take cover!' It wasn't exactly hilarious."

Robinson could feel that anger, that sense of betrayal, kneeling in the on-deck circle, looking at Kucks. Thanks to that 9-0 score, the same as a forfeit, Robinson wondered how many sarcastic sportswriters would note it in their dispatches the next day. Many did.

Robinson thought about the other times he'd faced the Yankees in the World Series. Five different times in a 10-year career. He lost in five games in 1941 and 1949 and lost in seven in 1947 and 1952. Now this. A Game Seven loss in 1956. Damn.

He looked up to see Snider rifle a shot back through the box, only the Dodgers' third hit off Kucks. It was now up to him. He dug in, looked out at the right-hander, saw Berra behind him, Newcombe's tormentor, and tried to focus. It went by too quickly.

*"Dodger despair: Robinson goes down swinging"*

Suddenly he had two strikes on him and Kucks's pitch was on its way, sinking and twisting. Robinson swung and missed.

The ball hit the dirt, Berra trapped it and Robinson had to run. He got a couple steps off, saw Berra's throw snap into Bill Skowron's mitt, and stopped. It was over. All over. The Yankees were world champs again. Brooklyn's reign as world champs lasted but a year. A flukey year. Robinson's heart ached as he watched the Yankees celebrate again. On his field.

A little over two months later—64 days to be exact—the Dodgers, figuring it was time to break up their aging club, dealt Robinson—with no warning or previous discussion—to the New York Giants for Dick Littlefield and $30,000. Everyone, including Jackie, was shocked by the move.

"It is impossible to think of Robinson except as a Dodger," wrote Red Smith in the *Herald-Tribune*. "Other players move from team to team and can change uniform as casually as the Madison Avenue space cadet sheds his weekday flannels for his weekend Bermuda shorts. His arrival in Brooklyn was a turning point in the history and the character of the game; it may not be stretching things to say it was a turning point in the history of this country."

One month later, Robinson had decided to retire. Instead of sharing the news with the New York press, he cashed in his chips and sold his exclusive story to *Look* magazine, stiffing the voracious newspapermen who, throughout his career, had built him into a folk hero.

*"Dodgers great Robinson ends series, season, career with whiff"*

Smith, naturally, was one of the first to let off steam.

"The fact that he gave [The Dodgers] full value on the field and the fact that after 11 years, they sold his contract without consulting him, these do not alter the fact that everything he has he owes to the club," he wrote. "If it is true that Jackie Robinson has, for a price, deliberately crossed his friends and employers past and present, then it requires an eloquent advocate, indeed to make a convincing defense for him. From here, no defense at all is discernible."

That was nothing. The next year, the team left Brooklyn forever.

The strikeout was somewhat unusual for Robinson, a player who fanned just 291 times in 4,877 big-league at-bats. It was a heck of a way to end a World Series, a season, a career.

It was also, some fans noted later, Kucks's only strikeout of the game.

# Sorry, Jackie

## 7th Game

### NEW YORK ( A. )

| | ab. | r. | h. | po. | a. |
|---|---|---|---|---|---|
| Bauer, rf | 5 | 1 | 1 | 0 | 0 |
| Martin, 2b | 5 | 2 | 2 | 2 | 6 |
| Mantle, cf | 4 | 1 | 1 | 0 | 0 |
| Berra, c | 3 | 3 | 2 | 1 | 1 |
| Skowron,1b | 5 | 1 | 1 | 16 | 1 |
| Howard, lf | 5 | 1 | 2 | 2 | 0 |
| McDougald, ss | 4 | 0 | 1 | 3 | 3 |
| Carey, 3b | 3 | 0 | 0 | 2 | 2 |
| Kucks, p | 3 | 0 | 0 | 1 | 2 |
| **TOTALS:** | 37 | 9 | 10 | 27 | 15 |

### BROOKLYN ( N. )

| | ab. | r. | h. | po. | a. |
|---|---|---|---|---|---|
| Gilliam, 2b | 4 | 0 | 0 | 6 | 2 |
| Reese, ss | 2 | 0 | 0 | 2 | 5 |
| Snider, cf | 4 | 0 | 2 | 1 | 0 |
| Robinson, 3b | 3 | 0 | 0 | 0 | 1 |
| Hodges, 1b | 3 | 0 | 0 | 10 | 2 |
| Amoros, lf | 3 | 0 | 0 | 0 | 0 |
| Furillo, lf | 3 | 0 | 1 | 0 | 0 |
| Campanella, c | 3 | 0 | 0 | 8 | 0 |
| Newcombe, p | 1 | 0 | 0 | 0 | 1 |
| Bessent, p | 0 | 0 | 0 | 0 | 0 |
| **a** Mitchell | 1 | 0 | 0 | 0 | 0 |
| Craig, p | 0 | 0 | 0 | 0 | 0 |
| Roebuck, p | 0 | 0 | 0 | 0 | 0 |
| **b** Walker | 1 | 0 | 0 | 0 | 0 |
| Erskine, p | 0 | 0 | 0 | 0 | 0 |
| **TOTALS:** | 28 | 0 | 3 | 27 | 11 |

**a** Grounded out for Bessent in sixth.  **b** Grounded out for Roebuck in eighth.

| | | |
|---|---|---|
| New York [A] | 2 0 2   1 0 0   4 0 0 | 9 |
| Brooklyn [N] | 0 0 0   0 0 0   0 0 0 | 0 |

E: Reese. RBI: Berra 4, Howard, Skowron 4. 2B: Mantle, Howard. HR: Berra 2, Howard, Skowron. SB: Bauer. S: Kucks. DP: Kucks, Martin, Skowron; McDougald, Skowron. LOB: New York [A] 6, Brooklyn [N] 4.

## PITCHING

BB: Newcombe 1 (Carey), Bessent 1 (Berra), Craig 2 (Mantle, Berra), Kucks 3 (Reese 2 , Robinson). SO: Newcombe 4 (Martin, Mantle 2, Skowron), Bessent 1 (Kucks), Roebuck 3 (Carey, Martin, Mantle), Kucks 1 (Robinson). HO: Newcombe 5 in 3 (faced one batter in 4th). Bessent 2 in 3. Craig 2 in 0 (faced five batters in 7th). Roebuck 0 in 2. Erskine 0 in 1. R-ER: Newcombe, 5-5; Bessent 0-0; Craig 4-4; Roebuck 0-0; Erskine 0-0; Kucks 0-0. WP: Craig. W: Kucks. L: Newcombe. U: Boggess [N] plate; Napp [A] first base; Pinelli [N] second base; Soar [A] third base; Gorman [N] left field; Runge [A] right field. T: 2:19. A: 33,782  (paid). Receipts (net): $223,828.80.

## JACK ROOSEVELT ROBINSON

Born January 31, 1919, at Cairo, Ga.
Died October 24, 1972, at Stamford, Conn.
Height 5-11½ Weight 225
Threw and batted right-handed.
Named to Hall of Fame, 1962.

| YEAR | CLUB | LEAGUE | POS. | G. | AB. | R. | H. | 2B. | 3B. | HR. | RBI. | B.A. | PO. | A. | E. | F.A. |
|------|------|--------|------|-----|------|-----|------|-----|-----|-----|------|------|------|------|-----|------|
| 1946 | Montreal | Int. | 2B | 124 | 444 | 113 | 155 | 25 | 8 | 3 | 66 | .349 | 261 | 385 | 10 | .985 |
| 1947 | Brooklyn | Nat. | 1B | 151 | 590 | 125 | 175 | 31 | 5 | 12 | 48 | .297 | 1323 | 92 | 16 | .989 |
| 1948 | Brooklyn | Nat. | INF | 147 | 574 | 108 | 170 | 38 | 8 | 12 | 85 | .296 | 514 | 342 | 15 | .983 |
| 1949 | Brooklyn | Nat. | 2B | 156 | 593 | 122 | 203 | 38 | 12 | 16 | 124 | .342 | 395 | 421 | 16 | .981 |
| 1950 | Brooklyn | Nat. | 2B | 144 | 518 | 99 | 170 | 39 | 4 | 14 | 81 | .328 | 359 | 390 | 11 | .986 |
| 1951 | Brooklyn | Nat. | 2B | 153 | 548 | 106 | 185 | 33 | 7 | 19 | 88 | .338 | 390 | 435 | 7 | .992 |
| 1952 | Brooklyn | Nat. | 2B | 149 | 510 | 104 | 157 | 17 | 3 | 19 | 75 | .308 | 353 | 400 | 20 | .974 |
| 1953 | Brooklyn | Nat. | INF-OF | 136 | 484 | 109 | 159 | 34 | 7 | 12 | 95 | .329 | 238 | 126 | 6 | .984 |
| 1954 | Brooklyn | Nat. | INF-OF | 124 | 386 | 62 | 120 | 22 | 4 | 15 | 59 | .311 | 166 | 109 | 7 | .975 |
| 1955 | Brooklyn | Nat. | INF-OF | 105 | 317 | 51 | 81 | 6 | 2 | 8 | 36 | .256 | 100 | 183 | 10 | .966 |
| 1956 | Brooklyn (a) | Nat. | INF-OF | 117 | 357 | 61 | 98 | 15 | 2 | 10 | 43 | .275 | 169 | 230 | 9 | .978 |
| Major League Totals | | | | 1382 | 4877 | 947 | 1518 | 273 | 54 | 137 | 734 | .311 | 4007 | 2728 | 117 | .983 |

a Traded to New York Giants for pitcher Dick Littlefield and reported $35,000, December 13, 1945; Robinson announced retirement from game, January 5, 1957, canceling trade.

### WORLD SERIES RECORD

| YEAR | CLUB | LEAGUE | POS. | G. | AB. | R. | H. | 2B. | 3B. | HR. | RBI. | B.A. | PO. | A. | E. | F.A. |
|------|------|--------|------|-----|------|-----|------|-----|-----|-----|------|------|------|------|-----|------|
| 1947 | Brooklyn | Nat. | 1B | 7 | 27 | 3 | 7 | 2 | 0 | 0 | 3 | .259 | 49 | 6 | 0 | 1.000 |
| 1949 | Brooklyn | Nat. | 2B | 5 | 16 | 2 | 3 | 1 | 0 | 0 | 2 | .188 | 12 | 9 | 1 | .955 |
| 1952 | Brooklyn | Nat. | 2B | 7 | 23 | 4 | 4 | 0 | 0 | 1 | 2 | .174 | 10 | 20 | 0 | 1.000 |
| 1953 | Brooklyn | Nat. | OF | 6 | 25 | 3 | 8 | 2 | 0 | 0 | 2 | .320 | 8 | 0 | 0 | 1.000 |
| 1955 | Brooklyn | Nat. | 3B | 6 | 22 | 5 | 4 | 1 | 1 | 0 | 1 | .182 | 4 | 18 | 2 | .917 |
| 1956 | Brooklyn | Nat. | 3B | 7 | 24 | 5 | 6 | 1 | 0 | 1 | 2 | .250 | 5 | 12 | 0 | 1.000 |
| World Series Totals | | | | 38 | 137 | 22 | 32 | 7 | 1 | 2 | 12 | .234 | 88 | 65 | 3 | .981 |

His once-great arm gone, Walter Johnson could still hit and in his final major-league start, swatted a home run before getting the hook. It would have been a nice way to end a career.

Photo courtesy of National Baseball Hall of Fame Library, Cooperstown, New York.

# WALTER JOHNSON

## *The Big Train Reaches the Station*

**DATE:** September 12, 1927

**SITE:** Griffith Park, Washington, D.C.

**OPPONENT:** Sam Jones of the St. Louis Browns

**RESULT:** Knocked out of box in fourth inning

**September 12, 1927, Washington, D.C.**—He could see Bucky Harris get up from the bench. Walter Johnson sighed. It was over.

He looked over at St. Louis Browns' outfielder little Harry Rice at first, saw the 6-1 Browns' lead, and waited for Senators' manager Harris to get to the hill. After all those innings—5,925—stretched over 21 mostly brilliant seasons, the Big Train had reached the station.

Johnson had faced his final big-league hitter, just two years after he'd pitched the Senators to their only World Series title.

The lowly Browns had chased him with a three-run fourth on hits by Spencer Adams, doubles by Wally Gerber and pitcher Sad Sam Jones and Rice's RBI single. The express train of the Johnson fastball had slowed like a trolley. After 802 games, after nine straight 300-inning seasons—as just 13 innings away from a dozen straight years of 300-plus innings of work—the arm was finally gone. The numbers in this final outing—nine hits and six runs in three and a third innings of work—were just not the kind of thing you expected from Walter Johnson.

"Senators' 'Big Train' derailed by Browns early"

Two weeks from the end of the year, everyone could see that this would be his final season. His numbers—a 5-6 record, a 5.08 ERA, nearly three runs per game higher than his career totals (2.17) only 48 strikeouts in 107.2 innings—those weren't Walter Johnson numbers.

Remember, this was a guy who, in 1913, amassed one of the most extraordinary pitching records in baseball history, a 36-7 record with 29 complete games, 11 shutouts, 346 innings of work and most amazing of all, just 38 walks—in the entire season!

This last season hadn't been much fun for the veteran. A line drive off the bat of Joe Judge had broken his leg in preseason and the combination of that injury and his age, Johnson never regained his old form.

Though Harris gave him one last shot to even his record after a lengthy rest, Johnson didn't have enough stuff left to squeeze by the Browns, one of the weakest teams in the American League. He found that out early.

St. Louis reached Johnson for a run in the second inning, thanks to errors by Harris and Goose Goslin, Spencer Adams's single, and Gerber's sacrifice fly. The Browns added two more in the third on a single by Homer Rice, a George Sisler double, and a Ken Williams single.

Once Johnson was chased in the third, he heard the crowd applauding politely as he walked into the dugout. It wasn't much of a way to wind up a career.

He didn't get the loss though, thanks to St. Louis' atrocious defense, by far the worst in the majors in that 1927 season. The Browns made 248 errors and committed four against the Senators that afternoon, allowing Harris's club to rally for a win. By then, Johnson was just an onlooker.

Happily, his teammates rallied right away after he was knocked out of the box, making sure that he would not go out as the losing pitcher. The Senators pounced on St. Louis starter "Sad" Sam Jones for six runs to take back the lead.

There was one nice thing about what would be the final pitching performance of Johnson's career. When he stepped up to the plate in the third inning, he belted a

Jones pitch into the left-field seats, his second home run of the season and 24th and last of his big-league career.

So if this was to be his final season, he had homered in what looked like his final at-bat, just like Ted Williams would do—to considerably more fanfare—33 years later.

At the time, Johnson was batting .350 and ranked second among American League pitchers in hitting. He played 15 games as an outfielder for the Senators throughout his long career.

As it turned out, that wasn't Johnson's final at-bat. His very last big-league appearance came in a historic game against the New York Yankees on September 30, when Johnson was sent up as a pinch-hitter for Senators' starter Tom Zachary in the ninth inning.

The Senators were 85-68, a respectable third-place club, facing the Murderers' Row Yankees, who had won a record 109 ballgames. The Senators had to close out the season in New York while Babe Ruth was on a home run rampage. With a typically dramatic finish, Ruth had been clubbing home runs at a record pace. He came into the next-to-last game of the regular season having tied his own major-league mark of 59 home runs.

Senators' left-hander Zachary was the man charged with trying to keep Ruth from breaking the record. And he made it through seven innings without giving Ruth anything worth hitting. The Babe had managed two scratch singles and a walk.

"Johnson homers but knocked out of box; Senators rally"

But in the eighth, Ruth came up for what surely would be the final time that next-to-last day of the regular season. Amazingly, he picked a Zachary screwball off his shoetops and put it in the right-field bleachers for his record-setting 60th. The Yankee Stadium crowd erupted.

As W. B. Hanna described it in the *New York Tribune*, "This one broke over the plate and was a screwball until it met the Babe's unruly bat. After that, it was a minie ball. It didn't go high and it did go on a line. Bill Dineen, the umpire, crouched on the foul line and peered carefully into the distance to see whether it was fair or foul. It buried itself in the bleachers 15 rows from the top and was fair by not more than six inches. Still, it was fair, and the record was broken."

After Ruth had crossed home plate, the Bronx crowd started in on Zachary, a 31-year-old left-hander who'd been traded to the Senators from the Browns. They didn't let up, even after he got the third out and headed for the Senators dugout. He was due up in the ninth but Harris spared him any further humiliation. "Walter, go up and hit for him," Senators manager Bucky Harris said. And Johnson went to get his bat. He lifted a medium-range fly ball to the guy who had just gotten the New York crowd into a frenzy, Babe Ruth.

Two outs later, the game was over and so was Johnson's big-league playing career.

When he retired, he was second in lifetime wins (413), first in shutouts (110) and strikeouts (3,506), seventh in earned run average (2.17), fifth in complete games (532), third in innings pitched (5,923), and fourth in games pitched (802).

Some 74 years after his 110th shutout, he still has a 20-shutout lead on his closest rival, Hall of Famer Grover Cleveland Alexander, who threw 90. Of modern era pitchers, Warren Spahn heads the list with 63.

Johnson went on to manage the Senators from 1929 to 1932 and the Cleveland Indians from 1933 to 1935. He was elected to the Baseball Hall of Fame in 1936 and died of a brain tumor 10 years later.

In his prime, his peers said there was nobody better.

"Did you ever see those pitching machines they have?" asked former Detroit Tigers outfielder Sam "Wahoo" Crawford in *The Glory of Their Times*. "That's what Walter Johnson always reminded me of, one of those compressed air pitching machines. Boy, what a pitcher [he] was. He was the best I ever faced."

*"Senators' rally saves Johnson from final-game loss"*

His Tiger teammate, Davy Jones—the first batter to face Johnson in a big-league game—agreed.

"Boy, could he fire that ball. He had those long arms, absolutely the longest arms I ever saw. They were like whips; that's what they were. He'd whip that ball in there."

Yet he had a gentle spirit. Shirley Povich, the esteemed baseball writer of the *Washington Post* who had seen Johnson's entire career, said this at his passing.

"Walter Johnson, more than any other ballplayer, probably more than any other athlete, professional or amateur, became the symbol of gentlemanly conduct in the battle heat. Here was the man who never argued with an umpire, never cast a frowning look at an error-making teammate, never presumed that it was his right to win, was as unperturbed in defeat."

Povich marveled at his kindness with fans with a story that has lived on—just like the Big Train.

"Joe Judge, Johnson's roommate, had persuaded the 'Big Train' to go to a movie after dinner," he wrote. "Leaving the dining room, Johnson was button-holed by a fan in the lobby. Judge, standing apart, watched them talk for 15 minutes.

"When Johnson finally broke away, Judge was exasperated. 'We might not make the last show now. What on earth were you two talking about?'

"That fellow," said Johnson, "said he was from Kansas and was asking about my sister. I had to be nice to him."

"I never knew you had a sister," Judge said.

"That's right," said Walter, "I don't, but I had to be nice to him."

# Big Train Comes to a Halt

## ST. LOUIS

| | ab. | r. | h. | po. | a. | e. |
|---|---|---|---|---|---|---|
| O'Rourke, 3b ... | 3 | 0 | 1 | 3 | 1 | 0 |
| Mellilo, 2b ..... | 2 | 0 | 0 | 3 | 3 | 0 |
| H. Rice, rf ..... | 5 | 2 | 2 | 2 | 2 | 0 |
| Sisler, 1b ...... | 5 | 1 | 4 | 7 | 1 | 1 |
| Williams, lf, cf . | 5 | 0 | 1 | 2 | 0 | 0 |
| Bennett, cf, lf ... | 4 | 0 | 1 | 2 | 0 | 0 |
| Dixon, c ....... | 3 | 1 | 0 | 2 | 1 | 0 |
| Adams, 2b, 3b .. | 4 | 1 | 2 | 0 | 1 | 2 |
| Gerber, ss ...... | 2 | 1 | 1 | 2 | 5 | 1 |
| Jones, p ....... | 4 | 1 | 1 | 1 | 1 | 0 |
| **TOTALS:** | **37** | **7** | **13** | **24** | **15** | **4** |

## WASHINGTON

| | ab. | r. | h. | po. | a. | e. |
|---|---|---|---|---|---|---|
| S. Rice, rf .. | 5 | 1 | 2 | 2 | 0 | 0 |
| Harris, 2b .. | 5 | 1 | 2 | 3 | 3 | 1 |
| Ganzel, lf .. | 5 | 0 | 2 | 4 | 0 | 0 |
| Goslin, cf .. | 4 | 1 | 0 | 3 | 0 | 1 |
| Judge, 1b ... | 5 | 0 | 2 | 6 | 0 | 0 |
| Tate, c ..... | 5 | 1 | 1 | 6 | 3 | 0 |
| Bluege, 3b .. | 2 | 1 | 1 | 1 | 1 | 0 |
| Gillis, ss ... | 3 | 2 | 0 | 2 | 2 | 0 |
| Johnson, p .. | 1 | 1 | 1 | 0 | 0 | 0 |
| Burke, p ... | 0 | 0 | 0 | 0 | 0 | 0 |
| Braxton, p .. | 1 | 1 | 1 | 0 | 0 | 0 |
| **a** Speaker .. | 1 | 0 | 0 | 0 | 0 | 0 |
| **b** McNeely . | 0 | 1 | 0 | 0 | 0 | 0 |
| **TOTALS:** | **37** | **10** | **12** | **27** | **9** | **2** |

**a** Batted for Burke in fourth.    **b** Ran for Speaker in fourth.

```
St. Louis ......  0 1 2   3 0 0   1 0 0—7
Washington ...  0 0 1   6 2 1   0 0 x—10
```

2B: Sisler, Harris, Gerber, Jones, Tate, Braxton, H. Rice. HR: Johnson. SB: Sisler, Judge. S: Gerber, Goslin. DP: Harris to Gillis to Judge. LOB: St. Louis 6, Washington 7. BB: Off Jones 2, off Braxton 2. SO: By Jones 2, by Johnson 2, by Braxton 5. Hits: Off Johnson 9 in 1 1/3 innings, off Burke 0 in 2/3 inning, off Braxton 4 in 5 innings. HBP: By Jones (Bluege). W: Braxton. U: Van Graflan, Rowland, Geisel. T: 2:00.

## WALTER PERRY (BARNEY) JOHNSON
Born November 6, 1887, at Humboldt, Kan.
Died December 10, 1993, at Washington, D.C.
Height 6-1  Weight 200
Threw and batted right-handed.
Named to Hall of Fame, 1936.

| YEAR | CLUB | LEAGUE | G. | IP. | W. | L. | Pct. | ShO. | H.. | R. | ER. | SO. | BB. | ERA. |
|------|------|--------|----|-----|----|----|------|------|-----|----|-----|-----|-----|------|
| 1907 | Washington | Amer. | 14 | 111 | 5 | 9 | .357 | 2 | 100 | 35 | — | 70 | 16 | — |
| 1908 | Washington | Amer. | 36 | 257 | 14 | 14 | .500 | 6 | 196 | 75 | — | 160 | 52 | — |
| 1909 | Washington | Amer. | 40 | 297 | 13 | 25 | .342 | 4 | 247 | 112 | — | 164 | 84 | — |
| 1910 | Washington | Amer. | 45 | 374 | 25 | 17 | .595 | 8 | 262 | 92 | — | 313 | 76 | — |
| 1911 | Washington | Amer. | 40 | 322 | 25 | 13 | .658 | 6 | 292 | 119 | — | 207 | 70 | — |
| 1912 | Washington | Amer. | 50 | 368 | 32 | 12 | .727 | 7 | 259 | 89 | — | 303 | 76 | — |
| 1913 | Washington | Amer. | 48 | 346 | 36 | 7 | .837 | 12 | 232 | 56 | 44 | 243 | 38 | 1.14 |
| 1914 | Washington | Amer. | 51 | 372 | 28 | 18 | .609 | 10 | 287 | 88 | 71 | 225 | 74 | 1.72 |
| 1915 | Washington | Amer. | 47 | 337 | 27 | 13 | .675 | 8 | 258 | 83 | 58 | 203 | 56 | 1.55 |
| 1916 | Washington | Amer. | 48 | 371 | 25 | 20 | .556 | 3 | 290 | 105 | 78 | 228 | 82 | 1.09 |
| 1917 | Washington | Amer. | 47 | 328 | 23 | 16 | .590 | 8 | 259 | 105 | 83 | 188 | 67 | 2.28 |
| 1918 | Washington | Amer. | 39 | 325 | 23 | 13 | .639 | 8 | 241 | 71 | 46 | 162 | 70 | 1.27 |
| 1919 | Washington | Amer. | 39 | 290 | 20 | 14 | .588 | 7 | 235 | 73 | 48 | 147 | 51 | 1.49 |
| 1920 | Washington | Amer. | 21 | 144 | 8 | 10 | .444 | 4 | 135 | 68 | 50 | 78 | 27 | 3.13 |
| 1921 | Washington | Amer. | 35 | 264 | 17 | 14 | .548 | 1 | 265 | 122 | 103 | 143 | 92 | 3.51 |
| 1922 | Washington | Amer. | 41 | 280 | 15 | 16 | .484 | 4 | 283 | 115 | 93 | 105 | 99 | 2.99 |
| 1923 | Washington | Amer. | 42 | 261 | 17 | 12 | .586 | 3 | 263 | 112 | 101 | 130 | 69 | 3.48 |
| 1924 | Washington | Amer. | 38 | 278 | 23 | 7 | .767 | 6 | 233 | 97 | 84 | 158 | 77 | 2.72 |
| 1925 | Washington | Amer. | 30 | 229 | 20 | 7 | .741 | 3 | 211 | 95 | 78 | 108 | 78 | 3.07 |
| 1926 | Washington | Amer. | 33 | 262 | 15 | 16 | .484 | 2 | 259 | 120 | 105 | 125 | 73 | 3.61 |
| 1927 | Washington | Amer. | 18 | 108 | 5 | 6 | .455 | 1 | 113 | 70 | 61 | 48 | 26 | 5.08 |
| 1928 | Newark | Int. | 1 | 0 | 0 | 0 | .000 | 0 | 0 | 0 | 0 | 0 | 1 | 0.00 |
| Major League Totals | | | 802 | 5924 | 416 | 279 | .599 | 113 | 4920 | 1902 | 1103 | 3508 | 1353 | — |

### WORLD SERIES RECORD

| YEAR | CLUB | LEAGUE | G. | IP. | W. | L. | Pct. | H. | R. | ER. | SO. | BB. | ERA. |
|------|------|--------|----|-----|----|----|------|----|----|-----|-----|-----|------|
| 1924 | Washington | Amer. | 3 | 24 | 1 | 2 | .333 | 30 | 10 | 6 | 20 | 11 | 2.25 |
| 1925 | Washington | Amer. | 3 | 26 | 2 | 1 | .667 | 26 | 10 | 6 | 15 | 4 | 2.08 |
| World Series Totals | | | 6 | 50 | 3 | 3 | .500 | 56 | 20 | 12 | 35 | 15 | 2.16 |

Ironically enough, the final hit of Shoeless Joe Jackson's big-league career, a double, won a game for teammate Dickie Kerr, the only White Sox pitcher able to win in the fixed 1919 World Series with the Cincinnati Reds.

Photo courtesy of National Baseball Hall of Fame Library, Cooperstown, New York.

# JOE JACKSON

*Shoeless Joe Gets Called Out*

**DATE:** September 27, 1920

**SITE:** Comiskey Field, Chicago, Illinois

**PITCHER:** George Hauss of the Detroit Tigers

**RESULT:** Game-winning double

**September 27, 1920, Chicago**—By now, the noise was deafening. So persistent, so unmistakable, there seemed to be no way to keep it quiet any longer.

"Shoeless Joe" Jackson stepped out of the dugout at Comiskey Field and looked around him. He could just feel it.

The season was almost over. They were just a game behind the Cleveland Indians, just one game, and they could do it. Here it was, the sixth inning of a scoreless duel with Detroit and a win might put them right at the top of the standings.

He hefted his trusty 48-ounce bat, "Black Betsy" and looked out at George "Hooks" Dauss, the Detroit Tigers' starter, who had just hit Buck Weaver with a pitch.

With No. 3 hitter Eddie Collins up next, maybe Collins could get Weaver into scoring position and Jackson would get a chance to give his club, charging hard at the American League pennant, the lead. Not only in this game but also in the American League race.

Jackson hefted the bat again. It was hard to think about only baseball. He wasn't reading the newspapers, that was for sure. Shoeless Joe couldn't read. But he could hear the talk. Everywhere he went. He knew this kettle was about to boil over.

Ever since Jackson and the rest of Kid Gleason's heavily favored Chicago "Black Sox" had fumbled away the 1919 World Series to the Cincinnati Reds, there had been talk in town that things weren't on the square. Of course, they weren't.

And now, thanks to the damn Cubs and their gambling talk, it was everywhere. It wouldn't go away. Ever.

Back at the start of the month, there was a story in the *Chicago Tribune* about an attempted fix of a midweek game between the Cubs and Phillies. Cubs management, eager to dispel that notion that there was anything shady about that game—they'd seen the World Series the year before—pitched ace Grover Cleveland Alexander out of turn and even offered him a $500 bonus if he won. But Alexander lost. The stench from the story seemed to linger in the Windy City. A week later, with the White Sox surging, the *Tribune*'s I. E. Sanborn was able to write like a prophet.

"Procrastination has proven the thief of something more valuable than time in the case of professional baseball versus gambling," he wrote. "It has cost the game a considerable portion of its good reputation. . . . If the promoters of professional baseball had heeded the warnings dinned into their ears for years against the inroads of the betting fraternity on their business they would have headed off much of the trouble that has come to them, and which is still coming to them."

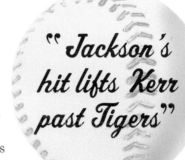

"*Jackson's hit lifts Kerr past Tigers*"

Jackson heard the talk in the locker room. He was worried. He knew he shouldn't have come to the big league all those years ago.

He first played in Philadelphia. He was 19. Why, it took him three tries to get to the big city.

Playing for the Greenville, South Carolina, team, he was summoned to play for the Philadelphia Athletics. Jackson was scared by the size of the town, the *Chicago Tribune* said.

"The Athletics' scout, on the first attempt to get Jackson north, succeeded in piloting him as far as Charlotte, North Carolina, when the boy decided he has gone far enough and leaving the train, he hid from Ossee Schreckengost. A day later, the boy showed up in Piedmont country.

"What's the matter, Joe? Don't you want to be a big leaguer?" friends of the young star asked.

"No, them places is too big," Jackson said. "Pelzer, Piedmont, and Newberry just about suits me."

On the second trip, the A's scout got Jackson 200 miles closer, getting him into rural Virginia. But one look around at the cotton fields and smokestacks and Joe got lonesome for South Carolina again and left.

On the third try, he made it to Philadelphia and played for Connie Mack, who let him go to Cleveland the next year. He'd been in Chicago since 1915. Hell, he thought, I should of stayed in South Carolina. What a jam he was in now.

It wasn't the first time that shady things had happened in baseball. There had always been talk about gamblers and players laying down. Hal Chase himself was good for a scandal or two a year. There was always that kind of talk around the game, gamblers asking who was hurt, whose arm was ailing, who was hitting? Sure, sometimes strange things happened at the end of a season. Just nine years earlier, Cleveland's Napoleon Lajoie thought he won himself a car (and the American League batting title) by collecting eight hits, including seven straight bunts in a final-day doubleheader to slip past Ty Cobb of the Detroit Tigers, who chose to sit out the last two games and protect his lead. Or so he thought.

It turned out that Lajoie tripled his first time up. Then St. Louis Browns' third baseman Red Corriden, a rookie, and St. Louis Browns' manager Jack O'Connor got the word to him that he should simply bunt. He didn't have to go through all the trouble of hitting triples. It was also hinted that the Browns' strategy was greeted with the strong encouragement of the rest of the Detroit Tigers, who didn't want the hated Cobb to get the car.

So Lajoie got his hits and was so eager for the car and the batting title that after the game, he actually called the game's official scorer Richard Collins, to ask him if he didn't think one of the fumbled bunts by Corriden should have been ruled a hit, which would have given him nine on the afternoon. According to a story in the *Chicago Tribune*, Harry Howell, a former Browns' pitcher, even offered Collins a $40 suit if he'd change the call to help Lajoie out. But Collins refused.

*"Shoeless Joe gets game-winner, will testify in Series scandal"*

Ultimately, Cobb was declared the winner, thanks to a clerical error by the American League office, where one of Cobb's games was counted twice. Lajoie's hits—legit or not—stayed on his lifetime record. Corriden, a rookie, was forgiven. Manager O'Connor got himself suspended indefinitely. Jackson knew about all that stuff. There was plenty more. All the stuff Hal Chase did. There were so many. But the one he was involved in, he couldn't shake.

Blowing a World Series was a different story. And for most of the season, it seemed that guilt hung over the White Sox players like a shroud.

Though it had four eventual 20-game winners and Joe Jackson was hitting .382, a 31-point improvement, the White Sox struggled early in 1920. Buck Weaver was up

37 points to .333 and Hap Felsch and Jackson were among the top 10 in the league in home runs: Felsch had 14, Jackson 12.

Yet for most of the season, it was Cleveland and New York battling it out for the lead. The reigning American League champion White Sox, with the whole team back, were having a tough time.

Near the end of the season, as the rumors grew louder, something clicked. Maybe it was a shot at redemption.

Nobody knows for sure, but Gleason's club took off and made a run at Tris Speaker's eventual pennant winners in Cleveland, winning 10 of its last 11 games, climbing within a half-game of the American League lead. Why, if they could just get back to the Series, they could make it all right again.

In mid-September, the last time Jackson played against Babe Ruth and his Yankees, Eddie Cicotte, the same Eddie Cicotte who let himself get lit up in the World Series as part of the fix held Ruth (who'd hit 54 homers that year) to a harmless single and the White Sox pounded New York, then the AL leaders, 15-9. The Yankees were worried.

Nothing, it seemed, could stop these Black Sox. They all talked about getting back into the World Series, winning the damn thing and it'd be done with. It seemed as if that was indeed fueling Gleason's club, who were roaring. But a grand jury investigation had begun. Everybody on the Black Sox got nervous. They knew someone would talk about gambling and baseball. Their dirty not-so-secret would soon be out.

"Baseball is more than a national game," the jury foreman said at the time, "it is an American institution, (our great teacher of) respect for authority, self-confidence, fair-mindedness, quick judgment, and self-control." And as the trial gathered, the talk in town was rampant.

A few days later, a letter to the *Chicago Tribune* from Fred Loomis, a heartsick White Sox fan, seemed to speak for all of Chicago. And you can imagine how the hearts of these Black Sox sank as his letter hit the press. Jackson heard all the guys talking about it. They weren't a close bunch, really, but now, this was going to be troublesome.

"Widespread circulation has been given to reports from various sources that the World Series of last fall between the Chicago White Sox and the Cincinnati Reds was deliberately and intentionally lost through an alleged conspiracy between certain unnamed members of the Chicago White Sox and certain gamblers. . . ." Loomis wrote. And the buzz continued.

By September 20, Gleason's White Sox had passed the Yankees and were within a game of trying to win themselves an American League pennant by outdueling the red-hot Cleveland Indians, taking two out of three.

In that last game in Cleveland, where Jackson first became a big-league regular, the crowd was nasty. Jackson had hit his final big-league homer in the fifth inning and with the crowd chanting nastily "Shipyard, shipyard"—mocking Jackson for refusing to enlist in the army for World War I, preferring instead to work in a shipyard in Cleveland.

Feeling the pressure of everything mounting on him, Jackson lost his cool and made an obscene gesture when he hit third base, then did it again when he crossed home plate. Things were turning ugly.

On September 23, the dam broke. The banner headline in the *Chicago Tribune* would echo through history. "'Fixed' World Series. Five White Sox men involved Hoyne aid says."

The investigation of the Alexander fix attempt had stirred a hornet's nest. It turned out too many people were asking too many questions. Cubs infielder Charles Herzog and Art Wilson, a Boston Braves reserve catcher, were the first two players to give affidavits about the rigged series.

*"Shoeless Joe's two-bagger breaks tie, Chisox to face grand jury"*

Meanwhile, the White Sox kept playing against a clock they knew was running out. Next up were these Tigers here in a midweek series. If they could just catch Cleveland, maybe they could put off this trial.

Jackson heard the Comiskey Park crowd roar as Collins's single drove Weaver over to third. Here was his chance. It was up to him and "Black Betsy." He looked over in the dugout to the White Sox pitcher that afternoon, fresh-faced Dickie Kerr, who was working on a six-hitter.

Kerr, Jackson remembered, was the guy who didn't know the fix was on in the Series and won two games against the Reds in spite of it.

Now he had a chance to win one for him—legitimately. He unleashed that picture-perfect swing one last time and launched a shot into the right-center-field gap, just beyond Ty Cobb's reach. Weaver came charging around and when Cobb botched the relay throw, so did Collins. Jackson pulled into second, the noise of the Comiskey Park crowd ringing in his ears one last time. It was the 1,774th and final hit of Jackson's career, his 120th and 121st RBI of the season, the only time in his career he drove in more than 100 runs.

The game, a 2-0 White Sox win and Shoeless Joe Jackson's last big-league game, was over in just 75 minutes. When he got into the clubhouse at the end of the game, the guys were reading the papers from Philadelphia, where the story broke. Billy Maharg had talked and explained the whole deal. This wasn't good. The next day, Jackson, like the other seven White Sox players involved in the World Series scandal, was ordered to appear before the grand jury. They were just one game out. They could win this thing and get them all off their back. Why now? Why now?

When he got his turn before the grand jury, Jackson was blunt.

"I wanted $20,000 for my part in the deal and (Chick) Gandil told me I could get that much out of it," he said. "After the first game, (Lefty) Williams came to my room at the hotel and slipped me $5,000. He said the rest would come as soon as we showed the gamblers we were on the square with them. But that is all I ever got. I raised a howl several times as the games went on but it never got anywhere. I was hog-tied."

And when he talked about the games themselves, he explained how easily a game could be rigged.

"I am left fielder for the Sox," he told the jury. "When a Cincinnati player would bat a ball in my territory, I'd muff it if I could. But if it would look too much like crooked work to do that, I'd be slow and would make a throw to the infield that would be too short. My work netted the Cincinnati team several runs that they would never have made had I been playing on the square."

Once the players were on the grand jury list, White Sox owner Charles Comiskey had to indefinitely suspend those eight players for the rest of the regular season. The team didn't win another game. Other teams around baseball offered to lend Comiskey their players for the rest of the season. It was quite a show. Cleveland won the pennant and went on to thump Brooklyn in the World Series.

The jury ended up acquitting the "Black Sox," but it was a hollow victory. There had been so much dirt unearthed from the testimony that new commissioner Kenesaw Mountain Landis banned all eight of them—for life.

"Regardless of the verdict of juries," Landis wrote, "no player who throws a ball game, no player that undertakes or promises to throw a ballgame, no player that sits in confidence with a bunch of crooked players and gamblers where the ways and means of throwing a game are discussed and does not promptly tell the club about it, will ever play professional baseball."

Shoeless Joe Jackson's .382 final season was the fourth-highest of his career and strongest season in eight years, raised his career mark to .356, ranking him third on the all-time list. The 1920 campaign was the 33-year-old Jackson's final one in the big leagues.

His 13th season.

# Say It Ain't So, Joe

CHICAGO

| | ab. | r. | h. | po. | a. |
|---|---|---|---|---|---|
| Leibold, cf .... | 4 | 0 | 0 | 3 | 0 |
| Weaver, 3b .... | 3 | 1 | 1 | 0 | 4 |
| E. Collins, 2b .. | 4 | 1 | 1 | 2 | 5 |
| Jackson, lf ..... | 3 | 0 | 1 | 7 | 0 |
| Strunk, rf ..... | 2 | 0 | 0 | 1 | 0 |
| J. Collins, ss ... | 3 | 0 | 0 | 9 | 0 |
| Risberg, ss .... | 3 | 0 | 0 | 1 | 3 |
| Schalk, c ...... | 3 | 0 | 0 | 4 | 1 |
| Kerr, p ....... | 3 | 0 | 1 | 0 | 0 |
| **TOTALS:** | **28** | **2** | **4** | **27** | **13** |

DETROIT

| | ab. | r. | h. | po. | a. |
|---|---|---|---|---|---|
| Young, 2b .... | 4 | 0 | 0 | 2 | 2 |
| Bush, ss ...... | 3 | 0 | 0 | 1 | 3 |
| Cobb, cf ...... | 4 | 0 | 1 | 2 | 0 |
| Veach, lf ...... | 4 | 0 | 1 | 6 | 0 |
| Heilman, 1b ... | 4 | 0 | 1 | 8 | 1 |
| Flagstead, rf ... | 4 | 0 | 1 | 2 | 0 |
| Pinnell, 3b .... | 3 | 0 | 0 | 2 | 1 |
| Ainsmith, c ... | 3 | 0 | 1 | 1 | 0 |
| Dauss, p ...... | 2 | 0 | 1 | 0 | 0 |
| **a** Hale ....... | 1 | 0 | 0 | 0 | 0 |
| Ayers, p ...... | 0 | 0 | 0 | 0 | 0 |
| **TOTALS:** | **32** | **0** | **6** | **24** | **7** |

**a** Batted for Dauss in eighth.

Chicago ...... 0 0 0   0 0 2   0 0 0—2
Detroit ....... 0 0 0   0 0 0   0 0 0—0

E: Cobb, Ainsmith. SB: Weaver. LOB: Detroit 6, Chicago 4. BB: Off Kerr 1, Dause 4. Hits: Off Dauss 3 in 7 innings, Ayers 1 in 1. HBP: By Dauss (Weaver). SO: By Kerr 4, Ayers 1. L: Dauss. T: 1:15.

## JOSEPH JEFFERSON JACKSON
Nickname: Shoeless Joe
Born July 16, 1889, in Pickens County, S.C.
Died December 5, 1951 in Greenville, S.C.
Height: 6-1 Weight: 200
Threw right handed; batted left handed
Career total = 13 years

| Year | Club | Pos. | G | AB | R | H | 2B | 3B | HR | RBI | B.A. | A | E | F.A. |
|------|------|------|---|----|---|---|----|----|----|-----|------|---|---|------|
| 1908 | Athletics | CF | 5 | 23 | 0 | 3 | 0 | 0 | 0 | 3 | .130 | 1 | 1 | .875 |
| 1909 | Athletics | OF | 4 | 17 | 3 | 3 | 0 | 0 | 0 | 3 | .176 | 0 | 2 | .833 |
| 1910 | Naps | OF | 20 | 75 | 15 | 29 | 2 | 5 | 1 | 11 | .387 | 2 | 1 | .977 |
| 1911 | Naps | OF | 147 | 571 | 126 | 233 | 45 | 19 | 7 | 83 | .408 | 32 | 12 | .958 |
| 1912 | Naps | OF | 150 | 572 | 121 | 226 | 45 | 26 | 3 | 90 | .395 | 30 | 16 | .950 |
| 1913 | Naps | RF | 148 | 528 | 109 | 197 | 39 | 17 | 7 | 71 | .373 | 28 | 18 | .930 |
| 1914 | Naps | OF | 119 | 453 | 61 | 153 | 22 | 13 | 3 | 53 | .338 | 13 | 7 | .967 |
| 1915 | Indians | OF-1B | 50 | 303 | 42 | 99 | 16 | 9 | 3 | 45 | .327 | 6 | 3 | .961 |
| 1915 | Indians | 1B | 30 | — | — | — | — | — | — | — | — | 15 | 7 | .977 |
| 1915 | White Sox | OF | 45 | 158 | 21 | 43 | 4 | 5 | 2 | 36 | .272 | 6 | 5 | .947 |
| 1916 | White Sox | OF | 155 | 592 | 91 | 202 | 40 | 21 | 3 | 78 | .341 | 17 | 8 | .975 |
| 1917 | White Sox | OF | 145 | 538 | 91 | 162 | 20 | 17 | 5 | 75 | .301 | 18 | 6 | .984 |
| 1918 | White Sox | OF | 17 | 65 | 9 | 23 | 2 | 2 | 1 | 20 | .354 | 1 | 0 | 1.000 |
| 1919 | White Sox | OF | 139 | 516 | 79 | 181 | 31 | 14 | 7 | 96 | .351 | 15 | 9 | .967 |
| 1920 | White Sox | LF | 145 | 570 | 105 | 218 | 42 | 20 | 12 | 121 | .382 | 14 | 12 | .965 |
| Totals | | | 1332 | 4981 | 873 | 1772 | 307 | 168 | 54 | 785 | .356 | 198 | 107 | .964 |

The lithe, angular Dizzy Dean of these photos had given way to a much less streamlined model for his final big-league appearance for the St. Louis Browns.

Photo courtesy of Allied Photocolor.

# DIZZY DEAN

## *Ol' Diz Shuts 'Em Up One Last Time*

**DATE:** September 28, 1947

**SITE:** Sportsman's Park, St. Louis, Missouri

**OPPONENT:** Eddie Lopat of the Chicago White Sox

**RESULT:** Four scoreless innings

**September 28, 1947, St. Louis**—The phrase has roared through history like a Dizzy Dean fastball: "It ain't bragging," he once reasoned, "if you can do it."

As he strode out to the mound at Sportsman's Park, home of the worst team in baseball—the St. Louis Browns—for the final game of the 1947 season, it's a safe bet Dizzy Dean, one of the greatest pitchers in St. Louis Cardinals' history, was laughing.

What was he doing in a Browns uniform? What was he doing, about 40 pounds over his playing weight, on a baseball mound? Was he a baseball announcer or a pitcher? What had that big mouth of his gone and gotten him into this time? As great a character as ever strode across a big-league stage, Jerome Hanna "Dizzy" Dean was Davy Crockett in spikes, a twinkle-eyed braggart with a prodigious talent and a personality that jumped out of America's sports pages. There didn't seem to be anything that he wouldn't do or say. The stories, apocryphal or not, have been out there for 50 years.

After his younger brother, Paul, fired a no-hitter in the second game of a doubleheader—Dizzy won the opener—he quipped, "If I'd have knowed Paul was going to have throwed a no-hitter, I'd have throwed one, too." Or, the day after he was struck in the head by a throw in a World Series game, "They X-rayed my head and didn't find nothing."

Or when he was criticized for his grammatical mistakes as an announcer. "Never went fur in school," he said, wryly. "Didn't get out of the third grade, you know; didn't want to pass my father."

Or confronted with the fact that he gave three different writers three different birthdays and birthplaces on the same day: "Them ain't lies," he said. "Them's scoops."

Well, now it was Dizzy's time to do it. After retiring from baseball in 1940, Dean had gone into radio broadcasting and been a hit. He won a wide following throughout St. Louis for his colorful expressions and folksy manner. But on January 11, 1947, St. Louis Cardinals' owner Sam Breadon had decided to go to a two-state, six-station network to do Cardinals' games live. And he chose the announcing team of Harry Caray and Gabby Street. Dean, despite his popularity in St. Louis, was relegated to doing the worst team around, covering the St. Louis Browns with John O'Hara.

Dean went after Breadon on and off the air. He once described the Cardinals owner as "a shameless skinflint, so tight he even sends paper towels to the laundry and schemes to save further money by requiring the players to hitchhike between cities."

He was just as tough on the sad Browns, ripping their hitters, their strategy, and the fans. Once, with the stands nearly empty, Dean quipped, "The peanut vendors is going through the stands. They is not doing so good because there is more of them than there is of customers."

He saved his toughest criticism for the beleaguered Browns' pitching staff (a league-worst 4.33 team ERA) suggesting time and again that he could go down there and do as well. "I can beat nine of ten who calls themselves pitchers today."

With the season winding down, the offer to do just that came from Browns' owner Dick Muckerman, who was desperate to help attendance. The Browns had drawn just

350 fans a few days before Dean's stunt. So here came a $1 contract and a chance to pitch the home finale. Dizzy Dean jumped at it.

There was a bit of a brouhaha in the Browns' front office over the stunt. Muddy Ruel, the Browns' manager, refused to sit on the bench and actually left town. But Dizzy was going to have his day.

On September 17, the *St. Louis Post-Dispatch* ran a droll brief with a little more editorializing than usual, announcing that Dean would return. "Trying to brighten the waning days of the America League season for their cash customers, the Browns today signed Jerome Hanna "Dizzy" Dean to a player contract. Ed Smith, publicity director for the club announced that Dean, who recently in his baseball broadcasts had expressed the wish to test his arm against the hitters of today, would be given the chance in a Brownie uniform.

"According to Smith, the Browns, before signing Dizzy, had checked with American League president Will Harridge. Nothing was said about the company carrying Dean's insurance or Dizzy's beneficiaries."

A *St. Louis Post-Dispatch* columnist was somewhat kinder—if as noncommittal. "That fans were interested in Dizzy's view is evident from the fan mail so voluminous, we're told, that the Browns decided to sign Dizzy for a one-game test—with more to follow if, perhaps Diz can prove his point.

"At 37, defying Father Time, bursitis, and six or more years absence from a major-league uniform, probably neither the club nor Diz is expectant. . . . But his appearance will make a very interesting 'pot-boiler' to help swell a last-day attendance.

"Many of us will be present to again view this assertive and aggressive fellow who provided this city more baseball thrills and baseball color than any player since the days of Sisler and Hornsby."

Those were the days for Dizzy Dean, a 30-game winner for the Cardinals in 1934 and one of the most entertaining players in the history of the sport. A pitcher with untold confidence—and matchless results—he blew onto the scene like a Missouri twister, wreaked havoc for a few years and was gone.

Columnist Red Smith was there the September day in 1934 when Dean won his 30th game, pitching the Cardinals to the National League championship, beating the Cincinnati Reds.

"It was Dean's ballgame," he wrote. "He, more than anyone else, had kept the Cardinals in the pennant race throughout the summer. He had won two games in the last five days to help bring the Red Birds to the top of the league. Here, with the championship apparently hinging on the outcome of this game, was his chance to add the brightest jewel to his crown, and at the same time, achieve the personal triumph of becoming the first National League pitcher since 1917 to win 30 games in a season.

"And it was Dizzy's crowd. . . . They whooped when he rubbed resin on his hands. They yowled when he fired a strike past a batter. They stood and yelled when he lounged to the plate, trailing his bat in the dust. And when, in the seventh inning, with the game already won by eight runs, he hit a meaningless single, the roar that thundered from the stands was as though he had accomplished the twelve labors of Hercules."

That was the way Dizzy Dean captivated a crowd. And even though he'd been away from the game for a long time, he was confident he could do it again.

While Dean worked out, preparing himself for the game, he was met with more than a few scornful looks, some of which, no doubt, came from the Browns' pitching staff itself, who hardly wanted to stand for criticism from a washed-up big-leaguer. The day of the game, the *Post-Dispatch* advance was similarly tart. "If you like track and field events with your baseball and if you're interested in seeing Dizzy Dean try to pitch again, then Sportsman's Park's the place this afternoon, starting at 1:30 o'clock."

After five field events and a 60-yard sprint (won by White Sox Thurman Tucker), Dean toed the rubber against the White Sox, a 70-84, sixth-place club that had Rudy York (15 home runs) as its only power threat. Future Hall of Famer Luke Appling (.306) was at shortstop and Taffy Wright, who finished tied for the third in the AL batting race with Boston's Johnny Pesky (.324), was in left.

Once the game began, Dean, looking strange in a baggy Browns uniform, turned back the clock. He pitched effortlessly and worked through the White Sox lineup—Don Kolloway, Bob Kennedy, Dave Philley, Rudy York, the whole bunch—without a hit or a run.

The 15,916 on hand—by far the biggest Browns' crowd in months and third largest of the season—were loving it. He didn't have much velocity but he sure knew how to pitch.

As they reported in the *St. Louis Post-Dispatch* the next morning, it was impressive. "Not so fast as when he pitched 30 victories for the Cardinals in 1934, Dean was remarkably free and easy in his motion. He kept the ball so close to the strike zone that he forced the White Sox batters to swing. As a result, he made only 39 pitches in the four innings [he worked]."

"*Dizzy Dean comes back in style*"

And that wasn't all. When Dean came up in the third inning against White Sox left-hander Eddie Lopat, a roar rose through the stands. Dizzy was carrying a bat painted black and white. He called it his "Zebra model."

Home plate umpire Cal Hubbard called time and ordered Dean to go get another one. Dizzy nodded, walked back to the Browns' dugout, and came back with a different bat, this one "grotesquely painted with red bands on it. Hubbard laughed, let Dean use it and Lopat's first pitch, the veteran right-hander lashed a single, then later slid theatrically into second base.

His wife, Pat, seated next to the Browns' dugout, hollered in: "He proved his point. Now get the damned fool out of there before he kills himself."

Dean returned to the mound and worked one more scoreless inning. But in between innings, he told Coach Fred Hofmann, running the team in Ruel's absence, that he'd pulled a muscle running out his single and was through pitching for the afternoon. Dean got a terrific ovation from the crowd. His big-league career was over. It wasn't a bad way to go out.

In true Browns' fashion, reliever Glenn Moulder surrendered five runs in the ninth to ruin Dean's good work. The White Sox were 5-2 victors.

Dean wasn't about to make a comeback, though.

"I still think I could pitch well enough to win up here but I don't intend to try it," he said after the game. "I have a contract as a radio announcer and I intend to stick to that job."

*"From the booth to the mound, Dean still an ace"*

Which, of course, he did, eventually going all the way to nationwide fame, working for NBC Television, doing their *Game of the Week* baseball telecasts. Not bad for a guy who didn't get through third grade.

His pitching career was mighty brief by Hall of Fame standards—a 12-year run but only six seasons where he appeared in more than 20 games. Though he's most often compared to Sandy Koufax, the Dodgers' Hall of Fame great who retired at 30 from arm miseries, Koufax actually pitched in 80 more games—397 than Dean's 317.

Yet Dizzy Dean was elected to Baseball's Hall of Fame in 1953, going into Cooperstown in the very same year that Joe DiMaggio appeared on the ballot for the first time. DiMaggio finished a distant eighth in the balloting. In his induction speech, Dizzy Dean left the Cooperstown audience the way he left everybody throughout his 12-year run in the big leagues—laughing.

"The Good Lord was good to me," Dean said, winding up his talk. "He gave me a strong body, a good right arm, and a weak mind."

# Diz Leaves 'Em Laughing

| CHICAGO | ab. | r. | h. |
|---|---|---|---|
| Kolloway, 2b .... | 4 | 0 | 1 |
| Kennedy, rf ...... | 4 | 1 | 2 |
| Philley, lf ....... | 3 | 1 | 0 |
| York, 1b ....... | 3 | 0 | 0 |
| Tucker, cf ....... | 3 | 1 | 1 |
| Wallaesa, ss ...... | 1 | 1 | 1 |
| Michaels, 3b ..... | 3 | 1 | 1 |
| Tresh, c ......... | 3 | 0 | 1 |
| Lopat, p ........ | 4 | 0 | 1 |
| **TOTALS:** | **28** | **5** | **8** |

| ST. LOUIS (Browns) | ab. | r. | h. |
|---|---|---|---|
| Dillinger, 3b ..... | 5 | 1 | 2 |
| Lehner, cf ....... | 5 | 0 | 1 |
| Berardine, 2b .... | 5 | 0 | 4 |
| Heath, lf ........ | 3 | 0 | 1 |
| **b** Zarilla ........ | 1 | 0 | 0 |
| Stephens, ss ...... | 4 | 0 | 1 |
| Judnich, 1b ...... | 4 | 0 | 0 |
| Coleman, rf ...... | 4 | 0 | 1 |
| Moss, c ......... | 4 | 0 | 0 |
| Dean, p ......... | 1 | 0 | 1 |
| Moulder, p ....... | 2 | 0 | 2 |
| **a** Peters ........ | 1 | 1 | 1 |
| **TOTALS:** | **39** | **2** | **14** |

**a** Singled for Moulder in ninth.  **b** Flied out for Heath in ninth.

```
Chicago ........  000  000  005—5
St. Louis ......  000  000  002—2
```

E: None. RBI: Wallaesa, Michaels 3, Tresh, Lehner, Berardine. 2B: Berardine, Michaels. S: Michaels, York, Philley. DP: Stephens, Berardine, Judnich 2; Stephens, Judnich; Wallaesa, York; Berardine, Stephens, Judnich; Wallaesa, Kolloway, York. LOB: Chicago 4, St. Louis 11. BB: Off Dean 1, off Moulder 4, off Lopat 1. SO: Lopat 1. Hits: Off Dean 3 in 4 innings, off Moulder 5 in 5 innings. L: Moulder. U: Hubbard, Berry, Jones. T: 1:40. A: 15,916.

## JAY HANNA (DIZZY) DEAN
Born January 16, 1911, at Lucas Ark.
Died July 17, 1974, at Reno, Nev.
Height 6-3  Weight 202
Threw and batted right-handed.
Named to Hall of Fame, 1953

| YEAR | CLUB | LEAGUE | G. | IP. | W. | L. | Pct. | H. | R. | ER. | SO. | BB. | ERA. |
|------|------|--------|-----|-----|-----|-----|------|-----|-----|-----|-----|-----|------|
| 1930 | St. Joseph | Western | 32 | 217 | 17 | 8 | .680 | 204 | 118 | 89 | 134 | 77 | 3.69 |
| 1930 | Houston | Texas | 14 | 85 | 8 | 2 | .800 | 62 | 31 | 27 | 95 | 49 | 2.86 |
| 1930 | St. Louis | National | 1 | 9 | 1 | 0 | 1.000 | 3 | 1 | 1 | 5 | 3 | 1.00 |
| 1931 | Houston | Texas | 41 | 304 | 26 | 10 | .722 | 210 | 71 | 52 | 303 | 90 | 1.57 |
| 1932 | St. Louis | National | 46 | 286 | 18 | 15 | .545 | 280 | 122 | 105 | 191 | 102 | 3.30 |
| 1933 | St. Louis | National | 48 | 293 | 20 | 18 | .526 | 279 | 113 | 99 | 199 | 64 | 3.04 |
| 1934 | St. Louis | National | 50 | 312 | 30 | 7 | .811 | 288 | 110 | 92 | 195 | 75 | 2.65 |
| 1935 | St. Louis | National | 50 | 324 | 28 | 12 | .700 | 326 | 128 | 112 | 182 | 82 | 3.11 |
| 1936 | St. Louis | National | 51 | 315 | 24 | 13 | .649 | 310 | 128 | 111 | 195 | 53 | 3.17 |
| 1937 | St. Louis (a) | National | 27 | 197 | 13 | 10 | .565 | 200 | 76 | 59 | 120 | 33 | 2.70 |
| 1938 | Chicago | National | 13 | 75 | 7 | 1 | .875 | 63 | 20 | 15 | 22 | 8 | 1.80 |
| 1939 | Chicago | National | 19 | 96 | 6 | 4 | .600 | 98 | 40 | 36 | 27 | 17 | 3.38 |
| 1940 | Chicago | National | 10 | 54 | 3 | 3 | .500 | 68 | 35 | 31 | 18 | 20 | 5.17 |
| 1940 | Tulsa | Texas | 21 | 142 | 8 | 8 | .500 | 149 | 69 | 50 | 51 | 19 | 3.17 |
| 1941 | Chicago (b) | National | 1 | 1 | 0 | 0 | .000 | 3 | 3 | 2 | 1 | 0 | 18.00 |
| 1947 | St. Louis (c) (d) | American | 1 | 4 | 0 | 0 | .000 | 3 | 0 | 0 | 0 | 1 | 0.00 |
| American League Totals | | | 1 | 4 | 0 | 0 | .000 | 3 | 0 | 0 | 0 | 1 | 0.00 |
| National League Totals | | | 316 | 1962 | 150 | 83 | .644 | 1918 | 776 | 663 | 1155 | 457 | 3.04 |
| Major League Totals | | | 317 | 1966 | 150 | 83 | .644 | 1921 | 776 | 663 | 1155 | 458 | 3.04 |

a Traded to Chicago Cubs for pitchers Curt Davis and Clyde Shoun, outfielder Tuck Stainback and $185,000, April
16, 1938.
b Released as player and signed as coach with Chicago Cubs, May 14, 1941; retired as coach to accept baseball
broadcasting job in St. Louis, July 12, 1941.
c Signed by St. Louis Browns to pitch final game as gate attraction.
d Made promotional appearances with Sioux Falls and Denver in Western League and Fargo-Moorehead in
Northern in 1941; with Clovis in West Texas-New Mexico in 1949.

## WORLD SERIES RECORD

| YEAR | CLUB | LEAGUE | G. | IP. | W. | L. | Pct. | H. | R. | ER. | SO. | BB. | ERA. |
|------|------|--------|-----|-----|-----|-----|------|-----|-----|-----|-----|-----|------|
| 1934 | St. Louis | National | 3 | 26 | 2 | 1 | .667 | 20 | 6 | 5 | 17 | 5 | 1.73 |
| 1938 | Chicago | National | 2 | 8 1/3 | 0 | 1 | .000 | 8 | 6 | 6 | 2 | 1 | 6.48 |
| World Series Totals | | | 5 | 34 1/3 | 2 | 2 | .500 | 28 | 12 | 11 | 19 | 6 | 2.88 |

Long and lean and deceptively smooth, the great Satchel Paige used his
long arms and legs to bewilder hitters for nearly 40 years.

# SATCHEL PAIGE

## *Nothing Was Gainin' on Satchel Paige*

**DATE:** September 25, 1965

**SITE:** Municipal Stadium, Kansas City, Missouri

**OPPONENT:** Bill Monbouquette of the Boston Red Sox

**RESULT:** Three scoreless innings

**September 25, 1965, Kansas City**—He stood out on that little hill that to enemy hitters over the past 30 years always looked like a mountain.

For Satchel Paige, the view was always majestic. He could hear the buzz in the stands. Satchel always could. Right now, he laughed to himself, they were probably wondering how old he was.

Was he 59? Or 62? Or 64? Had it been any other 59-year-old man, somebody surely would have asked, "What are you doing on a major-league mound?" Nobody was going to ask Satchel Paige that. Not even at 59.

Another baseball season had come and almost gone. Only a couple regular-season games left. The A's were out of it. So were their visitors, the Boston Red Sox.

The owner of the Kansas City A's, Charles Finley, had noticed the lagging attendance at Muncipal Stadium and decided to do something about it.

He contacted Paige, who hadn't pitched in the big leagues since 1953—he'd retired after a 3-9 record in 117 innings for the St. Louis Browns in 1953 at age 47—and asked him if he'd like to come back to the big leagues and pitch the regular-season finale. Paige, who was always up for making a dollar, said sure.

*"Satchel holds Bosox scoreless, A's fall"*

Finley did the act up big-time. When Paige went out to the bullpen to warm up, there was a nurse there and a rocking chair.

Ever the showman, Paige sat down in the chair and commenced to rocking as the crowd of 9,289 began trickling in. The nurse even started rubbing liniment on his limber right arm and Paige went along with the gag.

But once his warm-ups were complete, the fans hooting and hollering, the lanky Paige, 6-foot 3-inches, all arms and legs, strode deliberately to the mound for the very last time. This time, it was just baseball.

There were nights where he'd tell the outfield to sit down so he could strike out the side, like he'd do in his barnstorming days. There were other nights he'd put up a 2 × 4 behind home plate with 10-penny nails in it and proceed to nail the board to the backstop with his pitches from the mound.

Tonight, he'd just pitch. He'd been doing this for a very long time, spanning baseball generations. He once struck out the great Rogers Hornsby five times in a single barnstorming game. Hornsby won his first batting title in 1920, his last in 1928. He had long since retired.

Then there was Joe DiMaggio. He'd called Satchel "the fastest pitcher I ever batted against. And the best." DiMaggio had been retired for nine years.

Former Cubs' slugger Hack Wilson said Satchel's fastball "started out like a baseball but by the time it got to the plate, it looks like a marble."

"(He) must be talking about my slowball," Paige replied. "My fastball looks like a fish egg."

Wilson had died in 1948. Satchel pitched on.

Why, Dizzy Dean, who used to barnstorm with Ol' Satchel, hadn't been on a major-league mound in 18 years. Now he was an announcer. Dizzy said Satchel was the best pitcher he ever saw, adding "my fastball looks like a change of pace compared to that pistol bullet that ol' Satchel sends up there."

Dean, Hornsby, Wilson, DiMaggio—all of them were gone now. Yet here was Satchel Paige, a baseball in that long, spidery hand, standing on the mound at Municipal Stadium, staring in at a stocky left-handed hitting rookie, Jim Gosger.

Paige was back in the big leagues. One last time. For the longest time, he wondered if he'd ever get the chance that Jackie Robinson did.

From the late 1920s on, the name Satchel Paige was known all across America. He'd been wowing them in the Negro Leagues and in barnstorming tours.

Some of that was because of his undeniable talent. Some of it was because he understood how to be colorful. He called his pitches different names: his be-ball ("because it be where I want it to be") his jump ball, trouble ball, Little Tom, Long Tom, his midnight rider, and his four-day creeper. Whether the hitter could actually distinguish between any of the pitches didn't matter. Paige could and the lore grew.

"I'm the easiest guy in the world to catch," Paige once told a rookie receiver. "I don't take to signals too good. All you have to do is show me a glove and hold it still. I'll hit it."

When barnstorming, Paige used to guarantee to strike out the first nine hitters. He was willing to go anywhere and pitch for a dollar. He jumped teams, jumped leagues, went wherever there was a little more money. Despite his magnificent talent, not all the black newspaper writers were sympathetic to his cause.

As Chester Washington wrote in the *Pittsburgh Courier*, "No player is bigger than a baseball club, and no player is certainly more important than the National Association of Negro Baseball Clubs.

"And this goes for Satchel Paige, too. . . . Despite his contract, Paige, who has in the past set a bad example for Negro baseball by his 'gallivantin'' tactics, repeatedly refused to join the Pittsburgh Crawfords training camp at Hot Springs; instead, he joined the Bismark [North Dakota] Club, where he expects to play 'free-lance' baseball."

Later, when Paige joined the Crawfords, then took off again in a contract dispute, black baseball's greatest pitcher was rapped by the black press. "Some owners and fans are genuinely glad to have Paige leave," they wrote then. "Others are sorry. Negro baseball has been very good to Paige. His phenomenal, well-publicized pitching ability could not be expressed in terms of finance. No colored club drew enough cash customers to pay him a salary commensurate with his ability. Then again, his unreliability was a factor which at all times kept him from being a valuable asset to any team."

Because of that reputation, when it came time to break the color barrier several years later, major-league owners weren't all that tempted to bring Paige along, even though, at his advanced age, he could probably still win.

Finally on July 9, 1948, the Cleveland Indians' maverick owner Bill Veeck signed the 42-year-old Paige. When he made his first big-league appearance, relieving Bob Lemon in the fifth inning of a game Cleveland trailed the St. Louis Browns, 4-1, all of baseball was watching to see how the legend would fare. Paige threw two scoreless innings.

He made his first start a month later and the Indians drew 72,000 to watch him pitch a night game against the Washington Senators. He won, 4-3.

Some baseball folks still talk about a game that Paige pitched on August 6, 1952, when he was at least 46 years old. For 12 innings, the ageless Paige shut the Detroit

Tigers out, finally winning the 0-0 game in the bottom of the 12th. He won 12 games that season.

But he retired after the 1953 season with a 3-9 record. But 3-9 for the Browns, that might have been the equivalent of a 15-win season for some teams. Even that year, when Paige maybe was 49 years old, he had his moments. In June, the sad Browns, losers of 14 straight, stumbled into New York to face the Yankees, who were riding an 18-game win streak.

With Duane Pichette inexplicably pitching superbly one Wednesday afternoon, holding a 3-1 lead into the eighth, Browns' skipper Marty Marion had a hunch to bring in ol' Satchel to try to close it out.

A New York AP sportswriter caught the moment perfectly.

"A lone figure disentangled itself from the little group out there, stepped over the low fence and headed for the mound. It wasn't exactly a march, although there was a certain dignity in the shuffling advance.

"His pants legs dangled almost to his ankles, his shirt hung on his bony shoulders like tired bunting the day after a celebration. Old Satch never was much for sartorial splendor on a ballfield.

"He took his warm-up pitches, then stood back and rubbed his hands with the rosin bag. You could almost hear his mind ticking, as if he was thinking 'Well, so you want a little action, hey boys?'"

Paige was magical. He got Joe Collins and Irv Noren to pop out to end the eighth, then in the ninth, got Mickey Mantle to hit a foul, trying to bunt a third strike ("Why for that boy to try that?" was Satch's quote the next day), induced Yogi Berra to pop out, gave up a single to Gene Woodling, then retired Gil McDougald on a pop-up to preserve the Browns win.

An ancient Satchel Paige (approximately mid-40s) pitching to a 22-year-old Mantle. Seems like a mismatch. But it wasn't.

Magically, it all came back for Satchel one last time this night 12 years later. Leading off the game, Boston outfielder Jim Gosger popped Paige's pitch up into foul territory. One out.

"At **59**, Paige blanks Bosox through three"

Next was another young lefty, Dalton Jones. He topped a slow roller to first baseman Santiago Rosario, who bobbled it.

Next up was Boston's talented Carl Yastrzemski, twice an American League batting champion. Paige's next pitch was in the dirt, scooting past catcher Bill Bryan, letting Jones go to second. When Paige's second pitch was also in the dirt, Jones lit out for third. Bryan threw him out. Two down. When the next pitch missed, Paige was behind in the count, 3-0, an unusual predicament for a guy whose control was so extraordinary, he convinced Cleveland Indians' owner Bill Veeck to sign him by throwing five straight pitches over the stub of Veeck's ground-out cigarette.

Paige fired a fastball on the outside corner and Yastrzemski swung and bounced it off the left-field wall. It was the last hit off the great Negro League legend. It also prompted much teasing in the Yastrzemski house. Yaz's dad, Carl Sr., had also gotten a hit off the great Paige, except he did it about 20 years earlier. Carl Sr. hit a triple.

Paige got 20-year-old Tony Conigliaro, who led the league in home runs that year, to end the inning. The Red Sox scoring threat had passed.

Before the night was out, Paige faced six more hitters— Lee Thomas, Felix Mantilla, Ed Bressoud, Mike Ryan, Boston's pitcher Bill Monbouquette—and got 'em all.

When he himself came to bat, the whole Municipal Stadium crowd rose and cheered him. Cheered him even louder when he struck out. And when A's manager Haywood Sullivan sent out Diego Segui to relieve Paige to begin the fourth inning, the cheers grew the loudest of all.

*"Old man Paige keeps rolling along"*

As Satchel went into the clubhouse to change, the fans in Municipal Stadium were urged to light matches in tribute and by the time Satchel came out of the locker room to the dugout in his regular clothes, the stadium lights had been turned down and as thousands began to sing, "The ol' grey mare she ain't what she used to be."

One of the greatest careers in the game was over. A little later than usual. Better late than never.

In the clubhouse afterwards, Paige sat in his long A's underwear and chatted with the newspapermen. It had been a cool night but Paige said he handled it okay.

"Naw, the cold was nothing," he told the *Kansas City Star*. "It ain't like it is when you're sitting around. When I got goin' I got hot, and there was nothing on my mind but baseball."

It didn't sound as if Paige planned on just sitting around.

"Everybody doubted me on the ballclub," he said. "They'll have more confidence in me now. Before, they only took my word for it. Don't forget, I ain't been up in this league for 15 years (actually, it was 12 years.) Now I'll stay in shape because they know what I can do."

Satchel Paige never did come back to pitch. But don't think it was because he couldn't. One of the greatest careers in the game was finally over. Better late, much better late, than never.

# Satchel Stops Time

| BOSTON | ab. | r. | h. | KANSAS CITY | ab. | r. | h. |
|---|---|---|---|---|---|---|---|
| Gosger, cf | 4 | 1 | 1 | Campaneris, ss | 4 | 0 | 0 |
| Jones, 3b | 3 | 0 | 0 | Tartabull, cf | 4 | 1 | 2 |
| Malzone, ph-3b | 1 | 0 | 0 | Causey, 3b | 3 | 0 | 0 |
| Yastrzemski, lf | 4 | 1 | 2 | Bryan, c | 4 | 1 | 2 |
| Conigliaro, rf | 3 | 2 | 2 | Green, 2b | 4 | 0 | 2 |
| Thomas, 1b | 3 | 1 | 1 | Rosario, 1b | 4 | 0 | 1 |
| Mantilla, 2b | 4 | 0 | 1 | Hershberger, rf | 3 | 0 | 0 |
| Bressoud, ss | 4 | 0 | 0 | Reynolds, lf | 3 | 0 | 0 |
| Ryan, c | 4 | 0 | 0 | Paige, p | 1 | 0 | 0 |
| Monbouquette, p | 4 | 0 | 0 | Segui, p | 1 | 0 | 0 |
|  |  |  |  | Stahl, ph | 1 | 0 | 0 |
| **TOTALS:** | 34 | 5 | 7 | **TOTALS:** | 32 | 2 | 7 |

```
Boston ..................... 000  000  230  5
Kansas City ............. 100  001  000  2
```

RBI: Conigliaro 2, Thomas 2, Bryan, Green. 2B: Yastrzemski, Bryan. HR: Thomas [*21], Cingliaro [*31]. E: Rosario. DP: Boston. LOB: Boston, 4; Kansas City, 5.

PITCHING SUMMARY:

| | IP | H | R | ER | BB | S |
|---|---|---|---|---|---|---|
| **BOSTON** | | | | | | |
| Monbouquette | 9 | 7 | 2 | 2 | 1 | 6 |
| **KANSAS CITY** | | | | | | |
| Paige | 3 | 1 | 0 | 0 | 0 | 1 |
| Segul | 4 | 3 | 2 | 2 | 1 | 4 |
| Mossi | 1/3 | 1 | 1 | 1 | 0 | 1 |
| Wyatt | 1/3 | 2 | 2 | 2 | 1 | 1 |
| Aker | 1 1/3 | 0 | 0 | 0 | 0 | 1 |

W: Monbouquette [10-18]. L: Mossl [5-7]. WP: Segui, Wyatt. PB: Bryan, 2. T: 2:14. A: 9,289.

*Total home runs to date.*

# LEROY ROBERT (SATCHEL) PAIGE

Born July 7, 1905, at Mobile, Ala.
Died June 8, 1982, at Kansas City, Mo.
Height 6-4  Weight 190
Threw and batted right-handed.
Named to Hall of Fame, 1971.

| YEAR | CLUB | LEAGUE | G. | IP. | W. | L. | Pct. | H. | R. | ER. | SO. | BB. | ERA. |
|------|------|--------|----|-----|----|----|------|----|----|-----|-----|-----|------|
| 1948 | Cleveland | American | 21 | 73 | 6 | 1 | .857 | 61 | 21 | 20 | 45 | 25 | 2.47 |
| 1949 | Cleveland | American | 31 | 83 | 4 | 7 | .364 | 70 | 29 | 28 | 54 | 33 | 3.04 |
| 1950 | | | | (Out of Organized Ball) | | | | | | | | | |
| 1951 | St. Louis | American | 23 | 62 | 3 | 4 | .429 | 67 | 39 | 33 | 48 | 29 | 4.79 |
| 1952 | St. Louis | American | 46 | 138 | 12 | 10 | .545 | 116 | 51 | 47 | 91 | 57 | 3.07 |
| 1953 | St. Louis | American | 57 | 117 | 3 | 9 | .250 | 114 | 51 | 46 | 51 | 39 | 3.54 |
| 1954-55 | | | | (Out of Organized Ball) | | | | | | | | | |
| 1956 | Miami | International | 37 | 111 | 11 | 4 | .733 | 101 | 29 | 23 | 79 | 28 | 1.86 |
| 1957 | Miami | International | 40 | 119 | 10 | 8 | .556 | 98 | 35 | 32 | 76 | 11 | 2.42 |
| 1958 | Miami | International | 28 | 110 | 10 | 10 | .500 | 94 | 44 | 36 | 40 | 15 | 2.95 |
| 1959-60 | | | | (Out of Organized Ball) | | | | | | | | | |
| 1961 | Portland | Pacific Coast | 5 | 25 | 0 | 0 | .000 | 28 | 12 | 8 | 19 | 5 | 2.88 |
| 1962-63-64 | | | | (Out of Organized Ball) | | | | | | | | | |
| 1965 | Kansas City | American | 1 | 3 | 0 | 0 | .000 | 1 | 0 | 0 | 1 | 0 | 0.00 |
| 1966 | Peninsula | Carolina | 1 | 2 | 0 | 0 | .000 | 5 | 2 | 2 | 0 | 0 | 9.00 |
| Major League Totals—6 years | | | 179 | 476 | 28 | 31 | .475 | 429 | 191 | 174 | 290 | 183 | 3.29 |

## WORLD SERIES RECORD

| YEAR | CLUB | LEAGUE | G. | IP. | W. | L. | Pct. | H. | R. | ER. | SO. | BB. | ERA. |
|------|------|--------|----|-----|----|----|------|----|----|-----|-----|-----|------|
| 1948 | Cleveland | American | 1 | 2/3 | 0 | 0 | .000 | 0 | 0 | 0 | 0 | 0 | 0.00 |

Teammate Yogi Berra (8) gives the glad hand to New York Yankee slugger Joe DiMaggio after a round-tripper. DiMaggio doubled in his final major-league at-bat in the World Series. Joe Collins (41) looks on.

Photo courtesy of National Baseball Hall of Fame Library, Cooperstown, New York.

# JOE DIMAGGIO

## *One Last Jolt from Joe*

| | |
|---|---|
| **DATE:** October 10, 1951 (Game Six of the 1951 World Series) | |
| **SITE:** Yankee Stadium, New York, New York | |
| **PITCHER:** Larry Jansen of the New York Giants | |
| **RESULT:** Double to right center | |

**October 10, 1951, New York City**—Of course, it really wasn't a secret.

Anybody that had been watching the New York Yankees really closely already knew that The Yankee Clipper, literally, was on his last legs.

But they didn't have to go and tell the whole world. Was that anyway to treat somebody like DiMaggio? The New York papers sure didn't ever treat him that way. Louie wasn't like that. And he was with the *New York Times*.

DiMaggio couldn't believe that *Life* magazine was going to go and blab it all. Why the hell couldn't they leave him alone and let him go quietly?

Was it the Dodgers way of getting back at the Yankees for beating them in all those World Series? *Life* could go to Hell.

He still got mad when he remembered that profile they did on him back in 1939, just as he was taking over as the Yankees' marquee player following Lou Gehrig's retirement.

"Instead of olive oil or smelly bear grease, he keeps his hair slick with water," the profile said. "He never reeks of garlic and prefers chicken chow mein to spaghetti."

Or how about "Joe DiMaggio's rise in baseball is a testimonial to the value of general shiftlessness? His inertia caused him to give up school after one year in high school. He is lazy, rebellious, and endowed with a bad stomach."

Even the caption of a photo of DiMaggio with then heavyweight champion Joe Louis was insulting. "Like Heavyweight Champion Joe Louis, DiMaggio is lazy, shy, and inarticulate."

Yeah, that was a nice story, wasn't it? But nobody remembered that stuff now. DiMaggio had gotten past it. He had 'em, all of the New York media, eating out of

*"DiMaggio bows out with grace"*

his hands. Jimmy Cannon listed DiMaggio as one of his best friends. Same thing for Red Smith.

But *Life* magazine? What was this?

As Joe DiMaggio walked out of the dugout and knelt in the on-deck circle in the eighth inning of Game Six of the 1951 World Series, there was a lot going through his mind. He was coming to the end of something. He knew it. Nobody else did. Yeah, he wasn't hitting anything when the Series started. He talked to his friend, the *Times*'s Louie Effrat about it, didn't he? He owned up. Louie handled it right, too. It looked good; it looked okay the way he did it. What was *Life* magazine doing? Was this any way to treat somebody like DiMaggio? After all he'd done? How would it look? That was the thing with Joe. Yankee players would talk about it, about how when DiMaggio came back to the dugout after making an out, he might ask, "How'd I look?" The answer was always one thing: "Great, Joe, great." DiMaggio tried to clear his mind. He knew this was it. And the moment meant a little more to him than he imagined.

Hampered by injuries ever since he came back from World War II, he'd struggled and played in just 116 games in 1951, hitting a career-low .263. He could see it all coming to a close. Then this *Life* magazine crap. What would people say?

Hefting his bat, he looked out at the Giants' Larry Jansen, a 23-game winner, on to pitch the eighth, trying to keep his club still alive in the series that the Yankees had stolen away once again. He watched him carefully, saw the delivery, imagined the ball and how it'd look coming out of his hand. Then he was distracted again. If only he'd had a chance to say something to that little bastard, Andy High. *Life* magazine, too. Since when did *Life* magazine give a good Goddamn about whether a guy could hit a high fastball or not? Or maybe he'd give him the DiMaggio stare, a spine-tingling look that made even the toughest reporter wince. Who did he think he was, writing like that about DiMaggio?

All these years, all the effort he put into being the perfect Yankee, the perfect ballplayer, the guy that nobody ever saw argue a call or dive for a ball or find himself looking bad in any way. And now this?

He hefted the bat again and swung it, still on one knee. Jansen, a 6-foot-2 right-hander with a new pitch, a slider, had held him hitless in Game Two. How did he work him? He thought about the pitch sequence, how Jansen's ball moved. He was going to miss this part of the game. Damn.

DiMaggio could see who would be the next star. That was okay. He took over for Babe Ruth and Lou Gehrig. Now someone would take over for him.

Bolstered by the arrival of a broad-shouldered, free-swinging rookie named Mickey Mantle, Casey Stengel's Yankees sailed through the regular season, winning by five games over Al Lopez's Cleveland Indians. DiMaggio, for once, didn't have much to do with this pennant.

Vic Raschi and Eddie Lopat each won 21 games, the Yankees led the league in pitching and homers and were one point away from leading the AL in batting average, too.

At first it looked as if Bobby Thomson's dramatic "Shot Heard 'round the World" was going to propel Leo Durocher's Giants past the Yankees in the Series, as the

Giants grabbed two of the first three games, Stengel's club had come around, led by—who else? DiMaggio.

Thank God, he did. The Yankees came back to take the next two to lead, 3-2. A win here would clinch it. They were almost there. Then Joe could walk away in style, looking good.

That would show that High son of a bitch. When he read what High, the Dodgers' key scout, had to say about his fading skills in the latest issue of *Life* magazine, he burned inside. The bastard.

What happened was this: The Dodgers had been leading the National League most of the year. So they sent High, their top scout, to watch the Yankees in the latter part of the season. They were expecting to play them in the World Series.

High took his job seriously, wrote copious notes, noticing exactly what DiMaggio's game had fallen to. But when Thomson's dramatic home run knocked the Dodgers out of the World Series, High's report was going to be filed somewhere, never to be read.

"Yanks win Series, DiMaggio leaves in style"

Except an out-of-work writer named Clay Felsker had heard about it. He knew the Dodgers had scouted the Yankees and he was trying to get a job with *Life* magazine. The brass at *Life* told him that if he got a copy of the report, he was in.

"So I went to Andy High's hotel room," Felsker said. "I asked him, and he gave me a copy of the report," High's assessment of the fading star was scalding.

Fielding: "He can't stop quickly and throw hard. Take the extra base on him if he is in motion. He won't throw on questionable plays. Challenge him even though he may throw a man out."

DiMaggio seethed. Somebody going to take an extra base on him? The great DiMaggio? Louie didn't get into that crap in the *Times*. He told them how poorly he was hitting and how he'd brought Lefty O'Doul in to help him fix it. They didn't need to know that other crap. Not after all Joe D. had done for the Yankees. Hell, all he'd done for baseball.

What was wrong with the way his pal Louie did it in the *New York Times*? Wasn't that good enough?

"Sympathy is merely a word in the dictionary to Joe DiMaggio," Louis Effrat wrote in the *Times* that week. "Powerless, hitless, runless in the series so far, the Yankee Clipper is not feeling sorry for himself. What's more, he doesn't want fans feeling sorry for him.

"I've just been lousy."

"Such self-censure by the man who many acknowledge as the greatest baseball player since Babe Ruth, the man who currently is playing in his 10th series, the man who has carried the Yankees to so many glorious victories, was characteristic of Joseph Paul DiMaggio.

"Always a perfectionist, with a burning desire to succeed, Joe cannot excuse himself. So far, he has flopped and no one is more aware of it than DiMaggio himself."

Louie's story went on to talk about Lefty O'Doul coming in and advising Joe he was swinging too hard, trying too hard. . . .

"Warm, friendly throughout the hour-long interview [Gee, Joe D. gave you an hour?], DiMaggio, comfortable in pajamas and lounging robe, sipped coffee and appeared to be completely at ease.

"He has been sleeping well, eating well, and is in the best physical condition of the year. He looks great everywhere except at the plate and that is a matter he hopes to correct."

That was how to write a story, DiMaggio thought. He said I wasn't hitting, that I had help, that I was trying. What more did they want? Do people need to read Andy High's crap?

The *Life* magazine article was comprehensive.

"Speed: He can't run and won't bunt."

Awful, he thought. And people are going to read this tripe?

"Hitting vs. Right-Handed Pitchers: His bat is slow and he can't pull a good fastball . . . throw him nothing but good fastballs. Don't slow up on him."

What kind of crap was that to write about a guy? Louie understood how to play the game between writers and players. Why Joe D. remembered the night he and Louie were out at Toots Shor's and Louie started to ask him about his contract.

"What are ya, trying to play newspaperman?" DiMaggio sneered at him. That ended that. You just had to put these newspaper guys in their place.

*"Two-bagger is Joltin' Joe's final blow"*

It was great to hang around with 'em—off the record. You could get 'em to write great stuff about you, never any negative stuff. If they got negative, they were done. Gone. Cut off. That was DiMaggio's way. If you were late for a dinner date, mentioned something he didn't want to hear, whatever, you were done. Gone. Forgotten.

For the first three games of this 1951 World Series, High looked like a prophet, it drove Joe even more. He could feel his ears burning every time he walked back to the bench.

With the Giants taking two of the first three games, beating both Raschi and Lopat, he wondered if the Yanks could turn it around, especially without Mantle, the heir apparent who'd gotten injured in the fifth inning of Game Two, trying to back up the elder center fielder.

Willie Mays had ripped one into the gap and DiMaggio was slow to react to it. Mantle, playing right field, saw that DiMaggio got a slow start and with his tremendous speed, dashed into the gap to try to get to the ball.

At the last second, without calling for the ball, DiMaggio came in and reached up to make the catch. Mantle, frantically turning away to avoid colliding with the Clipper, caught his knee in an outfield drain, tearing ligaments. He was out for the rest of the Series. The Yankees seemed poised to stumble.

Finally, in Game Four, DiMaggio found a way to kick himself—and his team—back into gear. In the fifth inning, he slashed a two-run homer off Sal Maglie—his eighth and final in World Series play—and the blow seemed to lift the Yankees. They'd won two more games. And now, the Yanks up 4-1 in the eighth, his club three outs from a title, it was down to that little game he loved so, pitcher vs. hitter: he and Jansen.

Maybe he wasn't hitting much in this Series (just 5-for-22) but hey, he was still DiMaggio. That still meant something.

He settled into the batter's box and looked out at Jansen. He was good. He was pitching his 10th inning of World Series work, and during the season was fourth in strikeouts (145), fifth in innings pitched (278.1), and tied for fifth in ERA (3.04.) The Giants had left their season up to him. But even he couldn't rescue them.

DiMaggio heard his name announced over the stadium loudspeakers for the last time and the applause rumbled through the stands. Of course, they would have been so much louder had they only known what they were witnessing.

He looked out at the mound, the great green expanse of center field that was his territory, the monuments out there, then took his stance, that spread-legged, erect pose, bat held way back, head unmoving, eyes focused on the pitcher.

Then without thinking, he swung one last time and connected and the ball roared off his bat out into the alley in right-center field. He knew it was two bases the minute he hit it and as he came hard around first base, the crowd's excitement ringing in his ears, he slowed to a magnificent trot as he approached the base.

By the time Joe DiMaggio actually got to second, the ball was still being relayed in from the outfield. So there he was, in the middle of the diamond, one last time. He stood and looked around him. He was going to miss all this.

Many years later, friends of DiMaggio admitted that he got as much of a bang out of that last at-bat as any hit in his career. "I bowed out with a two-bagger," he'd say, smiling happily. It was something DiMaggio didn't do very often.

A few pitches later, the game was over. The Yankees celebrated once again and DiMaggio headed for the locker room a champion once more. What would *Life* magazine have to say about that?

Though he didn't want to say anything publicly—and wouldn't for a couple months—once he was in the clubhouse, he finally did say something about it. The guys in there, they could just tell it was the end of something.

Reliever Spec Shea asked him point-blank. "What about it, Joe?" DiMaggio's voice was even, well thought out. "This is it," he told him. "I've played my last game of ball."

Two months later, after a farewell trip to Japan, Joe DiMaggio made it official. In Red Smith's column the next day, he called DiMaggio "The Real Amateur."

"'When baseball is no longer fun, it is no longer a game. . . . And so, I have played my last game of ball,'" Smith wrote, quoting DiMaggio. "That is the amateur view. It is the feeling which prevents a great commercial enterprise like baseball from ever becoming a commercial enterprise exclusively. Joe DiMaggio made a great deal of money playing baseball. Most of all, though, he played for fun, and now that it is no longer any fun, he isn't going to play any more."

Later on, Smith even got a little maudlin.

"This is a meandering way of approaching the simple flat fact that the greatest ballplayer of our day and one of the greatest of any day quit baseball yesterday. . . . They know he's quitting because he cannot stand mediocrity in anything, and least of all in himself. They [the fans] couldn't stand it either, not in Joe. On him, it couldn't look good."

# Joe's Last Jolt

## Game Six

### N.Y. GIANTS

| | ab. | r. | h. | po. | a. | e. |
|---|---|---|---|---|---|---|
| Stanky, 2b .... | 5 | 1 | 1 | 3 | 4 | 0 |
| Dark, ss ...... | 3 | 1 | 1 | 1 | 2 | 0 |
| Lockman, 1b .. | 5 | 0 | 3 | 10 | 0 | 0 |
| Irvin, lf ...... | 4 | 0 | 0 | 3 | 0 | 0 |
| Thomson, 3b .. | 4 | 0 | 1 | 2 | 0 | 0 |
| Thompson, rf . | 3 | 0 | 1 | 0 | 0 | 1 |
| c Yvars ...... | 1 | 0 | 0 | 0 | 0 | 0 |
| Westrum, c ... | 3 | 0 | 1 | 3 | 0 | 0 |
| b Williams ... | 0 | 0 | 0 | 0 | 0 | 0 |
| Jansen, p ..... | 0 | 0 | 0 | 0 | 1 | 0 |
| Mays, cf ..... | 3 | 1 | 2 | 2 | 0 | 0 |
| Koslo, p ...... | 2 | 0 | 0 | 0 | 1 | 0 |
| a Rigney ..... | 1 | 0 | 1 | 0 | 0 | 0 |
| Hearn, p ..... | 0 | 0 | 0 | 0 | 0 | 0 |
| Noble, c ...... | 1 | 0 | 0 | 0 | 1 | 0 |
| **TOTALS:** | **35** | **3** | **11** | **24** | **9** | **1** |

### N.Y. YANKEES

| | ab. | r. | h. | po. | a. | e. |
|---|---|---|---|---|---|---|
| Rizzuto, ss ..... | 4 | 0 | 1 | 4 | 4 | 0 |
| Coleman, 2b .... | 4 | 1 | 1 | 2 | 1 | 0 |
| Berra, c ........ | 4 | 1 | 2 | 4 | 0 | 0 |
| DiMaggio, cf ... | 2 | 1 | 1 | 1 | 0 | 0 |
| McDougald, 3b . | 4 | 0 | 0 | 1 | 3 | 0 |
| Mize, 1b ....... | 2 | 1 | 1 | 6 | 0 | 0 |
| Collins, 1b ..... | 1 | 0 | 0 | 0 | 0 | 0 |
| Bauer, rf ....... | 3 | 0 | 1 | 4 | 0 | 0 |
| Woodling, lf .... | 3 | 0 | 0 | 5 | 0 | 0 |
| Raschi, p ...... | 1 | 0 | 0 | 0 | 0 | 0 |
| Sain, p ........ | 1 | 0 | 0 | 0 | 0 | 0 |
| Kuzava, p ...... | 0 | 0 | 0 | 0 | 0 | 0 |
| **TOTALS:** | **29** | **4** | **7** | **27** | **8** | **0** |

a Singled for Koslo in seventh.   b Ran for Westrum in eighth.   c Flied out for Thompson in ninth.

```
N.Y. Giants  ..  0 0 0   0 1 0   0 0 2 —3
N.Y. Yankees .   1 0 0   0 0 3   0 0 x —4
```

RBI: McDougald, Stanky, Bauer 3, Irvin, Thomson. 2B: Lockman, Berra, DiMaggio. 3B: Bauer. DP: Rizzuto, Mize 2; Rizzuto, Coleman, Mize; Dark, Stanky, Lockman. LOB: Giants 12, Yankees 5. BB: Off Koslo 4 (DiMaggio 2, Raschi, Mize), Raschi 5 (Westrum, Dark 2, Irvin, Thomson), Sain 2 (Thompson, Mays). SO: By Raschi 1 (Dark), Sain 2 (Dark, Noble), Koslo 3 (Raschi, Bauer, Coleman). Hits and runs: Off Koslo 4 and 4 in 6 innings, Hearn 1 and 0 in 1, Jansen 1 and 0 in 1, Raschi 7 and 1 in 6 (none out in 7th), Sain 4 and 2 in 2 (none out in 9th), Kuzava 0 and 0 in 1. WP: Koslo. Passed ball: Berra. W: Raschi. L: Koslo.

# JOSEPH PAUL (YANKEE CLIPPER) DI MAGGIO

Born November 25, 1914, at Martinez, Calif.
Died March 8, 1999, at Hollywood, Calif.
Height 6-2  Weight 193
Threw and batted right-handed.
Named to Hall of Fame, 1955

| YEAR | CLUB | LEAGUE | POS. | G. | AB. | R. | H. | 2B. | 3B. | HR. | RBI. | B.A. | PO. | A. | E. | F.A. |
|------|------|--------|------|----|-----|----|----|-----|-----|-----|------|------|-----|----|----|------|
| 1932 | San Francisco | P.C. | OF | 3 | 9 | 2 | 2 | 1 | 1 | 0 | 2 | .222 | 4 | 7 | 1 | .917 |
| 1933 | San Francisco | P.C. | OF | 187 | 762 | 129 | 259 | 45 | 13 | 28 | 169 | .340 | 407 | 32 | 17 | .963 |
| 1934 | San Francisco | P.C. | OF | 101 | 375 | 58 | 128 | 18 | 6 | 12 | 69 | .341 | 236 | 11 | 8 | .969 |
| 1935 | San Francisco | P.C. | OF | 172 | 679 | 173 | 270 | 48 | 18 | 34 | 154 | .398 | 430 | 32 | 21 | .957 |
| 1936 | New York | Amer. | OF | 138 | 637 | 132 | 206 | 44 | 15 | 29 | 125 | .323 | 339 | 22 | 8 | .978 |
| 1937 | New York | Amer. | OF | 151 | 621 | 151 | 215 | 35 | 15 | 46 | 167 | .346 | 413 | 21 | 17 | .962 |
| 1938 | New York | Amer. | OF | 145 | 599 | 129 | 194 | 32 | 13 | 32 | 140 | .324 | 366 | 20 | 15 | .963 |
| 1939 | New York | Amer. | OF | 120 | 462 | 108 | 176 | 32 | 6 | 30 | 126 | .381 | 328 | 13 | 5 | .986 |
| 1940 | New York | Amer. | OF | 132 | 508 | 93 | 179 | 28 | 9 | 31 | 133 | .352 | 359 | 5 | 8 | .978 |
| 1941 | New York | Amer. | OF | 139 | 541 | 122 | 193 | 43 | 11 | 30 | 125 | .357 | 385 | 16 | 9 | .978 |
| 1942 | New York | Amer. | OF | 154 | 610 | 123 | 186 | 29 | 13 | 21 | 114 | .305 | 409 | 10 | 8 | .981 |
| 1943-44-45 | New York | Amer. | | | | | | | | (In Military Service) | | | | | | |
| 1946 | New York | Amer. | OF | 132 | 503 | 81 | 146 | 20 | 8 | 25 | 95 | .290 | 314 | 15 | 6 | .982 |
| 1947 | New York | Amer. | OF | 141 | 534 | 97 | 168 | 31 | 10 | 20 | 97 | .315 | 316 | 2 | 1 | .997 |
| 1948 | New York | Amer. | OF | 153 | 594 | 110 | 190 | 26 | 11 | 39 | 155 | .320 | 441 | 8 | 13 | .972 |
| 1949 | New York | Amer. | OF | 76 | 272 | 58 | 94 | 14 | 6 | 14 | 67 | .346 | 195 | 1 | 3 | .985 |
| 1950 | New York | Amer. | OF | 139 | 525 | 114 | 158 | 33 | 10 | 32 | 122 | .301 | 376 | 9 | 9 | .977 |
| 1951 | New York | Amer. | OF | 116 | 415 | 72 | 109 | 22 | 4 | 12 | 71 | .263 | 288 | 11 | 3 | .990 |
| Major League Totals | | | | 1736 | 6821 | 1390 | 2214 | 389 | 131 | 361 | 1537 | .325 | 4529 | 153 | 105 | .978 |

## WORLD SERIES RECORD

| YEAR | CLUB | LEAGUE | POS. | G. | AB. | R. | H. | 2B. | 3B. | HR. | RBI. | B.A. | PO. | A. | E. | F.A. |
|------|------|--------|------|----|-----|----|----|-----|-----|-----|------|------|-----|----|----|------|
| 1936 | New York | Amer. | OF | 6 | 26 | 3 | 9 | 3 | 0 | 0 | 3 | .346 | 18 | 0 | 1 | .947 |
| 1937 | New York | Amer. | OF | 5 | 22 | 2 | 6 | 0 | 0 | 1 | 4 | .273 | 18 | 0 | 0 | 1.000 |
| 1938 | New York | Amer. | OF | 4 | 15 | 4 | 4 | 0 | 0 | 1 | 2 | .267 | 10 | 0 | 0 | 1.000 |
| 1939 | New York | Amer. | OF | 4 | 16 | 3 | 5 | 0 | 0 | 1 | 3 | .313 | 11 | 0 | 0 | 1.000 |
| 1941 | New York | Amer. | OF | 5 | 19 | 1 | 5 | 0 | 0 | 0 | 1 | .263 | 19 | 0 | 0 | 1.000 |
| 1942 | New York | Amer. | OF | 5 | 21 | 3 | 7 | 0 | 0 | 0 | 3 | .333 | 20 | 0 | 0 | 1.000 |
| 1947 | New York | Amer. | OF | 7 | 26 | 4 | 6 | 0 | 0 | 2 | 5 | .231 | 22 | 0 | 0 | 1.000 |
| 1949 | New York | Amer. | OF | 5 | 18 | 2 | 2 | 0 | 0 | 1 | 2 | .111 | 7 | 0 | 0 | 1.000 |
| 1950 | New York | Amer. | OF | 4 | 13 | 2 | 4 | 1 | 0 | 1 | 2 | .308 | 8 | 0 | 0 | 1.000 |
| 1951 | New York | Amer. | OF | 6 | 23 | 3 | 6 | 2 | 0 | 1 | 5 | .261 | 17 | 0 | 0 | 1.000 |
| World Series Totals | | | | 51 | 199 | 27 | 54 | 6 | 0 | 8 | 30 | .271 | 150 | 0 | 1 | .993 |

New York Yankees slugger Lou Gehrig looks the picture of strength and intensity as he watches the flight of the ball to deep right field. Gehrig, perhaps the premier RBI man of all-time, stranded 10 runners in his final game as a Yankee.

# LOU GEHRIG

## *Sad Finish for the Iron Horse*

**DATE:** May 1, 1939

**SITE:** Yankee Stadium, New York, New York

**PITCHER:** Pete Appleton of Washington Senators

**RESULT:** Fly ball to Sammy West

**May 1, 1939, New York City**—He watched carefully as the ball came whistling out of the left hand of Washington Senators' pitcher Joe Krakauskas and headed toward the plate. He was always really focused up there.

Now it was a matter of survival. Literally.

"Inside," Lou Gehrig told himself in the split-second as the pitch bore in on him. "It's going to be inside. Gotta back up."

Snap! He heard the ball plop into the catcher's glove and felt it whistle as it went by. How did it miss him?

After his ground ball out, Gehrig trotted back to the bench, shaking his head slowly from side to side. How could this be happening to him? Two more stranded runners. Another failed at-bat. How could this be? He couldn't be washed up at 35, could he? And geez, look at that scoreboard. We're losing to the Senators? Every time up there were men on. Every time, he left 'em out there. The greatest RBI guy in baseball history.

He looked up and it was the eighth inning already. The guys were getting to this reliever, this well-traveled right-hander named Pete Appleton. "I knew him when he was Pete Jablonowski," Gehrig laughed to himself, remembering back in 1933 when Appleton decided to change his name.

As Gehrig walked to the plate, he kept telling himself to be quick, to see the ball hit the bat. The bases were loaded, just the way Lou liked 'em. With a home run, Gehrig would have himself 24 grand slams, an all-time baseball record, more even than The Babe. He remembered that last shot, a grand slam off Lee Ross of the A's last August. That gave him 23.

Even a nice sharp hit here, maybe that'd get him back on track. How could a reasonably young, almost impossibly strong, extraordinarily durable athlete weaken so? He could hardly rest, he was so worried.

There was talk in the locker room that something was seriously wrong with him. He couldn't wrestle with anybody any more. They talked in Spring Training about watching him walk across the grass, working as hard as a man on roller skates.

Grantland Rice, one of the country's most famous sportswriters, saw Gehrig couldn't even lift a large coffee pot with one hand the night before. What was wrong? Why now?

Appleton looked in at the forlorn figure there in pinstripes. Once the most feared man in baseball history with runners on base, now he was an easy out. Appleton fired one in and Gehrig swung weakly at it and lifted it to left. Sammy West trotted in, reached up, and made the catch. Gehrig trotted back to the dugout quietly. How many men was that left on today? Six? Eight?

He didn't know his stats exactly, but he knew he'd only struck out once. Nobody got him today, either. But gee, what did he have, four hits —all singles—in the team's first eight games? A grand .143 average. Worst of all, the number he knew that they were talking about up in the press box. One measly RBI. One.

Suddenly, the game was over. He could see the bat boys gathering the bats, lining them up in front of the dugout. He could see the Senators looking over at the Yankee dugout, talking. It was all slipping away. And damn, he couldn't stop it.

In the other clubhouse, the Senators' first pitcher of the day, Joe Krakaukas was shaking his head, talking to a sportswriter.

"They better get that Gehrig out of there before somebody kills him," he said. "I pitched him inside, across the letters today—just once! If Gehrig saw that ball he couldn't move away from it. The ball went through his arms. Not over or under 'em but through his arms."

Gehrig just couldn't get out of the way. And sitting in front of his stall across the way, smoking a cigarette—his one vice—he knew what he would have to do. The team was traveling to Detroit in a few hours to start a series with the Tigers. He knew what he was going to have to do.

Maybe he hadn't missed a game since 1925. Maybe that streak was important and everything. But Lou Gehrig just wasn't Lou Gehrig any more. In his mind, he kept hearing the voices of his teammates congratulating him on this routine play he made in the ninth inning, flipping the ball to Johnny Murphy. "Great play, Lou!" they told him. Great play, my butt.

Losing to the Washington Senators on a rainy Sunday afternoon was unsettling for Gehrig. How exactly did Krakauskas, who had a record of 11-17 that season or Appleton, who went 5-10 that year, get him out four times? And all four times with men on base, a Gehrig specialty. That'd be in the paper tomorrow, for sure.

It was, too. Sure enough, the next morning, he noticed that the *New York Times* duly noted "Lou Gehrig was up four times with men on base yesterday and didn't drive in a single run." That hurt.

That was Gehrig's pride in being a Yankee, driving in runs. Maybe he couldn't hit 'em as far as The Babe. Or as often. Except for that one game he whacked four, which he knew was kind of a fluke. His specialty was reliability, consistency, the guy you could always count on.

Why, he wouldn't even play golf. Was afraid it'd hurt his swing. Sitting there at his locker, he knew the saddest truth of all. The Yankees couldn't count on him any more.

In his prime, his numbers were amazing. Seven times he drove in more than 150 runs in a season, including his American League record 184 in 1931, a record that he figured would last a long time.

In 34 World Series games, he drove in 35 runs. Only Yankee successors Mickey Mantle and Yogi Berra would surpass Gehrig's total. It took Mantle 65 games to drive in 40 runs. Berra played in a record 75 World Series games and drove in 39 runs.

Gehrig was clutch, too, hitting .361 to Ruth's .326 in World Series games, twice hitting over .500. But he never was a headline guy, that's just how it was. Heck, the day he swatted the four homers it wasn't even big news because New York Giants' manager John McGraw decided to retire that day.

"Slow start prompts Gehrig to bench himself"

This would be headline news. The streak, Gehrig's 2,130 game monstrosity, had to end. He knew it. He had to do something to help the team.

He'd make the trip, sure. He wanted to be with the fellas. He was part of the team, still. But he knew he had to talk to Yankees' manager Joe McCarthy. He knew McCarthy would never take him out of the lineup. Why, he was careful about moving him down to No. 5 in the order, even with Gehrig hitting .142 with one measly RBI.

When he got to Detroit, he went up to McCarthy's room at the Box Cadillac Hotel and told him he was taking himself out of the lineup. It was time, he said.

At first, they thought it was lumbago, because if Gehrig had to bend over to catch a throw or field a ball, sometimes, he had a tough time straightening up. Yankee infielders resigned themselves to make sure they threw the ball around neck high, so Gehrig wouldn't have to stoop over to field the throw.

But now, he knew it was time. He had to wait in Detroit for McCarthy to arrive from Buffalo by plane. Once McCarthy arrived, Gehrig met with him and told him he was taking himself out of the lineup. McCarthy met immediately with the New York press and broke the news.

"Lou just told me he felt it would be best for the club if he took himself out of the lineup," McCarthy told the *New York Times*. "I asked him if he really felt that way. He told me he was serious. He feels blue. He is dejected.

"I told him it would be as he wished. Like everybody else, I'm sorry to see it happen. I told him not to worry. Maybe the warm weather will bring him around.

"He's been a great ballplayer. Fellows like him come along once in a hundred years. I told him that. More than that, he's been a vital part of the Yankee ballclub since he started with it. He's always been a perfect gentleman, a credit to baseball."

Gehrig met with the press, too. And it was hard to talk.

"I decided last Sunday night on this move," Gehrig told the *Times*. "I haven't been a bit of good to the team since the season started. It would not be fair to the boys, to Joe or to the baseball public for me to try to go on. In fact, it would not be fair to myself.

"It's tough to see your mates on base, have a chance to win a ballgame and not be able to do anything about it. . . . I knew in Sunday's game that I should get out of there.

"I went up there four times with men on base. . . . A hit would have won the game for the Yankees but I missed. . . . Maybe a rest would do me good."

*"Gehrig takes himself out of lineup, ends streak"*

The next day, May 2, Gehrig officially ended his consecutive games streak. He brought the lineup card out to home plate before the game, tipped his cap to the Detroit crowd who cheered wildly when they understood what was happening. And one of the game's greatest records was brought to a solemn end.

A little over a month later, on June 19, his 36th birthday, Gehrig got the news from the Mayo Clinic that he had a degenerative, incurable nerve disease.

His teammates were stricken, especially when the newspapers caught wind of it. They called the illness "infantile paralysis—polio" and many of the Yankees were petrified that Gehrig's disease was contagious.

One overzealous New York sportswriter even penned a column that said that the reason the Yankees were slumping in June was the team had contracted polio from Gehrig. He was later sued by several Yankees and ultimately settled out of court. Gehrig never returned to the lineup.

On July 4, the Yankees held Lou Gehrig Day at the Stadium. Mayor Fiorello La Guardia was on hand to speak. Postmaster General James Farley and many of Gehrig's teammates on the 1927 Yankees were present.

And Ruth. Yes, Babe Ruth was there, retired for four years himself. He went up and threw his big meaty arms around Gehrig, a teammate and ex-pal. The two hadn't spoken in years, not since Ruth inadvertently criticized Gehrig's mother.

After the speeches were concluded, it was Gehrig's turn to talk, but he was too choked up. He couldn't do it. Master of Ceremonies Sid Mercer saw it and spoke up.

"I shall not ask Lou Gehrig to make a speech. I do not believe that I should."

They started to take the microphones away and Gehrig started toward the Yankee dugout. Then, suddenly, he stopped and walked back toward the microphone. The crowd of 60,000 hushed. He held up a hand and spoke from his heart.

"'Iron Horse' heads for Yankee dugout"

"Fans, for the past two weeks, you have been reading about a bad break I got. Yet today, I consider myself the luckiest man on the face of the Earth. I have been in ballparks for 17 years and I have never received anything but kindness and encouragement from you fans.

"Look at these grand men. Which of you wouldn't consider it the highlight of his career just to associate with them for even one day?

"Sure I'm lucky. Who wouldn't have considered it an honor to have known Jacob Ruppert? Also, the builder of baseball's greatest empire, Ed Barrow? To have spent six years with that wonderful little fellow Miller Huggins? Then to have spent the next nine years with that outstanding leader, that smart student of psychology, the best manager in baseball today, Joe McCarthy?

"Sure, I'm lucky. When the New York Giants, a team you would give your right arm to beat and vice versa, sends you a gift, that's something.

"When everybody down to the groundskeepers and those boys in white coats remember you with trophies, that's something. When you have a mother and father who work all their lives so that you can have an education and build your body, it's a blessing.

"When you have a wife who has been a tower of strength and shown more courage than you dreamed existed, that's the finest I know. So I close in saying that I might have been given a bad break, but I've got an awful lot to live for."

Gehrig died two years and one month from the very day his 2,130-game streak ended in Detroit—June 2, 1941.

# Lou Leaves Quietly

| WASHINGTON | ab. | r. | h. | po. | a. | e. |
|---|---|---|---|---|---|---|
| Case, cf ...... | 4 | 0 | 0 | 5 | 0 | 0 |
| Lewis, 3b ..... | 4 | 0 | 3 | 0 | 3 | 0 |
| West, lf ...... | 5 | 0 | 0 | 4 | 0 | 0 |
| Wright, rf ..... | 5 | 0 | 1 | 1 | 0 | 0 |
| Myer, 2b ..... | 5 | 0 | 1 | 2 | 3 | 0 |
| Travis, ss ..... | 5 | 1 | 1 | 1 | 1 | 0 |
| Wasdell, 1b ... | 4 | 1 | 4 | 0 | 1 | 1 |
| Ferrell, c ..... | 1 | 0 | 1 | 3 | 0 | 0 |
| Krakauskas, p . | 2 | 0 | 0 | 0 | 0 | 0 |
| **a** Gelbert ..... | 0 | 1 | 0 | 0 | 0 | 0 |
| Appleton, p ... | 0 | 0 | 0 | 0 | 0 | 0 |
| Carrasquel, p .. | 0 | 0 | 0 | 0 | 0 | 0 |
| **TOTALS:** | **35** | **3** | **11** | **27** | **8** | **1** |

| NEW YORK | ab. | r. | h. | po. | a. | e. |
|---|---|---|---|---|---|---|
| Crosetti, ss ... | 6 | 0 | 0 | 0 | 1 | 0 |
| Rolfe, 3b ..... | 4 | 1 | 1 | 1 | 4 | 0 |
| Powell, cf .... | 3 | 0 | 0 | 6 | 0 | 0 |
| Henrich, cf ... | 1 | 0 | 0 | 0 | 0 | 0 |
| Dickey, c ..... | 2 | 0 | 1 | 3 | 1 | 0 |
| Gehrig, 1b .... | 4 | 0 | 0 | 7 | 2 | 0 |
| Gallagher, rf .. | 3 | 1 | 1 | 2 | 0 | 0 |
| Keller, rf ..... | 0 | 0 | 0 | 0 | 0 | 0 |
| Selkirk, lf .... | 3 | 0 | 0 | 3 | 0 | 0 |
| Gordon, 2b ... | 3 | 0 | 0 | 3 | 2 | 0 |
| Hildebrand, p . | 2 | 0 | 1 | 1 | 1 | 0 |
| Murphy, p .... | 0 | 0 | 0 | 1 | 0 | 0 |
| **b** Ruffing .... | 1 | 0 | 0 | 0 | 0 | 0 |
| **TOTALS:** | **31** | **2** | **4** | **27** | **11** | **0** |

**a** Batted for Krakauskas in eighth.   **b** Batted for Murphy in ninth.

```
Washington ..  0 0 0   0 0 0   0 2 0—2
New York ....  0 0 0   0 0 0   1 1 0—2
```

RBI: Hildebrand, Case, Lewis 2, Selkirk. 2B: Wasdell. S: Hildebrand, Ferrell, Case. DP: Dickey, Gordon. LOB: New York 9, Washington 12. BB: Off Hildebrand 5, Krakauskas 2, Appleton 4. SO: By Krakauskas 4, Hildebrand 3, Appleton 1. Hits: Off Krakauskas 4 in 7 innings, Appleton 0 in 2/3, Carrasquel 0 in 1 1/3, Hildebrand 11 in 8, Murphy 0 in 1. WP: Hildebrand. W: Krakauskas. L: Hildebrand. U: Pipgras, Basil, Ormsby, and Summens. T: 2:17. A: 22,712.

# HENRY LOUIS (LOU or IRON HORSE) GEHRIG
Born June 19, 1903, at New York, N.Y.
Died June 2, 1941, at Riverdale, N.Y.
Height 6-1  Weight 212
Threw and batted left-handed.
Named to Hall of Fame, 1939.

| YEAR | CLUB | LEAGUE | POS. | G. | AB. | R. | H. | 2B. | 3B. | HR. | RBI. | B.A. | PO. | A. | E. | F.A. |
|------|------|--------|------|----|-----|-----|-----|-----|-----|-----|------|------|------|-----|-----|------|
| 1921 | Hartford * | East | 1B | 12 | 46 | 5 | 12 | 1 | 2 | 0 | - | .261 | 130 | 4 | 2 | .985 |
| 1922 | - | - | - | | | | | | (Not in Organized Ball) | | | | | | | |
| 1923 | New York | Amer. | 1B-PH | 13 | 26 | 6 | 11 | 4 | 1 | 1 | 9 | .423 | 53 | 3 | 4 | .933 |
| 1923 | Hartford | East. | 1B | 59 | 227 | 54 | 69 | 13 | 8 | 24 | - | .304 | 623 | 23 | 6 | .991 |
| 1924 | New York | Amer. | PH-1-O | 10 | 12 | 2 | 6 | 1 | 0 | 0 | 6 | .500 | 10 | 1 | 0 | 1.000 |
| 1924 | Hartford | East. | 1B | 134 | 504 | 111 | 186 | 40 | 13 | 37 | - | .369 | 1391 | 66 | 23 | .984 |
| 1925 | New York | Amer. | 1B-OF | 126 | 437 | 73 | 129 | 23 | 10 | 20 | 68 | .295 | 1126 | 53 | 13 | .989 |
| 1926 | New York | Amer. | 1B | 155 | 572 | 135 | 179 | 47 | 20 | 16 | 107 | .313 | 1565 | 73 | 15 | .991 |
| 1927 | New York | Amer. | 1B | 155 | 584 | 149 | 218 | 52 | 18 | 47 | 175 | .373 | 1662 | 88 | 15 | .992 |
| 1928 | New York | Amer. | 1B | 154 | 562 | 139 | 210 | 47 | 13 | 27 | 142 | .374 | 1488 | 79 | 18 | .989 |
| 1929 | New York | Amer. | 1B | 154 | 553 | 127 | 166 | 33 | 9 | 35 | 126 | .300 | 1458 | 82 | 9 | .994 |
| 1930 | New York | Amer. | 1B-OF | 154 | 581 | 143 | 220 | 42 | 17 | 41 | 174 | .379 | 1298 | 89 | 15 | .989 |
| 1931 | New York | Amer. | 1B-OF | 155 | 619 | 163 | 211 | 31 | 15 | 46 | 184 | .341 | 1352 | 58 | 13 | .991 |
| 1932 | New York | Amer. | 1B | 156 | 596 | 138 | 208 | 42 | 9 | 34 | 151 | .349 | 1293 | 75 | 18 | .987 |
| 1933 | New York | Amer. | 1B | 152 | 593 | 138 | 198 | 41 | 12 | 32 | 139 | .334 | 1290 | 64 | 9 | .993 |
| 1934 | New York | Amer. | 1B-SS | 154 | 579 | 128 | 210 | 40 | 6 | 49 | 165 | .363 | 1284 | 80 | 8 | .994 |
| 1935 | New York | Amer. | 1B | 149 | 535 | 125 | 176 | 26 | 10 | 30 | 119 | .329 | 1337 | 82 | 15 | .990 |
| 1936 | New York | Amer. | 1B | 155 | 579 | 167 | 205 | 37 | 7 | 49 | 152 | .354 | 1377 | 82 | 9 | .994 |
| 1937 | New York | Amer. | 1B | 157 | 569 | 138 | 200 | 37 | 9 | 37 | 159 | .351 | 1370 | 74 | 16 | .989 |
| 1938 | New York | Amer. | 1B | 157 | 576 | 115 | 170 | 32 | 6 | 29 | 114 | .295 | 1483 | 100 | 14 | .991 |
| 1939 | New York | Amer. | 1B | 8 | 28 | 2 | 4 | 0 | 0 | 0 | 1 | .143 | 64 | 4 | 2 | .971 |
| Major League Totals | | | | 2164 | 8001 | 1888 | 2721 | 535 | 162 | 493 | 1991 | .340 | 19511 | 1087 | 193 | .991 |

* Played under name of Lewis with Hartford in 1921.

## WORLD SERIES RECORD

| YEAR | CLUB | LEAGUE | POS. | G. | AB. | R. | H. | 2B. | 3B. | HR. | RBI. | B.A. | PO. | A. | E. | F.A. |
|------|------|--------|------|----|-----|-----|-----|-----|-----|-----|------|------|------|-----|-----|------|
| 1926 | New York | Amer. | 1B | 7 | 23 | 1 | 8 | 2 | 0 | 0 | 3 | .348 | 78 | 1 | 0 | 1.000 |
| 1927 | New York | Amer. | 1B | 4 | 13 | 2 | 4 | 2 | 2 | 0 | 5 | .308 | 41 | 3 | 0 | 1.000 |
| 1928 | New York | Amer. | 1B | 4 | 11 | 5 | 6 | 1 | 0 | 4 | 9 | .545 | 33 | 0 | 0 | 1.000 |
| 1932 | New York | Amer. | 1B | 4 | 17 | 9 | 9 | 1 | 0 | 3 | 8 | .529 | 37 | 2 | 1 | .975 |
| 1936 | New York | Amer. | 1B | 6 | 24 | 5 | 7 | 1 | 0 | 2 | 7 | .292 | 45 | 2 | 0 | 1.000 |
| 1937 | New York | Amer. | 1B | 5 | 17 | 4 | 5 | 1 | 1 | 1 | 3 | .294 | 50 | 1 | 0 | 1.000 |
| 1938 | New York | Amer. | 1B | 4 | 14 | 4 | 4 | 0 | 0 | 0 | 0 | .286 | 25 | 3 | 0 | 1.000 |
| World Series Totals | | | | 34 | 119 | 30 | 43 | 8 | 3 | 10 | 35 | .361 | 309 | 12 | 1 | .997 |

With flashbulbs popping from one side of Camden Yards to the other, Baltimore Orioles' folk hero Cal Ripken Jr. takes his final cut in a major-league game.

©DIAMOND IMAGES®

# CAL RIPKEN JR.

*Sweet Finale for Cal*

| | |
|---|---|
| **DATE:** | October 6, 2001 |
| **SITE:** | Camden Yards, Baltimore, Maryland |
| **PITCHER:** | David Cone of the Boston Red Sox |
| **RESULT:** | Fly out to left fielder Trot Nixon |

**October 6, 2001, Baltimore**—How do you say goodbye to a legend?

It wasn't an easy thing for the Baltimore Orioles to do. Cal Ripken, in many ways, was the embodiment of the Oriole franchise. The guy who never missed a game was going to play his last one.

This would be a night to remember. Former president Bill Clinton showed up to say thanks. David Letterman sent in a video tribute, a Top 10 list that included the bulletin that Ripken ended his consecutive game streak at 2,632 so he could catch a *Golden Girls* marathon on the Lifetime Network.

There was baseball stuff there, too. The kind of gesture that showed just how Ripken had touched everyone who'd worn the Orioles uniform. Just as he was about to run onto the field for his 3,001st and final game, the entire Orioles lineup from his very first big-league game (August 12, 1981) emerged from the third-base dugout, wearing 1981 Orioles uniforms.

That is, all of them except for Mark Belanger, the O's shortstop who'd died of cancer a few years ago. His place was taken by his son.

By the end of the night, Cal had been treated to a chauffeured trip around the ballpark in the back of a cherry red Corvette, and given a spotlighted Farewell Address that General McArthur would have approved of. There were fireworks, music, and more sentimentality than *Terms of Endearment*.

The only way Cal Ripken could have correctly finished off this magnificent final night would have been to climb aboard a rocket ship and fly directly to the Moon, where first, he'd unfurl a giant Orioles logo, then inscribe the numbers 2,632 with a Cal Ripken-model Louisville Slugger on the lunar surface.

Was this the right way to say goodbye? Was it too much? What do you do for a cultural monument who happens to still be alive when you want to honor him?

The Orioles did about everything they could think of. There wasn't much else left in their season. Why not make an event out of it? Cash in. The media did the same thing, with TV specials and memorial editions, and hour-long tributes. If Channel 5 did it, Channel 2 had to.

The thing is, what do you do? You can't ignore someone who lasted as long and played as well as Ripken did. But where do you draw the line? Or do you draw a line?

Speaking strictly from a baseball standpoint, Ripken's career had been on a downslide for five years. He hadn't been the same player and had slowed quite a bit. The thing was, he loved playing. The age-old question that plagues every superstar was starting to get asked around the Orioles offices. Who was going to ask him to leave?

In mid-June, Ripken solved that problem nicely. He off-handedly slipped word of his impending retirement to Dave Sheinin of the *Washington Post*. Ripken, hitting just .132 over his previous 10 games, was beginning to feel the pressure to move on. But he wanted to finish what he started. When you've played in 2,632 consecutive games, you're not about to quit in midseason. Maybe this move—get it off his chest—would help.

Within minutes, it seemed word of Ripken's retirement at the end of the season was out. Front page of the *Baltimore Sun*. Top story on ESPN's *Baseball Tonight*. Talk radio. Everywhere.

The next day, there was a hastily assembled press conference in Baltimore. Ripken, wearing a bright blue short-sleeved shirt and black slacks with a portable microphone pack on his waist, seemed glad to see everyone and talk on his own terms.

He walked in with wife, Kelly, at his side. He had the air of someone who'd just won an election. He stole her line to open things.

"I don't have a formal statement," he told the media. "I do have an observation, though. I guess maybe I'll give Kelly the credit for it. She said 'It feels like we're getting married all over again.' That's my statement."

It all happened so fast, his teammates found out about Cal's decision from the newspapers or TV. With three full months of baseball left, including the All-Star Game, it was an open invitation for America to show Cal their love.

America came through.

First, he and Tony Gywnn, who was also retiring at the end of the season, were invited to the All-Star Game and given awards right in the middle of the game. Then Ripken, with his flair for the dramatic, like so many of the game's all-time greats, gave everyone something to smile about.

In his final All-Star at-bat, he had barely stepped into the box and stared out at Dodgers starter Chan Ho Park when the ball was on its way. Ripken cut loose with a mighty swing.

Before you could say "Goodbye," Ripken caught a belt-high fastball in front of the plate with a resounding crack. There was no doubt about where it was headed.

And as he trotted toward first base, watching it all the way, he saw it descend into the bullpen. Home run. And he smiled.

Ripken had also homered on the night he broke Lou Gehrig's record. He'd also been a hero in several All-Star Games, including winning MVP in the 1991 All-Star Game, the night after he hit 12 home runs out of 22 swings in the Home Run Derby to win that title. This was a guy who knew how to step up. Now he was showing he could step down, too.

Named the All-Star Game's Most Valuable Player, Ripken seemed nourished by the love of a nation. The next day, the Ripken Farewell Tour began in earnest. Ripken seemed revitalized.

Though there were endless autograph sessions—which he initiated—endless interview requests before and after games; somehow he never got tired of it. Amazingly, he also began to hit.

In one game against the Atlanta Braves, he collected six hits in six trips, including a pair of homers. His batting average climbed all the way to .261. He continued to play well in the field and looked as if he were enjoying every single inning, like he had in the old days.

That was something people didn't understand about Ripken's consecutive game streak. Everybody around him saw it as work. He saw it as play. Even as hard as he worked, it was still play to him.

By late September, though, Ripken was worn out. The crowds didn't care, of course, and he wasn't about to come out of the lineup. The average dipped.

As he came out of the dugout for his first at-bat on that final Sunday night, Ripken had managed just two hits in his previous 45 at-bats, an .044 batting average. His seasonal mark had dipped to .242.

Maybe he would rise to the occasion on this final night. He had so many times before. Both teams were excited about it.

Why, Boston's David Cone had skipped a turn in the rotation just to pitch this game. He decided to throw Ripken nothing but fastballs.

"Ripken finale a sweet night at Camden Yards"

"I didn't throw him any cookies, though," Cone said later.

In his first trip, after taking Ball One, Ripken crushed Cone's second pitch, scorching a shot to left field that was gloved. One out.

"I really, really hit that ball hard," Ripken said later.

His next time up, still facing Cone, Ripken let a fastball get in on his hands and popped up to shortstop, angrily flinging the bat away like some guy who'd just spent a fortune on batting lessons and somehow forgot Lesson One: Hit a strike.

Ripken came up one last time, in the eighth, and everyone at Camden Yards knew, finally, this was going to be it.

Flashbulbs were going off all over the stadium from the instant he stepped out of the dugout like a Hollywood premiere. It amazed him. Hadn't everyone who wanted a picture of him already taken one? Surely, they'd already had an autograph. Or two or three. What more could they want? What could he do in this last at-bat that would send everyone home happy?

He stood there calmly, acknowledging the cheers that filled the park. How was he going to leave this game, after all?

So many other great players had left quietly. Lou Gehrig with a fly ball. Babe Ruth with a nubber to first. Mickey Mantle a pop out to short.

Ripken stepped in and swung the bat back and forth. He'd come a long way since 1981. He'd had 3,184 hits, 431 home runs, 1,695 RBI. Pretty nice numbers. This was game No. 3001.

Cone wound and gave him a medium-height fastball that he swung at and just missed. The high, harmless fly ball dropped in Trot Nixon's glove in left-center field. Ripken peeled off back toward the Oriole dugout. There was an inning to go. Three more outs.

Amazingly, in the bottom of the ninth, these dead-in-the-water Orioles rallied in a game that Boston seemed to have salted away. Trailing by a run, with one out, Brady Anderson moved into the on-deck circle. He turned to Ripken, who was next.

"You want to hit again?"

Ripken smiled and nodded. Of course, he wanted to hit again. He was Cal Ripken, wasn't he?

"OK," Anderson told him. "I'll make that happen."

Boston's Ugueth Urbina was throwing hard and when Anderson stepped in, there were two out. A "We Want Cal!" chant rose up from the crowd. Flashbulbs still popped. Ripken knelt in the on-deck circle and waited. Would he get three last swings?

Anderson put up a mighty fight. With a full count, he chased a fastball in his eyes to end it. Urbina pumped a fist on the mound. Ripken stood and greeted his teammate. It was okay, he said.

A little while later, no one had left. With the stadium darkened, except for a spotlight on him, Ripken walked back out to a podium, as if giving a State of the Union Address. Which, in a way, he was. Who better to speak for the state of the game than its most celebrated participant?

"As a kid, I had this dream," Ripken said. "And I had parents that encouraged that dream.

"Then I became part of this organization that helped me fulfill this dream. Imagine playing for my hometown team for my whole career.

"Tonight, we close the chapter on this dream, my playing career."

What was strange was his voice. So calm. So collected. So . . . reasoned. He *was* ready to retire. And it was hard to believe. Harder to accept.

"Cal Ripken: King of Camden Yards"

"I've been asked, how do I want to be remembered?" Ripken said, the words echoing through the ballpark and hearts of every true baseball fan all across America.

"My answer has been simple. To be remembered at all is pretty special."

# A Perfect Goodbye

## BOSTON

| | ab. | r. | h. | bi. | bb. | so. | avg. |
|---|---|---|---|---|---|---|---|
| Offerman, 2b .. | 5 | 1 | 2 | 2 | 0 | 1 | .267 |
| D. Lewis, rf ... | 5 | 0 | 1 | 0 | 0 | 2 | .280 |
| T. Nixon, cf ... | 4 | 0 | 1 | 0 | 0 | 1 | .280 |
| Daubach, 1b ... | 3 | 1 | 0 | 0 | 1 | 1 | .263 |
| Bichette, dh ... | 4 | 1 | 2 | 2 | 0 | 1 | .286 |
| O'Leary, lf .... | 4 | 0 | 1 | 0 | 0 | 1 | .240 |
| Stynes, 3b .... | 4 | 0 | 0 | 0 | 0 | 2 | .280 |
| Merloni, ss .... | 4 | 1 | 2 | 0 | 0 | 1 | .267 |
| J. Oliver, c .... | 4 | 1 | 3 | 1 | 0 | 1 | .250 |
| **TOTALS:** | **37** | **5** | **12** | **5** | **1** | **11** | |

## BALTIMORE

| | ab. | r. | h. | bi. | bb. | so. | avg. |
|---|---|---|---|---|---|---|---|
| Raines, Jr., cf .... | 3 | 1 | 0 | 0 | 1 | 1 | .174 |
| Matos, rf ....... | 3 | 0 | 0 | 0 | 0 | 2 | .214 |
| Raines, ph ...... | 1 | 0. | 0 | 0 | 0 | 0 | .273 |
| Blake, 1b ....... | 0 | 0 | 0 | 0 | 0 | 0 | .243 |
| Conine, 1b-rf .... | 3 | 0 | 0 | 1 | 0 | 1 | .311 |
| Richard, dh ..... | 4 | 0 | 1 | 0 | 0 | 1 | .265 |
| T. Batista, ss .... | 4 | 0 | 0 | 0 | 0 | 2 | .238 |
| B. K. Anderson, lf | 4 | 0 | 2 | 0 | 0 | 1 | .202 |
| Ripken, 3b ...... | 3 | 0 | 0 | 0 | 0 | 0 | .239 |
| Gil, c .......... | 3 | 0 | 1 | 0 | 0 | 0 | .293 |
| Hairston, 2b ..... | 2 | 0 | 0 | 0 | 1 | 1 | .233 |
| **TOTALS:** | **30** | **1** | **4** | **1** | **2** | **9** | |

```
Boston  ......  0 2 0   0 2 0   0 0 1—5
Baltimore ....  1 0 0   0 0 0   0 0 0—1
```

| | IP | H | R | ER | BB | SO | NP | ERA |
|---|---|---|---|---|---|---|---|---|
| **BOSTON** | | | | | | | | |
| Cone (W, 9-7) | 8 | 3 | 1 | 0 | 2 | 7 | 95 | 4.31 |
| Urbina ..... | 1 | 1 | 0 | 0 | 0 | 2 | 18 | 2.25 |
| **BALTIMORE** | | | | | | | | |
| Bauer (L, 0-5) | 7 | 7 | 4 | 4 | 1 | 5 | 105 | 4.64 |
| BRyan ...... | 1 | 2 | 0 | 0 | 0 | 3 | 17 | 4.25 |
| Groom ..... | 1/3 | 0 | 0 | 0 | 0 | 1 | 7 | 3.55 |
| Julio ....... | 2/3 | 3 | 1 | 1 | 0 | 2 | 19 | 3.80 |

E: J. Oliver (2), Cone (2). LOB: Boston 6, Baltimore 5. 2B: J. Oliver (2), Richard (31), B. K. Anderson (12). HR: Offerman (9) off Bauer, Bichette (12) off Bauer. RBI: Offerman 2 (49), Bichette 2 (49), J. Oliver (3), Conine (97). SB: Raines, Jr. (3). SF: Conine. DP: Baltimore 2. T: 2:43. A: 48,807 (48,190).

## CALVIN EDWARD RIPKEN, JR.
Nickname: The Iron Man
Born August 24, 1960, in Havre de Grace, Md.
Height: 6-4 Weight: 225
Threw and batted right-handed
Career total = 21 years

| YEAR | CLUB | POS. | G. | AB. | R. | H. | 2B. | 3B. | HR. | RBI. | B.A. | A. | E. | F.A. |
|------|------|------|----|-----|-----|-----|-----|-----|-----|------|------|-----|-----|------|
| 1981 | Orioles | SS | 12 | 39 | 1 | 5 | 0 | 0 | 0 | 0 | .128 | 24 | 2 | .946 |
| 1981 | Orioles | 3B | 6 | — | — | — | — | — | — | — | — | 6 | 1 | .889 |
| 1982 | Orioles | 3BSS | 94 | 598 | 90 | 158 | 32 | 5 | 28 | 93 | .264 | 289 | 13 | .972 |
| 1982 | Orioles | 3B | 71 | — | — | — | — | — | — | — | — | 151 | 6 | .973 |
| 1983 | Orioles | SS | 162 | 663 | 121 | 211 | 47 | 2 | 27 | 102 | .318 | 534 | 25 | .970 |
| 1984 | Orioles | 3B | 162 | 641 | 103 | 195 | 37 | 7 | 27 | 86 | .304 | 583 | 26 | .971 |
| 1985 | Orioles | SS | 161 | 642 | 116 | 181 | 32 | 5 | 26 | 110 | .282 | 474 | 26 | .967 |
| 1986 | Orioles | SS | 162 | 627 | 98 | 177 | 35 | 1 | 25 | 81 | .282 | 482 | 13 | .982 |
| 1987 | Orioles | SS | 162 | 624 | 97 | 157 | 28 | 3 | 27 | 98 | .252 | 480 | 20 | .973 |
| 1988 | Orioles | SS | 161 | 575 | 87 | 152 | 25 | 1 | 23 | 81 | .264 | 480 | 21 | .973 |
| 1989 | Orioles | SS | 162 | 646 | 80 | 166 | 30 | 0 | 21 | 93 | .257 | 531 | 8 | .990 |
| 1990 | Orioles | SS | 161 | 600 | 78 | 150 | 28 | 4 | 21 | 84 | .250 | 435 | 3 | .996 |
| 1991 | Orioles | SS | 162 | 650 | 99 | 210 | 46 | 5 | 34 | 114 | .323 | 528 | 11 | .986 |
| 1992 | Orioles | SS | 162 | 637 | 73 | 160 | 29 | 1 | 14 | 72 | .251 | 445 | 12 | .984 |
| 1993 | Orioles | SS | 162 | 641 | 87 | 165 | 26 | 3 | 24 | 90 | .257 | 495 | 17 | .977 |
| 1994 | Orioles | SS | 112 | 444 | 71 | 140 | 19 | 3 | 13 | 75 | .315 | 321 | 7 | .985 |
| 1995 | Orioles | SS | 144 | 550 | 71 | 144 | 33 | 2 | 17 | 88 | .262 | 409 | 7 | .989 |
| 1996 | Orioles | SS | 158 | 640 | 94 | 178 | 40 | 1 | 26 | 102 | .278 | 467 | 14 | .980 |
| 1996 | Orioles | 3B | 6 | — | — | — | — | — | — | — | — | 16 | 0 | 1.000 |
| 1997 | Orioles | 3B | 162 | 615 | 79 | 166 | 30 | 0 | 17 | 84 | .270 | 314 | 22 | .949 |
| 1997 | Orioles | SS | 3 | — | — | — | — | — | — | — | — | 0 | 0 | 1.000 |
| 1998 | Orioles | 3B | 161 | 601 | 65 | 163 | 27 | 1 | 14 | 61 | .271 | 265 | 8 | .979 |
| 1999 | Orioles | 3B | 85 | 332 | 51 | 113 | 27 | 0 | 18 | 57 | .340 | 142 | 13 | .932 |
| 2000 | Orioles | 3B | 73 | 309 | 43 | 79 | 16 | 0 | 15 | 56 | .256 | 134 | 5 | .974 |
| 2000 | Orioles | DH | 10 | | — | — | — | — | — | — | — | — | — | — |
| 2001 | Orioles | 3B | 111 | 477 | 43 | 114 | 16 | 0 | 14 | 68 | .239 | 209 | 14 | .956 |
| Totals | | | 3001 | 11551 | 1647 | 3184 | 603 | 44 | 431 | 1695 | .276 | 8214 | 294 | .977 |

Durable catcher Carlton Fisk wound up playing more years as a White Sox than a Red Sox. Yet the White Sox released him a few days after breaking the game's all-time mark for games caught. When it came time for him to be inducted in Cooperstown, Fisk chose to go in as a member of the Boston Red Sox.

Photo courtesy of National Baseball Hall of Fame Library, Cooperstown, New York.

# CARLTON FISK

*Thanks for the Memories, Carlton*

**DATE:** June 22, 1993

**SITE:** Comiskey Park, Chicago, Illinois

**PITCHER:** Kenny Rogers of Texas Rangers

**RESULT:** Fly out to Dave Hulse

**June 22, 1993, Chicago**—You can see him sitting at his stall in his underwear, feet in stirrups, baseball undershirt and jock on, scanning that morning's *Tribune*.

"That piss ant," he would say, reaching down for a paper cup, spitting with extra emphasis, though the Chicago White Sox locker room was mostly empty. The game with the Texas Rangers wouldn't begin for a few hours yet.

As Carlton Fisk read the remarks from the California Angels' diminutive outfielder Luis Polonia one more time, he could feel the back of his neck getting hot. If he had only known this when that little son-of-a— came to the plate last night.

"You know, he's not the same," Polonia said in the *Tribune*. "You lose a lot when you get old. He's almost done, ready to retire."

There was that word again, retire. Even on a day that would put Fisk into the record books—Most Games Caught, Lifetime, Carlton Fisk, Boston (A), Chicago (A) 2,225—there was no escaping it.

At 45, with a batting average well below the Mendoza line, teams were running against him at will. Hell, 20 steals in a row, the newspaper cheerfully pointed out. What else could anybody say?

*"Fisk breaks all-time mark; gets release"*

He straightened up in his canvasback chair—his extraordinarily erect posture always made him look two inches taller—and ran a hand through his thick brown hair, still parted in the middle like some 18th-century blacksmith or Methodist minister. He was a native New Englander and looked it, too. He was just as stubborn as ever.

Maybe *they* wanted to retire him but Carlton Fisk would retire when he was good and ready and not a second before. He wasn't ready. The White Sox management had been trying to get him to retire for years now. How many times had he fought back? There were too many to count.

He remembered back when Jim Fregosi was the White Sox manager. Once in mid-August, Fregosi said that Fisk, then 38, would be benched for the rest of the season so they could get a look at Ron Karkovice, the 23-year-old prospect who'd moved up from Double-A. Fisk was hitting just .215, so there wasn't much he could say, Fregosi thought. But management knew better. They knew Fisk.

Through the cooperation of former *Tribune* baseball writer Jerome Holtzman, the White Sox brass sent Fisk a hint in Holtzman's notes column the next day.

"What happens to Carlton from here on," Holtzman's unnamed source said, "will depend on his reaction. . . ."

Fisk's reaction? Give me a break.

He laughed as he remembered the way he handled it.

"Why they are doing this now, I have no idea," he said in a story that ran on the top of the page in sports the next day. "What have I done? I've played hard and I've worked hard. It's been fairly evident for close to a year that they thought I should be somewhere else. I don't understand why. I feel like from Day One, my situation has been approached less than honorably."

That was seven years ago. He was still here. But for how much longer?

What is management supposed to do when they have an icon that has outlasted his usefulness? Or somebody who simply won't go along with what they tell him he should do for the team?

Even before the season started, the White Sox management tried to get Fisk to accept a minor league contract for $500,000 so they could protect another prospect on their 40-man major league roster. Most 44-year-olds, happy to have a major league job, would have agreed. Fisk said no.

He'd hit more home runs than anyone in White Sox history, had been essential in reestablishing the franchise as a viable contender in the 1980s after coming over from Boston when Red Sox management blundered and let an angry Fisk get away. So no, he didn't trust management. Still. Not after 24 years in the major leagues. He knew how it all worked, what a meat market it was.

He could hear the noise rising around him as the clubhouse began to fill up with young millionaires.

"Today, one, two, three-million dollar salaries are assumed," he would say a couple years later. "Some of the guys would kid me because I grew up in such a different era. They can't even fathom what it was like to be expected to do chores and work for the family and not get paid for it."

He felt very distant from just about all of them, and that made this management crap worse. Fisk didn't have anything in common with any of these guys. He clearly came from a different time.

"I enjoyed coming out and hitting," he said later. "Even warming up the pitchers, talking to those who would listen . . . but the rest, it became difficult."

He didn't like the way the game was turning, either. The last blitz of national media Fisk got before this, for the games caught record, was back in 1990 when he dressed down then New York Yankee outfielder Deion Sanders for not running out a popup at Yankee Stadium, The House that Ruth Built.

Sanders, a National Football League All-Star defensive back in the offseason, barely moved toward first and had peeled off toward the Yankee dugout when he heard Fisk, mask balanced on top of his head, screaming at him (and really every other overpaid rookie hot shot who were ruining his game).

"Run it out, you piece of shit," Fisk said.

Sanders was shocked. Unlike his usual manner, didn't say anything back.

On his next trip to the plate, Deion couldn't help himself. He muttered something to Fisk.

"What?" Fisk shot back, hoping, maybe even praying for a confrontation.

"The days of slavery are over," Sanders, a two-sport millionaire, said.

Fisk stood up and was at full bellow before you could say "Go."

*"Fisk, 45, gets walking papers from Chisox"*

"Let me tell you something you little son-of-a- . There is a right way and a wrong way to play this game. You're playing it the wrong way. And the rest of us don't like it. Someday you're going to get this game shoved right down your throat."

Or up somewhere else, he had to be thinking. The umpire leaped between the two players and both benches emptied. All over Fisk's moral crisis.

To some, he was a hero for that. And frankly, he hadn't given them much to cheer about for some time now.

And when he came up out of the dugout for the pregame ceremony that night, he could hear the cheers from all corners of Comiskey Park. Cheers of relief.

He saw a few signs. "The Commander" and "Fisk Forever." Forever. Well, at 45, he almost got there, he laughed.

When the team and management gathered around him out in front of the mound a little while later, he was proud and as always, unyielding.

His teammates gave him a motorcyle; Bo Jackson himself rode it in from center field. The White Sox gave him a shadow box of home plate, gave his wife, Linda, a diamond bracelet, and had some orchids (one of his off-field hobbies) planted in Fisk's name at Chicago's Botanical Garden.

But the unpleasant undercurrent between him and management was still there and you could hear it in Fisk's voice when he began to speak.

"This record isn't something that just happened," he said. "It is more an example of perseverance and endurance. I always dreamed and expected it to end on a productive note."

White Sox management looked around, at the ground, preparing for the other spike. And here it came.

"I find it has been increasingly difficult to maintain a competitive edge," Fisk said, his voice strong and defiant. "I feel as though I've played hard, played with intensity, and played with enthusiasm.

"But most importantly, I've played to win. I've given a lot to this game and the game has taken a lot. The game has been fun sometimes and sometimes it hasn't.

When the old rooster crows, the young rooster learns, and I've crowed a lot in my life."

Which was part of what made Carlton Fisk such an extraordinary figure in baseball history. He was a modern-era player with old-school values. And, as that 12th-inning "wave it fair" World Series home run showed, someone who understood that baseball was meant to be "play-ed" not performed.

And he could be cranky. "I really resent that old phrase about the 'tools of ignorance,'" Fisk told writer Roger Angell one spring late in his career. "No catcher is ignorant. I've caught for pitchers who thought that if they won it's because they did such a great job, and if they lost, it's because you called the wrong pitch. A lot of pitchers need to be led—taken to the point where they're told what pitch to throw, where to throw it, when to throw it and what to do after they've thrown it.

"I worked with Luis Tiant as well as anybody, and if he threw a fastball waist-high down the middle— well, it was nobody's fault but his own and he was the first to say so. Not many fans know the stats about catchers, but smart pitchers notice after a while that they'll have a certain earned-run average with one catcher and that it'll be a point and a half higher with another catcher on the same club. Then they've begun to see that it isn't just their talent that's carrying them out there."

"Fisk sets record, White Sox say goodbye"

At 45, though, his sermons were mostly falling on ears already plugged with headphones or adorned with earrings. He felt as much of an outsider as a rookie.

It was a relief to get the game going. When Fisk stepped to the plate in the second inning, the plane he'd hired flew over Comiskey Park carrying a banner that read "Thanks for your support, Sox fans No. 72." Facing Texas' lefty Kenny Rogers, he lifted a fly ball to deep center to Dave Hulse.

In the fifth, he put down a nice sacrifice bunt to move Lance Johnson to second base. Johnson then scored on Craig Grebeck's single.

In the seventh, Fisk came up for the final time that night—and the final at-bat of his career, as it turned out. He again lofted a deep fly ball to Hulse in center field.

When White Sox manager Gene LaMont sent out Mike Lavalliere, another New Hampshire boy, to catch for Fisk in the eighth, his night was over. So was his career.

Though there had been plenty of hints dropped in the Chicago papers about the White Sox needing to make a roster move and that the aging Fisk was a likely candidate, he read over it.

He sat on the bench the next five nights. Then, six days after he'd set the record for most games caught, lifetime, a testament to his stubborn pride and extraordinary endurance and persistence, the White Sox pulled into Cleveland to begin a series with the Tribe.

Fisk was summoned to General Manager Ron Schueler's room on the 13th floor of the team hotel as soon as the White Sox arrived in town. He told him that the White Sox had given him his release.

"He thought I was calling him to talk about his role on the team," Schueler told the press. "I don't think he expected it. He still thought he was going to be here all season. It was a rough thing to do but I feel I owe it to the fans, the city of Chicago and the White Sox organization to try and bring home a winner."

The White Sox, then battling the Kansas City Royals for the American League West lead, did go on and win the West but fell in six games in the American League Championship Series to Baltimore.

Carlton Fisk never played again. Though he ended up playing longer in Chicago than he did in Boston, when he was inducted to the Baseball Hall of Fame in the summer of 2000, he chose to go in as a member of the Red Sox.

# Farewell for Fisk

## TEXAS

| | ab. | r. | h. | bi. | bb. | so. | avg. |
|---|---|---|---|---|---|---|---|
| Hulse, cf . . . . . | 5 | 0 | 2 | 0 | 0 | 0 | .267 |
| Franco, dh . . . . | 5 | 1 | 1 | 0 | 0 | 1 | .251 |
| Palmeiro, 1b . . | 4 | 0 | 2 | 0 | 0 | 1 | .273 |
| Gonzalez, lf . . | 3 | 0 | 1 | 0 | 1 | 0 | .321 |
| Rodriguez, c . . | 1 | 0 | 0 | 0 | 0 | 0 | .284 |
| Petralli, c . . . . | 2 | 0 | 0 | 0 | 1 | 0 | .289 |
| Palmer, 3b . . . . | 4 | 1 | 1 | 0 | 0 | 0 | .242 |
| Strange, 2b . . . | 4 | 0 | 0 | 0 | 0 | 1 | .276 |
| Redus, rf . . . . . | 3 | 0 | 0 | 0 | 1 | 1 | .258 |
| Diaz, ss . . . . . . | 3 | 0 | 2 | 1 | 0 | 0 | .286 |
| **TOTALS:** | **34** | **2** | **9** | **1** | **3** | **4** | |

## WHITE SOX

| | ab. | r. | h. | bi. | bb. | so. | avg. |
|---|---|---|---|---|---|---|---|
| Cora, 2b . . . . . | 4 | 0 | 1 | 0 | 0 | 0 | .273 |
| Burks, rf . . . . . | 4 | 1 | 1 | 0 | 0 | 1 | .286 |
| Thomas, 1b . . . | 3 | 1 | 1 | 0 | 1 | 0 | .312 |
| Bell, dh . . . . . . | 4 | 0 | 2 | 0 | 0 | 0 | .232 |
| Ventura, 3b . . . | 4 | 0 | 1 | 1 | 0 | 1 | .258 |
| B. Jackson, lf . | 3 | 0 | 0 | 0 | 0 | 1 | .235 |
| a Raines, ph . . | 0 | 0 | 0 | 0 | 1 | 0 | .290 |
| L. Johnson, cf . | 4 | 1 | 2 | 1 | 0 | 0 | .293 |
| Fisk, c . . . . . . . | 2 | 0 | 0 | 0 | 0 | 0 | .189 |
| LaValliere, c . . | 0 | 0 | 0 | 0 | 0 | 0 | .500 |
| Grebeck, ss . . . | 3 | 0 | 1 | 1 | 0 | 2 | .228 |
| **TOTALS:** | **31** | **3** | **9** | **3** | **2** | **5** | |

Two outs when winning run scored.   **a** Walked for Jackson in ninth.

```
Texas . . . . . . .   0 1 0   0 0 1   0 0 0—2
White Sox . . .   1 0 0   0 1 0   0 0 1—3
```

| | IP | H | R | ER | BB | SO | NP | ERA |
|---|---|---|---|---|---|---|---|---|
| **TEXAS** | | | | | | | | |
| Rogers . . . . . . . | 8 | 7 | 2 | 2 | 0 | 4 | 96 | 5.63 |
| Henke (L, 4-2) . | 2/3 | 2 | 1 | 1 | 2 | 1 | 28 | 2.78 |
| **WHITE SOX** | | | | | | | | |
| Fernandez . . . . | 8 | 9 | 2 | 1 | 2 | 3 | 130 | 2.85 |
| Pall (W, 2-2) . . | 1 | 0 | 0 | 0 | 1 | 1 | 15 | 2.72 |

E: Grebeck (3). LOB: Texas 9, White Sox 5. 2B: Palmeiro (13). 3B: Palmer (1). RBI: Diaz (2), Ventura (38), L. Johnson (21), Grebeck (5). SB: Petralli (1), Diaz (1). CS: Grebeck (2). S: Diaz, Fisk. GIDP: Franco, Burks, B. Jackson. DP: Texas 2 (Diaz, Strange, Palmeiro; Strange, Diaz, Palmeiro), White Sox 1 (Grebeck, Cora, Thomas). IBB: Off Fernandez (Petralli) 1. U: Barnett, Kosc, Clark, Morrison. T: 2:59. A: 36,757.

# CARLTON ERNEST FISK

Nickname: Pudge
Born December 26, 1947, in Bellows Falls, Vt.
Height: 6-2 Weight: 220
Threw and batted right-handed
Career total = 24 years
Named to Hall of Fame: 2000

| SEASON | TEAM | G | AB | R | H | 2B | 3B | HR | RBI | TB | BB | SO | SB | CS | BA |
|--------|------|---|----|----|----|----|----|----|-----|----|----|----|----|----|----|
| 1969 | Boston Red Sox | 2 | 5 | 0 | 0 | 0 | 0 | 0 | 0 | 0 | 0 | 2 | 0 | 0 | .000 |
| 1971 | Boston Red Sox | 14 | 48 | 7 | 15 | 2 | 1 | 2 | 6 | 25 | 1 | 10 | 0 | 0 | .313 |
| 1972 | Boston Red Sox | 131 | 457 | 74 | 134 | 28 | 9 | 22 | 61 | 246 | 52 | 83 | 5 | 2 | .293 |
| 1973 | Boston Red Sox | 135 | 508 | 65 | 125 | 21 | 0 | 26 | 71 | 224 | 37 | 99 | 7 | 2 | .246 |
| 1974 | Boston Red Sox | 52 | 187 | 36 | 56 | 12 | 1 | 11 | 26 | 103 | 24 | 23 | 5 | 1 | .299 |
| 1975 | Boston Red Sox | 79 | 263 | 47 | 87 | 14 | 4 | 10 | 52 | 139 | 27 | 32 | 4 | 3 | .331 |
| 1976 | Boston Red Sox | 134 | 487 | 76 | 124 | 17 | 5 | 17 | 58 | 202 | 56 | 71 | 12 | 5 | .255 |
| 1977 | Boston Red Sox | 152 | 536 | 106 | 169 | 26 | 3 | 26 | 102 | 279 | 75 | 85 | 7 | 6 | .315 |
| 1978 | Boston Red Sox | 157 | 571 | 94 | 162 | 39 | 5 | 20 | 88 | 271 | 71 | 83 | 7 | 2 | .284 |
| 1979 | Boston Red Sox | 91 | 320 | 49 | 87 | 23 | 2 | 10 | 42 | 144 | 10 | 38 | 3 | 0 | .272 |
| 1980 | Boston Red Sox | 131 | 478 | 73 | 138 | 25 | 3 | 18 | 62 | 223 | 30 | 62 | 11 | 5 | .289 |
| 1981 | Chicago White Sox | 96 | 338 | 44 | 89 | 12 | 0 | 7 | 45 | 122 | 38 | 37 | 3 | 2 | .263 |
| 1982 | Chicago White Sox | 135 | 476 | 66 | 127 | 17 | 3 | 14 | 65 | 192 | 46 | 60 | 17 | 2 | .267 |
| 1983 | Chicago White Sox | 138 | 488 | 85 | 141 | 26 | 4 | 26 | 86 | 253 | 46 | 88 | 9 | 6 | .289 |
| 1984 | Chicago White Sox | 102 | 359 | 54 | 83 | 20 | 1 | 21 | 43 | 168 | 26 | 60 | 6 | 0 | .231 |
| 1985 | Chicago White Sox | 153 | 543 | 85 | 129 | 23 | 1 | 37 | 107 | 265 | 52 | 81 | 17 | 9 | .238 |
| 1986 | Chicago White Sox | 125 | 457 | 42 | 101 | 11 | 0 | 14 | 63 | 154 | 22 | 92 | 2 | 4 | .221 |
| 1987 | Chicago White Sox | 135 | 454 | 68 | 116 | 22 | 1 | 23 | 71 | 200 | 39 | 72 | 1 | 1 | .256 |
| 1988 | Chicago White Sox | 76 | 253 | 37 | 70 | 8 | 1 | 19 | 50 | 137 | 37 | 40 | 0 | 0 | .277 |
| 1989 | Chicago White Sox | 103 | 375 | 47 | 110 | 25 | 2 | 13 | 68 | 178 | 36 | 60 | 1 | 0 | .293 |
| 1990 | Chicago White Sox | 137 | 452 | 65 | 129 | 21 | 0 | 18 | 65 | 204 | 61 | 73 | 7 | 2 | .285 |
| 1991 | Chicago White Sox | 134 | 460 | 42 | 111 | 25 | 0 | 18 | 74 | 190 | 32 | 86 | 1 | 2 | .241 |
| 1992 | Chicago White Sox | 62 | 188 | 12 | 43 | 4 | 1 | 3 | 21 | 58 | 23 | 38 | 3 | 0 | .229 |
| 1993 | Chicago White Sox | 25 | 53 | 2 | 10 | 0 | 0 | 1 | 4 | 13 | 2 | 11 | 0 | 1 | .189 |
| **Career Totals** | | 2499 | 8756 | 1276 | 2356 | 421 | 47 | 376 | 1330 | 3999 | 849 | 1386 | 128 | 58 | .269 |

Cranky, irascible, an inveterate horse player, Rogers Hornsby was one of the first managers in baseball history to receive a vote of confidence from management and be fired shortly thereafter.
Photo courtesy of National Baseball Hall of Fame Library, Cooperstown, New York.

# ROGERS HORNSBY

## *Rajah Leaves on a Sour Note*

| | |
|---|---|
| **DATE:** | July 20, 1937 |
| **SITE:** | Sportsman's Park, St. Louis, Missouri |
| **PITCHER:** | Frank Makosky of the New York Yankees |
| **RESULT:** | Ground out to pitcher Frank Makosky |

**July 20, 1937, St. Louis**—The trouble had started about a month ago with a quote.

He was a pithy, brutally honest assessment of the bat-handling capabilities (or liabilities) of the rag-tag collection of ballplayers under his direction. It was exactly what one would expect Rogers Hornsby to say. That was the problem.

Presently his St. Louis Browns were one-half game out of the American League cellar. Back in early July, player-manager Hornsby, in talking with an out-of-town newspaper guy named Pat Robinson over breakfast, reportedly called his team "a bunch of banjo hitters."

It was true. That was the thing.

But in those days, a manager, even one as crusty as Hornsby, wouldn't come right out and say such a thing. And if he did say it, no writer worth his salt would dare write it. Certainly no St. Louis writer.

No manager rips his own players, deserved or not, and expects to read it in that afternoon's newspaper. Not when there's a whole season of baseball ahead and that writer planned to keep on covering the team. But that's just what happened. And the mess wouldn't disappear.

In his fifth season with the Browns and 12th overall as a player-manager, everybody knew Hornsby, one of the game's greatest hitters, didn't have a lot to work with. The team was going nowhere. There wasn't much else to write. Somehow, this "banjo hitters" controversy wouldn't go away. It was everywhere you went.

Finally, on July 2, Hornsby addressed the issue with the *St. Louis Post-Dispatch*.

"That story from New York in which I was quoted about 'banjo hitters' was signed by Pat Robinson," he said. "I haven't seen Robinson in at least a year. The last time I saw him he was in a group that included Dan Daniel of the *New York World-Telegram*, Frankie Graham of the *New York Sun*, Charlie O'Leary, and myself.

"We were talking about the pennant race and somebody brought up the subject of umpires. I said that perhaps umpires made an occasional mistake, but that so did we . . .

"O'Leary said something about umpires who always favored the home team and the next day, Robinson wrote a story quoting me as saying the American League umpires were 'a lot of homers. . . .'"

Ah yes, the old "I was misquoted" trick. Excepting that anyone who knew the caustic old National Leaguer Hornsby didn't doubt for a second that he probably said that about American League umpires. And "banjo hitters."

Heck, as one of the game's greatest right-handed hitters, Hornsby could speak with some authority on who was a banjo hitter and who wasn't. The thing was, nobody was used to insults at that time, not in the newspaper, anyway.

The next day, the talk was still all around. So Hornsby went into greater detail with a guy he'd known from his Cardinal years, J. Roy Stockton, the *Post-Dispatch*'s baseball writer.

"I never said anything about banjo hitters," he said. "You know me long enough that I don't care what anybody writes or says about me, but I would like to clear up that story. . . ."

This time, he told a different story, one about having breakfast with a New York writer who noted that the Browns weren't getting many big hits.

"I told him that yes, we were getting lots of hits," Hornsby said, "but that our best hitters were having trouble getting long ones right then and that it was tough to win when you were getting mostly singles and them scattered through a lot of innings. I told him Clift was the only one on the club getting his share of extra-base hits. . . ."

In other words, Hornsby was saying, "No wonder we're losing. I've got a bunch of banjo hitters here, whattya expect?" He just never actually came right out and said those actual words.

"I never had used the expression 'banjo hitters,'" Hornsby explained. "I hadn't put the slug on any of my players and I didn't know what that banjo hitter stuff was all about until I got back to St. Louis and they showed me a clipping of a story in which another New York writer, whom I didn't talk to about it at all, quoted me as saying I had a bunch of 'banjo hitters' on my club." The Rajah was turning a one-day story into the elephant in the living room. Or maybe the clubhouse.

Now, it was true that sometimes, writers would spread the word and it would get out. There might be three or four of 'em sitting around talking over beers and one of them might pipe up and say "Talked to Hornsby the other day. He's getting fed up managing the Browns. He can't get decent pitching and he's got a bunch of banjo hitters on his team, so how can you win with a lineup like that?" Something like that.

Then one of those guys would get back to the office, has nothing else—he's covering the Browns, remember?—and write it up. Even though he never actually heard Hornsby say those words himself. Happened all the time.

The hullabaloo even got Donald Barnes, the president of the Browns, going.

"I'd like to spike these rumors that are being circulated," Barnes told the *Post-Dispatch*, "to the effect that Hornsby is in trouble with us and is going to be released. . . . Of course, when a man has been in the public eye as long as Hornsby has, he usually has a few enemies. . . . There are a few snipers right here in St. Louis who welcome every chance to take a shot at Hornsby. But he has been 100 percent with us and we are backing him the same way.

"We are well satisfied with the way things are going this year. Naturally, we'd like to win more games but we don't blame Hornsby. . . . In fact, I personally am pleased to find that we have a better ball club than the one we bought."

It was a vote of confidence. The sure kiss of death.

A little over two weeks later, the Browns were still struggling. They'd lost 12 of 14 games and with the New York Yankees in town for a Tuesday afternoon game, things came to a head.

**"Rajah, Browns owner in squabble"**

The "banjo hitters" were getting to him. Hornsby was really agitated. Nobody could get a big hit for them when it counted. They could get singles all right, heck they had 11 hits through nine, the Yankees just four.

Yet here was poor Oral Hildebrand, pitching probably one of his best games of an 8-17 season, holding the Yankees to just four hits, the big blow a three-run homer by Joe DiMaggio in the fifth. And the Browns finally got him three runs in the eighth to tie it, but no more. Here we were in the 10th.

Hildebrand opened the inning by walking Frank Crosetti, but got Red Rolfe to bounce one right at Tim "Scoops" Carey at second, Hornsby's old spot, a nice spot for a double-play ball. But Carey kicked it.

Hildebrand got DiMaggio to bounce out and next up was Lou Gehrig. And wouldn't you know it? Gehrig tops a slow roller to Carey who again, can't make a play. Crosetti comes around to score to break the tie.

In the Browns' dugout, Hornsby was irate. Though he wasn't remembered as a great fielding second baseman, he could get an out when he needed it, for cryin' out loud. He looked down the lineup and saw that Carey was up in the tenth. He couldn't wait.

Now, Carey was generally a decent glove man; he only made eight errors all season, tops in the league for second baseman. But Hornsby was hot.

When the team came in and told Hildebrand that they'd get that run back for him, Hornsby was still seething. Beau Bell led off with a single and moved to third on Bill Knickerbocker's double off Yankee reliever Frank Makosky. Maybe they could do it after all.

Yankee manager Joe McCarthy didn't like the looks of that, so he had Makosky walk "Sunny Jim" Bottomley, a pinch-hitter to load the bases. Let's see how the Browns' "banjo hitters" would do in a tough spot.

"Carey, sit down," Hornsby cried out to his second baseman, who was ready to go up and hit.

There was quiet in the dugout as Hornsby picked out his bat and walked to the plate for the 8,173rd time of his 23-year career. He'd show his team what clutch hitting was like. Let's see Makosky get *him* out.

Sportsman's Park grew quiet with anticipation as Hornsby dug in. He was, after all, not only a career .358 hitter, he'd led the National League with lifetime grand slams with 12.

But this at-bat was a letdown. He took a mighty cut at Makosky's first pitch and topped it in front of the plate. Yankee catcher Bill Dickey pounced on it and stepped on home. One out.

As Hornsby returned to a quiet Browns' dugout, pinch-hitter Ethan Allen rocketed one right at right fielder Tommy Heinrich for out No. 2. Knickerbocker tagged and tried to score but a fine throw had him easily at the plate to end the ballgame.

The final was New York 5, St. Louis 4.

The next day, Hornsby was called to meet with Browns' business manager Bill DeWitt. He knew what it was. And it didn't have anything to do with baseball.

He'd been warned against spending too much time and money at the horse tracks. Once, when he was strictly a player, he'd gotten himself into debt and had to borrow money from some disagreeable people. So the word was out there.

Problem was, when it came to gambling, Hornsby couldn't help himself. Besides, nobody was going to tell Rogers Hornsby what to do.

"Have you been playing the horses again?" DeWitt asked. Hornsby didn't flinch. "I have," he said.

"You're through," DeWitt said. And that was that. Goodbye, Rogers Hornsby.

It was announced that Jim Bottomley would take over Hornsby's 46-108 club. Bottomley went 21-58 for the rest of the year. "Sunny Jim" who likely wouldn't have earned that nickname had he only been a St. Louis Brown, never managed again.

In the days to come, the St. Louis papers tried to get Barnes to say why Hornsby was let go but Barnes wouldn't say. "Just say he was released for cause," he said. "Draw your own conclusions."

Some time later, Hornsby spoke his piece.

"My betting at no time interfered with my handling of the club," he said. "Hell, I never promised anybody I wouldn't play the horses. The money is as good as the money you take from the loan shark business [Barnes's principal line of work]. It's better than taking interest from widows and orphans."

A few months later, Hornsby pulled a writer aside. He sounded worried.

"I don't know what I'll do," he said. "Maybe there's still a place for me in the game. I don't know any other business. I don't want to. Baseball is the best. But it's like everything else, I guess, some players for you, some against you.

"I'm a tough guy, a gambler on horses, a slave driver and in general, a disgrace to the game. I wish I knew why. I only wanted to win."

On the field and at the horse track.

# Out as a Player, Out as a Manager

## YANKEES

| | ab. | r. | h. | po. | a. | e. |
|---|---|---|---|---|---|---|
| Crosetti, ss ............. | 4 | 2 | 0 | 3 | 5 | 0 |
| Rolfe, 3b ................ | 5 | 0 | 0 | 0 | 5 | 1 |
| DiMaggio, cf............ | 4 | 2 | 1 | 3 | 1 | 0 |
| Gehrig, 1b ............... | 5 | 0 | 1 | 13 | 0 | 0 |
| Dickey, c ................. | 4 | 0 | 0 | 4 | 0 | 0 |
| Henrich, rf.............. | 4 | 0 | 2 | 1 | 1 | 0 |
| Powell, lf................ | 4 | 0 | 1 | 2 | 0 | 0 |
| Lasseri, 2b............... | 3 | 1 | 0 | 4 | 3 | 0 |
| Pearson, P .............. | 3 | 0 | 0 | 0 | 0 | 0 |
| Makosky, P.............. | 1 | 0 | 0 | 0 | 0 | 0 |
| **TOTALS:** | **37** | **5** | **5** | **30** | **15** | **1** |

## BROWNS

| | ab. | r. | h. | po. | a. | e. |
|---|---|---|---|---|---|---|
| Davis, 1b ................ | 4 | 1 | 1 | 8 | 0 | 0 |
| West, cf .................. | 4 | 1 | 2 | 4 | 0 | 0 |
| Vosmik, lf............... | 5 | 1 | 2 | 7 | 0 | 0 |
| Clift, 3b ................. | 5 | 1 | 2 | 2 | 2 | 0 |
| Bell, rf .................... | 5 | 0 | 3 | 1 | 0 | 0 |
| Knickerbocker, ss..... | 5 | 0 | 2 | 3 | 4 | 2 |
| Hemsley, c .............. | 4 | 0 | 1 | 3 | 0 | 0 |
| Carey, 2b ................ | 3 | 0 | 0 | 2 | 4 | 1 |
| Hildebrand, P........... | 4 | 0 | 0 | 0 | 0 | 0 |
| **a** Bottomley ............... | 0 | 0 | 0 | 0 | 0 | 0 |
| **b** Hornsby .................. | 1 | 0 | 0 | 0 | 0 | 0 |
| **c** Allen ....................... | 1 | 0 | 0 | 0 | 0 | 0 |
| **TOTALS:** | **41** | **4** | **13** | **30** | **10** | **3** |

**a** Batted for Hemsley in ninth.   **b** Batted for Carey in the ninth.   **c** Batted for Hildebrand in ninth.

| Innings. | 1 2 3 | 4 5 6 | 7 8 9 10 | |
|---|---|---|---|---|
| New York ................ | 0 0 0 | 1 3 0 | 0 0 0 1 | — 5 |
| Browns .................... | 0 0 2 | 0 1 0 | 0 1 0 0 | — 4 |

2B: Vosmik, West, Henrich, Knickerbocker 2. 3B: Henrich. HR: DiMaggio. RBI: Vosmik, Bell, Henrich, DiMaggio 3, Clift, Knickerbocker, Gehrig. DP: Lazzeri to Crosetti to Gehrig; DiMaggio to Dickey. BB: Pearson, 2; Makosky, 2; Hildebrand, 4. SO: Pearson, 2; Hildebrand, 3. Pitching record—off Pearson, 11 hits and 4 runs in 7 innings (none out in eighth): off Makosky, 2 hits and no runs in 3 innings. LOB: New York, 6; Browns, 11. Umpires— Kells Hubbard, Dineen. W: Makosky. T: 2:08.

## ROGERS (RAJAH) HORNSBY

Born April 27, 1896, at Winters, Tex.
Died January 5, 1963, at Chicago, Ill.
Height 5-11½  Weight 200
Threw and batted right-handed.
Named to Hall of Fame, 1942.

| YEAR | CLUB | LEAGUE | POS. | G. | AB. | R. | H. | 2B. | 3B. | HR. | RBI. | B.A. | PO. | A. | E. | F.A. |
|------|------|--------|------|----|-----|----|----|-----|-----|-----|------|------|-----|-----|-----|------|
| 1914 | Hugo-Denison | Tex.-Ok | SS | 113 | 393 | 47 | 91 | 12 | 3 | 3 | — | .232 | 208 | 285 | 45 | .916 |
| 1915 | Denison | W.A. | SS | 119 | 429 | 75 | 119 | 26 | 2 | 4 | — | .277 | 267 | 354 | 58 | .915 |
| 1915 | St. Louis | Nat. | SS | 18 | 57 | 5 | 14 | 2 | 0 | 0 | 4 | .246 | 48 | 46 | 8 | .922 |
| 1916 | St. Louis | Nat. | INF | 139 | 495 | 63 | 155 | 17 | 15 | 6 | 60 | .313 | 325 | 315 | 45 | .934 |
| 1917 | St. Louis | Nat. | SS | 145 | 523 | 86 | 171 | 24 | 17 | 8 | 70 | .327 | 268 | 527 | 52 | .939 |
| 1918 | St. Louis | Nat. | SS-OF | 115 | 416 | 51 | 117 | 19 | 11 | 5 | 59 | .281 | 211 | 434 | 46 | .933 |
| 1919 | St. Louis | Nat. | INF | 138 | 512 | 68 | 163 | 15 | 9 | 8 | 68 | .318 | 185 | 367 | 34 | .942 |
| 1920 | St. Louis | Nat. | 2B | 149 | 589 | 96 | 218 | 44 | 20 | 9 | 94 | .370 | 343 | 524 | 34 | .962 |
| 1921 | St. Louis | Nat. | INF-OF | 154 | 592 | 131 | 235 | 44 | 18 | 21 | 126 | .397 | 305 | 477 | 25 | .969 |
| 1922 | St. Louis | Nat. | 2B | 154 | 623 | 141 | 250 | 46 | 14 | 42 | 152 | .401 | 398 | 473 | 30 | .967 |
| 1923 | St. Louis | Nat. | 2B | 107 | 424 | 89 | 163 | 32 | 10 | 17 | 83 | .384 | 192 | 283 | 19 | .962 |
| 1924 | St. Louis | Nat. | 2B | 143 | 536 | 121 | 227 | 43 | 14 | 25 | 94 | .424 | 301 | 517 | 30 | .965 |
| 1925 | St. Louis | Nat. | 2B | 138 | 504 | 133 | 203 | 41 | 10 | 39 | 143 | .403 | 287 | 416 | 34 | .954 |
| 1926 | St. Louis (a) | Nat. | 2B | 134 | 527 | 96 | 167 | 34 | 5 | 11 | 93 | .317 | 245 | 433 | 27 | .962 |
| 1927 | New York (b) | Nat. | 2B | 155 | 568 | 133 | 205 | 32 | 9 | 26 | 125 | .361 | 299 | 582 | 25 | .972 |
| 1928 | Boston (c) | Nat. | 2B | 140 | 486 | 99 | 188 | 42 | 7 | 21 | 94 | .387 | 295 | 450 | 21 | .973 |
| 1929 | Chicago | Nat. | 2B | 156 | 602 | 156 | 229 | 47 | 7 | 40 | 149 | .380 | 286 | 547 | 23 | .973 |
| 1930 | Chicago | Nat. | 2B | 42 | 104 | 15 | 32 | 5 | 1 | 2 | 18 | .308 | 44 | 76 | 11 | .916 |
| 1931 | Chicago | Nat. | 2B-3B | 100 | 357 | 64 | 118 | 37 | 1 | 16 | 90 | .331 | 128 | 255 | 22 | .946 |
| 1932 | Chicago (d) | Nat | 3B-OF | 19 | 58 | 10 | 13 | 2 | 0 | 1 | 7 | .224 | 17 | 10 | 4 | .871 |
| 1933 | St. Louis | Nat. | 2B | 46 | 83 | 9 | 27 | 6 | 0 | 2 | 21 | .325 | 24 | 35 | 2 | .967 |
| 1933 | St. Louis | Amer. | PH | 11 | 9 | 2 | 3 | 1 | 0 | 1 | 2 | .333 | 0 | 0 | 0 | .000 |
| 1934 | St. Louis | Amer. | 3B-OF | 24 | 23 | 2 | 7 | 2 | 0 | 1 | 11 | .304 | 2 | 3 | 0 | 1.000 |
| 1935 | St. Louis | Amer. | INF | 10 | 24 | 1 | 5 | 3 | 0 | 0 | 3 | .208 | 38 | 5 | 0 | 1.000 |
| 1936 | St. Louis | Amer. | 1B | 2 | 5 | 1 | 2 | 0 | 0 | 0 | 2 | .400 | 10 | 0 | 0 | 1.000 |
| 1937 | St. Louis | Amer. | 2B | 20 | 56 | 7 | 18 | 3 | 0 | 1 | 11 | .321 | 30 | 41 | 4 | .947 |
| 1938 | Baltimore | Int. | 2-1B-OF | 16 | 27 | 2 | 2 | 0 | 0 | 0 | 0 | .074 | 22 | 2 | 0 | 1.000 |
| 1939 | Chattanooga | South | 2B | 3 | 3 | 1 | 2 | 0 | 0 | 1 | 2 | .667 | 0 | 0 | 0 | .000 |
| 1940 | Oklahoma City | Tex. | PH | 1 | 1 | 0 | 1 | 0 | 0 | 0 | 0 | 1.000 | 0 | 0 | 0 | .000 |
| 1942 | Ft. Worth | Tex. | 2B | 1 | 4 | 0 | 1 | 0 | 0 | 0 | 2 | .250 | 2 | 2 | 0 | 1.000 |

| | | | | | | | | | | | | | | | | |
|------|------|--------|------|----|-----|----|----|-----|-----|-----|------|------|-----|-----|-----|------|
| National League Totals | | | | 2192 | 8056 | 1566 | 2895 | 532 | 168 | 299 | 1550 | .359 | 4201 | 6767 | 492 | .957 |
| American League Totals | | | | 67 | 117 | 13 | 35 | 9 | 0 | 3 | 29 | .299 | 80 | 49 | 4 | .970 |
| Major League Totals | | | | 2259 | 8173 | 1579 | 2930 | 541 | 168 | 302 | 1579 | .358 | 4281 | 6816 | 496 | .957 |

a Traded to New York Giants for infielder Frank Frisch and pitcher Jimmy Ring, December 20, 1926.
b Traded to Boston Braves for outfielder Jimmy Welsh and catcher Francis Hogan, January 10, 1928.
c Traded to Chicago Cubs for infielder Fred Maguire, catcher Doc Leggett, pitchers Percy Jones, Harry Seibold and Bruce Cunningham and $200,000, November 7, 1928.
d Signed with St. Louis Cardinals, October 24, 1932.

### WORLD SERIES RECORD

| YEAR | CLUB | LEAGUE | POS. | G. | AB. | R. | H. | 2B. | 3B. | HR. | RBI. | B.A. | PO. | A. | E. | F.A. |
|------|------|--------|------|----|-----|----|----|-----|-----|-----|------|------|-----|-----|-----|------|
| 1926 | St. Louis | Nat. | 2B | 7 | 28 | 2 | 7 | 1 | 0 | 0 | 4 | .250 | 15 | 21 | 0 | 1.000 |
| 1929 | Chicago | Nat. | 2B | 5 | 21 | 4 | 5 | 1 | 1 | 0 | 1 | .238 | 9 | 11 | 1 | .952 |
| World Series Totals | | | | 12 | 49 | 6 | 12 | 2 | 1 | 0 | 5 | .245 | 24 | 32 | 1 | .982 |

Relentlessly confident, Cincinnati player-manager Pete Rose sent himself up to pinch hit against flame-throwing Goose Gossage in his last at-bat. He struck out.
©DIAMOND IMAGES®

# PETE ROSE

## *A Late Scratch*

| | |
|---|---|
| **DATE:** | August 17, 1986 |
| **SITE:** | Riverfront Stadium, Cincinnati, Ohio |
| **PITCHER:** | Rich "Goose" Gossage of San Diego Padres |
| **RESULT:** | Strikeout |

**August 17, 1986, Cincinnati**—He got up from his spot in the dugout and went to the bat rack in the bottom of the ninth. Nobody said a word.

Here it was, mid-August, and Pete Rose's fourth-place Cincinnati Reds were trailing the San Diego Padres, the worst team in the National League, 9-5.

It didn't look as if things were going to improve any time soon. Padres' reliever Rich "Goose" Gossage was in his second inning of relief and still throwing aspirin tablets. Looking down the dugout, it was hard to find any volunteers.

Earlier in the game, Rose, in his second year as player-manager, had already made some moves. He'd already sent Tony Perez and John Milner up as pinch-hitters. He was running out of choices.

With the top of the order coming up here in the ninth, he needed somebody else to get on base. Why not him? Nobody else was offering.

The dog days of August were setting in and Rose's Reds seemed to be going nowhere. They were already 10-and-a-half games behind Houston, five games under .500. Following Rose's encouraging second-place finish last year—he took over the team after being dealt from Montreal in midseason—many thought this year's club would win it all.

"Reds keep skidding, Rose whiffs"

But the year was a bust. Rose was on the disabled list when the year began. The Reds couldn't sort out their pitching, dropped 19 of their first 25 games and for months, couldn't seem to get rolling.

Worse, Rose, now 45 years old, couldn't step in and help. He'd played in just 72 of the team's first 116 games and seemed relegated to pinch hitting and playing the occasional day game after a night game.

At the start of the month, Rose's skidding average had bottomed out at a miserable .204. Had he not been the manager, there's no doubt he would have been shamed into retirement. This was not the way a Hall of Famer ought to go out.

Yet Rose had one surprise left.

One marvelous Monday night, Rose turned back the clock for the last time. He found his stroke and went 5-for-5 (including the final extra-base hit of his career, his 746th double), off three different San Francisco Giants' pitchers—Mike LaCoss, Mark Davis, and Frank Williams.

While Rose's five hits mattered little in a 13-4 San Francisco win, how could you not write about Pete Rose?

Author Roger Kahn, at work on a book on Rose, was there to document the scene. It was like feeding drugged canaries to a manic cat.

A sportswriter asked Rose if he knew how many five-hit games he'd had.

"That would be 10," Rose said.

What about the National League record, someone else asked?

"I got it now, if I'm not mistaken," Rose said. "The old record was nine. Belonged to Max Carey."

"And the major-league record?" came a third voice.

"Again, if I'm not mistaken," Rose said, "that would be Cobb. You guys remember Cobb. Supposed to have been a mean guy, but he got a lot of hits."

A reporter asked what this achievement meant to him. Rose smiled.

"A slightly larger stone on my grave," he said.

It was his first five-hit game since April 28, four years earlier. It raised his average to a grand .218. The Reds were still 10 games out.

Fueled by his big night, Rose kept himself close to the bat rack for what would be his final active week.

Tuesday night, Rose sent himself up as a pinch-hitter against the Giants' Scott Garrelts in a 2-1 loss and grounded out. He did the same thing the next night in an 8-6 win.

Yet as he sat in his office, making out his lineup every night, it was beginning to be hard to know when to play and when to sit. When does a manager bench himself?

Both Joe Torre (with the Mets) and Frank Robinson (with the Indians) took a brief shot at playing and managing at the same time. But neither one lasted many games. As a manager, there were too many distractions. And Rose found he was sensitive to criticism.

He knew that not everybody recognized all that went into his job, but handling the second-guess, that was a pitch he wasn't ready to foul off. He explained as much to a visiting writer over batting practice one afternoon, after receiving a particularly nasty letter from a fan.

"Guy's writing that I should have brought in Ron Robinson to replace Ted Power," he said, "Well, I didn't have Ron Robinson to bring in. He couldn't pitch but the guy writing it 1,200 miles away doesn't know that.

"Same as the people who wrote that I put Ty Cobb's record ahead of the team last year. I play in only 119 games, but I'm second in the league in walks. I don't start myself against left-handers and I hit .354 against them. And I'm putting myself ahead of the Cincinnati Reds? I don't let that stuff annoy me but, man, I don't understand it."

As this final week finished, Rose collected what would be the final hit of his career. Facing the Giants' Kelly Downs and reliever Greg Minton, he batted second, played first base, and had three hits as John Denny threw a three-hit shutout against the Giants. Rose even drove in the game-winning run with a fifth-inning single.

By the weekend, something changed in the clubhouse and in Rose's mind. His old pal Tony Perez, back with the Reds, had already announced he'd retire at the end of the season. He wanted to play first.

Rose also had promising Nick Esasky, a strong right-handed power hitter in the dugout, too. With just 50 games to play, Rose knew he had to do something to get the Reds' attack rolling.

In Friday's twi-night doubleheader vs. the Padres, Rose did pinch hit and make an out in the first game, a 7-2 win, then played first base against his old pal Eric Show, the Padres' pitcher who had surrendered Rose's 4,192nd hit to surpass Cobb last summer and went 0 for-4.

He played on Saturday against Ed Whitson and Lance McCullers in a 4-1 Reds' win. But his 0-4 dropping his seasonal average to .219 and his career average to .303. The guy who'd won four National League batting titles, three of them with averages over .330, well, that guy wasn't stepping into batter's boxes these days. With another out or three, he'd be below .300 for his career, just like Mickey Mantle.

He'd been at this for so long now. There were so many other things to deal with as a manager. And distractions away from the field, too. After all this time in fame's fast lane, Pete Rose wasn't about to stop taking chances. But the batting average? That was history. You didn't screw with that.

There were other things tugging at Rose now, not just age. The fans could sense it, perhaps, but still hoped their hero would come through. They didn't realize the gambling fever was taking over.

Rose, like a lot of other baseball people from Rogers Hornsby all the way to Don Zimmer, loved to spend every spare moment at the track. It wasn't hard to figure why. They liked the action, the excitement, anything that got the adrenaline going.

But there were rumblings that this wasn't just gambling there. It wasn't only wagers on college football and basketball. Or the NFL. If the talk was right, this was more serious. There was talk that Rose was betting on his own sport, baseball.

There would be talk that when the Riverfront Stadium out of town scoreboard was out of action for a couple months, Rose had a pal in the stands keeping tabs on all the other games Pete had supposedly bet on. Supposedly, the two exchanged signals throughout the game so Pete could keep tabs on his bets.

Gambling on baseball is a sore subject in Cincinnati. It was the underdog Redlegs who were the beneficiaries of the 1919 World Series title supposedly thrown by the Chicago "Black Sox" and the town has understandably been sensitive on the subject ever since.

But if there were any questions about Pete's off-the-field behavior when he played for the Reds or when he came back to manage, nobody said a word about it. He was a folk hero in Cincinnati.

When Rose let it be known he wanted out of Montreal in 1984, Cincinnati president Bob Howsam got a call from Rose's agent Reuven Katz and the two talked about Rose becoming manager.

There were problems. One was Rose's $500,000 salary, which was more than the Reds could afford, Howsam said. The other was Howsam didn't think Rose could hit anymore.

Rose, never one to back down from a challenge, knew what he wanted to have happen. Like he explained to writer Roger Kahn some time later, Rose knew how to get things his way.

"There aren't many things I back away from," he said. "If they wouldn't let me play back home in Cincinnati, then I was damned if I was going to manage. I'd hang in at Montreal and take my chances, as a free agent, it looked like, the following year.

"But I wanted to come home to be with the Reds when they won a pennant. I wanted to come home like a kid who forgot his school lunch somewhere and is standing in the yard smelling his mother's cooking through a window. . . ."

There was another problem. The Major League Players Union has an across-the-board rule that no player's salary may be reduced more than 20 percent at one time. Howsam was offering Rose $225,000, less than half his salary in Montreal.

But Rose really wanted to come home. He applied to the union for a dispensation and they agreed.

The next day, Rose was in uniform and in his very first at-bat against the Phillies' Dick Ruthven, ripped a single to center field. When the ball was misplayed, Rose came around second and flew into third with a wonderful belly whomping, headfirst slide. Yesssssireeeee. Pete Rose was back. That was two years ago. A lot can happen in two years.

Rose looked around at the middling crowd of 27,175. There was no huge reaction from the crowd when he was announced. He'd stayed long enough to be overlooked.

Rose walked up to the plate, took his familiar crouch in the left-hand batter's box against Gossage and got ready for his 14,053rd and final major-league at-bat.

Zing. . . . Gossage's fastball blistered past Rose's feeble swing. Home-plate umpire Ed Montague signaled Strike One. Gotta be quicker, he thought. Damn. Quicker.

Gossage wound and with that wild, tottering delivery, fired again.

Zing. . . . Rose swung through another fastball. Goose was bringing it. Rose stepped out of the batter's box. I'm not going to catch up with that, he thought. Nobody had gotten a hit off Gossage yet. Or a walk. Didn't look like anybody would.

Rose peered out at the mound in that crouch, his chin tucked behind his right shoulder, trying to pick the ball up out of Gossage's windmill motion. He saw Gossage rock and let the ball go. There was no way, just no way to get a bat on it. He swung and missed and the ball popped into catcher Bruce Bochy's glove.

He never batted again.

A week later, the Reds rolled into Chicago and *Tribune* columnist Bob Verdi asked him why he wasn't playing.

"Want to get Esasky in there," Rose said. "My decision to retire or not depends on how I finish up and how we finish up. There's no hurry. I don't want to make it before the season ends so I can have a night in Riverfront. I've had enough hullabaloo in my career."

So there would be no Pete Rose Farewell Tour?

"If I knew that was going to happen to me, I would have done that," Rose told Kahn. "But I didn't know and I had my philosophy. You see, play, or manage, I was going to the ballpark every day. I was putting my uniform on. It was not like I was going to be away from it."

Besides, as we would find out later, Rose had many other problems at the time. Concentrating on managing and hitting and keeping up with all the off-the-field nonsense was too much.

Years later, Rose explained his sudden benching to author Roger Kahn this way.

"My buddy Tony Perez had shared first base with me. Tony was in his last year. He had announced his retirement. He was a couple of home runs behind Orlando Cepeda as the most productive home run hitter of all the Latin players.

"He did end up tying that record," Rose said. "As a matter of fact, in the last week of the season Tony played and he was player of the week in the National League. I let him play the whole month of September because he was swinging the bat good and I wanted him to get the record."

But Rose's term as manager was short-lived. The off-the-field stuff escalated to the point where it became scandalous. A *Sports Illustrated* story blew it wide open.

Three years and one week later, he was sent away from the game for good.

Four months after it was alleged that Rose had been betting on baseball (among other things), then-commissioner Bart Giamatti ended a long investigation with Rose signing an agreement that would permit him to step away without admitting to gambling.

Then Giamatti made an announcement.

"The banishment for life of Pete Rose from baseball is the sad end of a sorry episode," Giamatti said. "One of the game's greatest players has engaged in a variety of acts which have stained the game and he must now live with the consequences of those acts. . . ."

In the press conference afterward, Rose felt double-crossed. Giamatti and he had agreed on a deal, that the commissioner's office wouldn't say that Pete Rose bet on baseball and that Rose himself would leave quietly.

Yet when a reporter asked Giamatti if he believed that Rose bet on baseball, the commissioner said he believed Rose had.

Nine days later, Giamatti was dead. Of a heart attack. Rose stuck to the statements he made after the lifetime ban—namely, that he never bet on baseball.

As the ban pushed on into its 16th year, Rose, baseball's all-time hit leader, could see his chances for Hall of Fame induction vanishing. A player remains on the Baseball Writers Association ballot for 20 years. Since Rose was confident that many of the writers were in favor of him being elected to the Hall, if he could get himself off the permanently ineligible list and on their ballot, they might vote him in.

If the writers didn't put him in, it'd be up to the Veterans' Committee to select him and Rose wasn't sure how that would go. Many of those players are on record as being against Rose's induction. Some have even threatened to boycott future induction ceremonies if he's elected.

So Rose found someone to float the word: confession to the commissioner's office, his old teammate, Joe Morgan.

In November, he was summoned to a meeting with Commissioner Bud Selig in Milwaukee. Selig asked Rose the question he finally understood he had to answer.

**"Goose gets Rose's gander in Reds' loss"**

As recounted in Rose's 2004 book, *My Prison without Bars* and excerpted in *Sports Illustrated*'s January 12 issue, the meeting went like this: "Mr. Selig looked at me and said, 'I want to know one thing. Did you bet on baseball?'"

"Yes," Rose said. "I did bet on baseball."

"How often?" Selig asked.

"Four or five times a week," Rose replied. "But I never bet against my own team and I never made any bets from the clubhouse."

"Why?" Selig asked.

"I didn't think I'd get caught," Rose said.

# Pete Sent Packing

| SAN DIEGO | ab. | r. | h. | bi. |
|---|---|---|---|---|
| Royster, 3b | 5 | 2 | 2 | 0 |
| Gwynn, cf | 5 | 3 | 3 | 1 |
| Kruk, lf | 5 | 2 | 3 | 2 |
| Garvey, 1b | 4 | 1 | 1 | 1 |
| Bochy, c | 5 | 0 | 2 | 3 |
| Templeton, ss | 4 | 0 | 2 | 1 |
| Wynne, cf | 5 | 0 | 0 | 1 |
| Roberts, 2b | 4 | 0 | 0 | 0 |
| Lefferts, p | 0 | 0 | 0 | 0 |
| McCullers, p | 0 | 0 | 0 | 0 |
| Gossage, p | 1 | 0 | 0 | 0 |
| Hoyt, p | 2 | 1 | 0 | 0 |
| Walter, p | 0 | 0 | 0 | 0 |
| Flannery, 2b | 1 | 0 | 0 | 0 |
| **TOTALS:** | **41** | **9** | **13** | **9** |

| CINCINNATI | ab. | r. | h. | bi. |
|---|---|---|---|---|
| Daniels, lf | 5 | 0 | 1 | 1 |
| Venable, cf | 5 | 0 | 0 | 0 |
| Parker, rf | 4 | 0 | 1 | 0 |
| B. Diaz, c | 4 | 1 | 2 | 0 |
| Bell, 3b | 3 | 1 | 1 | 2 |
| Larkin, ss | 4 | 1 | 1 | 1 |
| Esasky, 1b | 4 | 0 | 0 | 0 |
| Oester, 2b | 4 | 2 | 2 | 1 |
| Welsh, p | 0 | 0 | 0 | 0 |
| R. Murphy, p | 0 | 0 | 0 | 0 |
| Perez, ph | 1 | 0 | 0 | 0 |
| Willis, p | 0 | 0 | 0 | 0 |
| Power, p | 0 | 0 | 0 | 0 |
| Milner, ph | 1 | 0 | 1 | 0 |
| R. Robinson, p | 0 | 0 | 0 | 0 |
| Rose, ph | 1 | 0 | 0 | 0 |
| Franco, p | 0 | 0 | 0 | 0 |
| **TOTALS:** | **36** | **5** | **9** | **5** |

```
San Diego  ......  0 0 1  0 4 3  0 1 0—9
Cincinnati ......  0 0 0  0 1 4  0 0 0—5
```

| SAN DIEGO | IP | H | R | ER | BB | SO |
|---|---|---|---|---|---|---|
| Hoyt (W, 7-8) | 5 2/3 | 7 | 5 | 5 | 2 | 4 |
| Walter | 1/3 | 1 | 0 | 0 | 0 | 0 |
| Lefferts | 2/3 | 1 | 0 | 0 | 1 | 1 |
| McCullers | 1/3 | 0 | 0 | 0 | 0 | 0 |
| Gossage | 2 | 0 | 0 | 0 | 0 | 2 |
| CINCINNATI | | | | | | |
| Welsh (L, 4-4) | 4 1/3 | 8 | 5 | 5 | 2 | 4 |
| R. Murphy | 2/3 | 0 | 0 | 0 | 0 | 0 |
| Willis | 2/3 | 4 | 3 | 3 | 1 | 0 |
| Power | 1/3 | 0 | 0 | 0 | 0 | 1 |
| R. Robinson | 2 | 1 | 1 | 1 | 0 | 1 |
| Franco | 1 | 0 | 0 | 0 | 0 | 0 |

Game-winning RBI: Garvey (7). E: Esasky, Daniels, Royster. LOB: San Diego 8, Cincinnati 7. 2B: Gwynn, Kruk, Oester, Bochy. HR: Bell (13), Larkin (1), Oester (6), Kruk (3). SB: Daniels (10). U: Montague, Brocklander, Rippley, Rennert. T: 2:38. A: 27,175.

## PETER EDWARD ROSE

Nickname: Charlie Hustle
Born April 14, 1941, in Cincinnati, Ohio
Height: 5-11 Weight: 200
Threw right-handed, batted left- and right-handed
Career total = 24 years

| SEASON | TEAM | G | AB | R | H | 2B | 3B | HR | RBI | TB | BB | SO | SB | CS | BA |
|---|---|---|---|---|---|---|---|---|---|---|---|---|---|---|---|
| 1963 | Cincinnati Reds | 157 | 623 | 101 | 170 | 25 | 9 | 6 | 41 | 231 | 55 | 72 | 13 | 15 | .273 |
| 1964 | Cincinnati Reds | 136 | 516 | 64 | 139 | 13 | 2 | 4 | 34 | 168 | 36 | 51 | 4 | 10 | .269 |
| 1965 | Cincinnati Reds | 162 | 670 | 117 | 209 | 35 | 11 | 11 | 81 | 299 | 69 | 76 | 8 | 3 | .312 |
| 1966 | Cincinnati Reds | 156 | 654 | 97 | 205 | 38 | 5 | 16 | 70 | 301 | 37 | 61 | 4 | 9 | .313 |
| 1967 | Cincinnati Reds | 148 | 585 | 86 | 176 | 32 | 8 | 12 | 76 | 260 | 56 | 66 | 11 | 6 | .301 |
| 1968 | Cincinnati Reds | 149 | 626 | 94 | 210 | 42 | 6 | 10 | 49 | 294 | 56 | 76 | 3 | 7 | .335 |
| 1969 | Cincinnati Reds | 156 | 627 | 120 | 218 | 33 | 11 | 16 | 82 | 321 | 88 | 65 | 7 | 10 | .348 |
| 1970 | Cincinnati Reds | 159 | 649 | 120 | 205 | 37 | 9 | 15 | 52 | 305 | 73 | 64 | 12 | 7 | .316 |
| 1971 | Cincinnati Reds | 160 | 632 | 86 | 192 | 27 | 4 | 13 | 44 | 266 | 68 | 50 | 13 | 9 | .304 |
| 1972 | Cincinnati Reds | 154 | 645 | 107 | 198 | 31 | 11 | 6 | 57 | 269 | 73 | 46 | 10 | 3 | .307 |
| 1973 | Cincinnati Reds | 160 | 680 | 115 | 230 | 36 | 8 | 5 | 64 | 297 | 65 | 42 | 10 | 7 | .338 |
| 1974 | Cincinnati Reds | 163 | 652 | 110 | 185 | 45 | 7 | 3 | 51 | 253 | 106 | 54 | 2 | 4 | .284 |
| 1975 | Cincinnati Reds | 162 | 662 | 112 | 210 | 47 | 4 | 7 | 74 | 286 | 89 | 50 | 0 | 1 | .317 |
| 1976 | Cincinnati Reds | 162 | 665 | 130 | 215 | 42 | 6 | 10 | 63 | 299 | 86 | 54 | 9 | 5 | .323 |
| 1977 | Cincinnati Reds | 162 | 655 | 95 | 204 | 38 | 7 | 9 | 64 | 283 | 66 | 42 | 16 | 4 | .311 |
| 1978 | Cincinnati Reds | 159 | 655 | 103 | 198 | 51 | 3 | 7 | 52 | 276 | 62 | 30 | 13 | 9 | .302 |
| 1979 | Philadelphia Phillies | 163 | 628 | 90 | 208 | 40 | 5 | 4 | 59 | 270 | 95 | 32 | 20 | 11 | .331 |
| 1980 | Philadelphia Phillies | 162 | 655 | 95 | 185 | 42 | 1 | 1 | 64 | 232 | 66 | 33 | 12 | 8 | .282 |
| 1981 | Philadelphia Phillies | 107 | 431 | 73 | 140 | 18 | 5 | 0 | 33 | 168 | 46 | 26 | 4 | 4 | .325 |
| 1982 | Philadelphia Phillies | 162 | 634 | 80 | 172 | 25 | 4 | 3 | 54 | 214 | 66 | 32 | 8 | 8 | .271 |
| 1983 | Philadelphia Phillies | 151 | 493 | 52 | 121 | 14 | 3 | 0 | 45 | 141 | 52 | 28 | 7 | 7 | .245 |
| 1984 | Cincinnati Reds | 26 | 96 | 9 | 35 | 9 | 0 | 0 | 11 | 44 | 9 | 7 | 0 | 0 | .259 |
| 1984 | Montreal Expos | 95 | 278 | 34 | 72 | 6 | 2 | 0 | 23 | 82 | 31 | 20 | 1 | 1 | .365 |
| 1985 | Cincinnati Reds | 119 | 405 | 60 | 107 | 12 | 2 | 2 | 46 | 129 | 86 | 35 | 8 | 1 | .264 |
| 1986 | Cincinnati Reds | 72 | 237 | 15 | 52 | 8 | 2 | 0 | 25 | 64 | 30 | 31 | 3 | 0 | .217 |
| **Career Totals** | | 3562 | 14053 | 2165 | 4256 | 746 | 135 | 160 | 1314 | 5752 | 1566 | 1143 | 198 | 149 | .303 |

Hometown hero Joe Morgan wound up a Hall of Fame career in Oakland with a double in his final at-bat.
Photo courtesy of National Baseball Hall of Fame Library, Cooperstown, New York.

# JOE MORGAN

## *Staying under the Radar*

**DATE:** September 29, 1984

**SITE:** Oakland Coliseum, Oakland, California

**PITCHER:** Mark Gubicza of Kansas City Royals

**RESULT:** Double to left center

**September 29, 1984, OAKLAND**—He could hear the mitt popping. Kansas City's Mark Gubicza, a 6-foot 5-inch rookie fireballer, was bringing the high, hard one as he took his warm-up pitches for his 29th and final regular-season start.

You could hear the pop of fastball after fastball all over Oakland Coliseum as a trickle of die-hard A's fans trekked in for Fan Appreciation Day. Some, maybe, came to say goodbye to Joe Morgan.

Inside the Oakland dugout, the old-timer was watching Gubicza's every pitch, smiling to himself. One more hard-throwing kid who thinks he can throw the ol' pill past Joe. We'll have to see about that.

His long haul through a 22-year major-league career was over. This was going to be Joe Morgan's last game. It'd be nice to go out with a hit.

With his mother and father in the stands, along with 23,036 other fans on a sunny Sunday afternoon just down the street from where he grew up, Joe wanted to wrap things up right. That's how he did things.

He had his dad, Leonard, throw him the ceremonial first pitch. He had friends and family in the stands to see him bow out in his hometown, the place he left some 20-odd years ago with the crazy notion that a 5-foot 5-inch, 150-pound high schooler could play major-league baseball and have a major impact.

Morgan did. Way more than his relatively modest (by Hall of Fame standards) career numbers would ever show.

On this final Sunday, Morgan's departure was hardly front-page news. There was no mention of his impending retirement in any of the country's major newspapers. No big feature stories bidding him a fond farewell. There was no ESPN, of course, no live up-to-the-minute coverage of his departure.

Heck, by the time the game was over and the Oakland reporters hit the A's locker room, all that Joe Morgan left behind was an empty locker. At 5-feet 7-inches (maybe), Morgan made a career out of flying under the radar.

That's how he liked it. Coming out of Oakland's Castlemont High, a baseball-rich area that produced big leaguers like Frank Robinson, Vada Pinson, and Willie Stargell, Morgan was a fine high school player. But nobody would look at him because of his size, or lack of it.

Only the National League expansion team from Houston, the Colt 45s, later the Astros, were interested. They signed him out of junior college for $3,000. They were so desperate for talent, Morgan found himself in the big leagues for eight games at age 20. He wasn't ready.

Two years later, he was back with the big club and stayed seven seasons with the Astros, all well under the radar. He was a solid major league player and Houston liked him. But Cincinnati saw something in him, something the Astros didn't suspect. They thought Morgan just might be the catalyst for the gathering collection of talent that would become the Big Red Machine.

He was smart, he was fast, he was always on base and better than anybody else in the game; he was one step ahead, mentally. But he was little. How long would he last?

The Astros now know the answer to that question. In leading the Reds to two World Championships in 1975 and 1976, Morgan won himself two MVP awards, amassed five Gold Gloves and seven All-Star berths. He played until he was 40.

But he never forgot that it all could have been different. He couldn't help but remember. Tony Perez was always reminding him, "If you had stayed in Houston," Perez would laugh, "nobody would know who you are."

Under the radar, indeed. Luck and timing had always been a key part of baseball. What if Babe Ruth had stayed in Boston? What if Stan Musial hadn't hurt his arm pitching and turned to outfielding? The history of the game was filled with "what ifs." Joe Morgan was one more.

After all the games and the end-of-career jumping around, from Cincinnati to Houston to San Francisco to Philadelphia, he'd finally landed back in Oakland. It hadn't been a wonderful year. His average hovered in the low .240s and the team—well, they would never really get it together.

Morgan had thought about retiring after teaming up with old Reds' teammates Pete Rose and Tony Perez to lead the Philadelphia Phillies into the 1983 World Series. He was going to retire on top. He wanted to wrap things up right.

But in the off-season, Morgan struck up a friendship with Oakland club president Roy Eisenhardt. Eisenhardt wanted Morgan to play with the A's, offered him a two-year deal. He figured Joe could bring some maturity and wisdom to a team in tatters after the Billy Martin regime.

Morgan wasn't sure it was the right thing to do. He'd been a career-long National Leaguer. Could he handle being a part-time player, being a designated hitter?

In the end, though, Morgan decided to play. Plus, there was one pretty big carrot out there for him. The all-time record for home runs by a second baseman was 264 by Rogers Hornsby. Morgan was two away. Now, he'd never been a real big stats guy. But Rogers Hornsby? That was tempting.

So, Morgan signed on with the A's and manager Steve Boros and his cast of excitables like Rickey Henderson, Dwayne Murphy, the always-cheery Dave Kingman, and his fiery protégé, Tony Phillips.

Problem was, all of the A's weren't as focused on the things Joe Morgan was. They were a second-division team with first-division talent.

On this, the final day of the season, the team in the other dugout, the Kansas City Royals, had an eight-game lead. They were thinking ahead to their playoff series with Detroit, which would start in Kansas City on Tuesday.

The Royals had beaten Oakland 6-5 on Friday night, clinching the West title behind Charlie Liebrandt and Dan Quisenberry. Morgan, who'd played about twice a week down the stretch, pinch hit and grounded out. Boros gave him Saturday off against Royals' ace Bret Saberhagen.

*"Hometown hero makes silent exit"*

Here on Sunday, he was back in his No. 2 spot in the batting order. He heard his name announced and strode toward the plate.

Even though it had been six years since he'd worn a Cincinnati Reds' uniform, somehow the No. 8—chosen in honor of friend Willie Stargell—didn't look right on the green uniform shirt. He waved the bat back and forth and did that strange little elbow flip with his arm, the one that always got people talking and pointing.

Then here it came—a fastball—and Morgan swung, a full, healthy cut and the ball screamed out into left center. Morgan, as always, was out of the box quickly and he sailed into second base with a double, the 449th of his career. His 2,518th hit.

The Coliseum faithful stood and cheered for the small man in green and white, who waved to them all, flashed that winning smile. He looked up and here came his protégé, another smallish second baseman, Tony Phillips, in to run for him. The baton was passed. Morgan headed for the dugout, his mission completed.

He wound up with a career batting average of .271, some 87 points lower than the career average for second-base icon Rogers Hornsby. Yet, five years later, Morgan was a first-ballot Hall of Famer, something Joe DiMaggio couldn't boast of.

"To make it in on the first ballot is unbelievable," Morgan said then. "Only players who are deemed great make it on the first ballot. I guess that makes me a great second baseman. I'm appreciative [the writers] took the time to look beyond the numbers."

To those who played with him, there was little debate about that issue. "He did it all and he did it all the time," teammate Johnny Bench said. "I always thought Joe was the best player I ever played with, and that takes in a lot of ground."

Oddly, Morgan had never thought about the Hall of Fame until about midway through his career. Then Sparky Anderson, his old Cincinnati Reds' manager said something to him.

"In 1975, at the end of the season," Morgan recalled, "Sparky said 'You're going to be Most Valuable in the league. Joe, you need one of those to get in the Hall of Fame.'

"That was the first time I thought about going to the Hall of Fame," Morgan said on the eve of his election in 1990. "I started thinking, maybe. I never thought for sure."

Funny enough, the guy who had everything in his career work out just about right was thrown a curve on his big day. The 1990 Hall of Fame Induction Ceremony was rained out. It ended up being held the next day in the Cooperstown High School gym.

That was okay with Morgan. He had education on his mind, anyway. He'd just completed his bachelor's degree, fulfilling a promise he'd made to his mother way back when he first signed a pro contract.

*"One last hit and Joe Morgan is gone"*

"It took me 22 years in the major leagues to get a plaque in the Hall of Fame and it took me 27 years to get my degree. But I'm thrilled to have them both."

When he finally was handed his Hall of Fame plaque, the little guy from Oakland who flew under the radar was amazed by his own ability to make such a perfect landing.

"Mays, Musial, and Morgan in the same breath," he said. "I'm not sure I'll ever get used to that."

# A Sweet Finish for Joe

| KANSAS CITY | ab. | r. | h. | bi. |
|---|---|---|---|---|
| U. Wshtn, ss | 4 | 1 | 2 | 0 |
| L. Jones, cf | 4 | 0 | 1 | 1 |
| McRae, dh | 3 | 0 | 1 | 0 |
| Roberts, ph | 1 | 0 | 1 | 1 |
| Balboni, 1b | 2 | 0 | 0 | 0 |
| D. Forg, rf | 2 | 0 | 0 | 0 |
| Motley, rf | 2 | 0 | 1 | 0 |
| Leeper, rf | 2 | 0 | 0 | 0 |
| Pryor, 3b | 2 | 0 | 0 | 0 |
| Scrantn, 3b | 2 | 0 | 0 | 0 |
| Wathan, lf | 3 | 0 | 0 | 0 |
| Pujois, c | 3 | 0 | 0 | 0 |
| Blancin, 2b | 3 | 1 | 1 | 0 |
| **TOTALS:** | **33** | **2** | **7** | **2** |

| OAKLAND | ab. | r. | h. | bi. |
|---|---|---|---|---|
| R. Hndsn, lf | 3 | 1 | 0 | 0 |
| Heath, lf | 1 | 0 | 1 | 0 |
| Morgan, 2b | 1 | 0 | 1 | 0 |
| Phillips, 2b | 3 | 2 | 1 | 3 |
| Kiefer, ss | 1 | 0 | 0 | 0 |
| Murphy, cf | 3 | 1 | 1 | 0 |
| Hancck, rf | 1 | 0 | 0 | 0 |
| Kngmn, dh | 1 | 0 | 0 | 0 |
| Meyer, ph | 1 | 0 | 0 | 0 |
| Burghs, ph | 1 | 0 | 0 | 0 |
| Essian, ph | 0 | 0 | 0 | 0 |
| Bochte, 1b | 2 | 1 | 1 | 1 |
| Almon, 1b | 2 | 0 | 0 | 0 |
| M. Davis, rf | 3 | 2 | 1 | 3 |
| Tettleton, c | 4 | 0 | 2 | 0 |
| D. Hill, ss | 4 | 1 | 4 | 1 |
| Wagner, 3b | 4 | 0 | 0 | 0 |
| **TOTALS:** | **35** | **8** | **12** | **8** |

```
Kansas City .............  000  000  0 0 2 2
Oakland ...................  400  300  1 0 x 8
```

Game winning RBI: Bochte (9). E: U. Washington, L. Jones. DP: Kansas City 2, Oakland 1. LOB: Kansas City 4, Oakland 8. 2B: Morgan, L. Jones. HR: M. Davis (9), Phillips (4).

| | IP | H | R | ER | BB | SO |
|---|---|---|---|---|---|---|
| **KANSAS CITY** | | | | | | |
| Gubicza (L, 10-14) | 3 | 6 | 4 | 4 | 1 | 2 |
| M. Jones | 2 | 3 | 3 | 3 | 1 | 2 |
| Beckwith | 1 | 0 | 0 | 0 | 1 | 2 |
| D. Jackson | 2 | 3 | 1 | 1 | 2 | 2 |
| | | | | | | |
| **OAKLAND** | | | | | | |
| Krueger (W, 10-10) | 6 | 3 | 0 | 0 | 0 | 3 |
| Warren | 1 | 0 | 0 | 0 | 0 | 0 |
| Leiper | 2 | 4 | 2 | 2 | 0 | 1 |

T: 2:11. A: 23,028.

## JOE LEONARD MORGAN

Nickname: —
Born September 19, 1943, in Bonham, Tex.
Height: 5-7, Weight: 160
Threw right-handed and batted left-handed
Career total = 22 years
Named to Hall of Fame: 1990

| YEAR | CLUB | POS. | G. | AB. | R. | H. | 2B. | 3B. | HR. | RBI. | B.A. | A. | E. | F.A. |
|------|------|------|-----|------|------|------|-----|-----|-----|------|------|------|-----|-------|
| 1963 | Colt .45s | 2B | 7 | 25 | 5 | 6 | 0 | 1 | 0 | 3 | .240 | 15 | 3 | .909 |
| 1964 | Colt .45s | 2B | 10 | 37 | 4 | 7 | 0 | 0 | 0 | 0 | .189 | 25 | 3 | .949 |
| 1965 | Astros | 2B | 157 | 601 | 100 | 163 | 22 | 12 | 14 | 40 | .271 | 492 | 27 | .969 |
| 1966 | Astros | 2B | 117 | 425 | 60 | 121 | 14 | 8 | 5 | 42 | .285 | 316 | 21 | .965 |
| 1967 | Astros | 2B | 130 | 494 | 73 | 136 | 27 | 11 | 6 | 42 | .275 | 344 | 14 | .979 |
| 1967 | Astros | LF | 1 | — | — | — | — | — | — | — | — | 0 | 0 | 1.000 |
| 1968 | Astros | 2B | 5 | 20 | 6 | 5 | 0 | 1 | 0 | 0 | .250 | 6 | 2 | .882 |
| 1968 | Astros | LF | 1 | — | — | — | — | — | — | — | — | 0 | 0 | 1.000 |
| 1969 | Astros | 2B | 132 | 535 | 94 | 126 | 18 | 5 | 15 | 43 | .236 | 328 | 18 | .972 |
| 1969 | Astros | OF | 14 | — | — | — | — | — | — | — | — | 0 | 0 | 1.000 |
| 1970 | Astros | 2B | 142 | 548 | 102 | 147 | 28 | 9 | 8 | 52 | .268 | 430 | 17 | .979 |
| 1971 | Astros | 2B | 157 | 583 | 87 | 149 | 27 | 11 | 13 | 56 | .256 | 482 | 12 | .986 |
| 1972 | Reds | 2B | 149 | 552 | 122 | 161 | 23 | 4 | 16 | 73 | .292 | 436 | 8 | .990 |
| 1973 | Reds | 2B | 154 | 576 | 116 | 167 | 35 | 2 | 26 | 82 | .290 | 440 | 9 | .990 |
| 1974 | Reds | 2B | 142 | 512 | 107 | 150 | 31 | 3 | 22 | 67 | .293 | 385 | 13 | .982 |
| 1975 | Reds | 2B | 142 | 498 | 107 | 163 | 27 | 6 | 17 | 94 | .327 | 425 | 11 | .986 |
| 1976 | Reds | 2B | 133 | 472 | 113 | 151 | 30 | 5 | 27 | 111 | .320 | 335 | 13 | .981 |
| 1977 | Reds | 2B | 151 | 521 | 113 | 150 | 21 | 6 | 22 | 78 | .288 | 359 | 5 | .993 |
| 1978 | Reds | 2B | 124 | 441 | 68 | 104 | 27 | 0 | 13 | 75 | .236 | 290 | 11 | .980 |
| 1979 | Reds | 2B | 121 | 436 | 70 | 109 | 26 | 1 | 9 | 32 | .250 | 329 | 12 | .900 |
| 1980 | Astros | 2B | 130 | 461 | 66 | 112 | 17 | 5 | 11 | 49 | .243 | 348 | 7 | .988 |
| 1981 | Giants | 2B | 87 | 308 | 47 | 74 | 16 | 1 | 8 | 31 | .240 | 258 | 4 | .991 |
| 1982 | Giants | 2B | 120 | 463 | 68 | 134 | 19 | 4 | 14 | 61 | .289 | 364 | 7 | .989 |
| 1982 | Giants | 3B | 3 | | — | — | — | — | — | — | — | 2 | 1 | .750 |
| 1983 | Phillies | 2B | 117 | 404 | 72 | 93 | 20 | 1 | 16 | 59 | .230 | 331 | 17 | .971 |
| 1984 | Athletics | 2B | 100 | 365 | 50 | 89 | 21 | 0 | 6 | 43 | .244 | 229 | 10 | .977 |
| 1984 | Athletics | DH | 5 | — | — | — | — | — | — | — | — | — | — | — |
| Totals | | | 2551 | 9277 | 1650 | 2517 | 449 | 96 | 268 | 1133 | .271 | 6969 | 245 | .981 |

Mickey Mantle unleashed his ferocious left-handed swing one final time in Boston's Fenway Park on a Saturday afternoon. He popped out to short.
©DIAMOND IMAGES®

# MICKEY MANTLE

## *A Quiet Farewell for the Mick*

**DATE:** September 27, 1968

**SITE:** Fenway Park, Boston, Massachusetts

**PITCHER:** Jim Lonborg of the Boston Red Sox

**RESULT:** Pop out to shortstop Rico Petrocelli

**September 27, 1968, Boston**—For years, they hated and admired him, all at the same time.

Another season was almost over. Boston's long-suffering Red Sox fans had suffered so much over the years, thanks to these New York Yankees, the idea of applauding for one of them, under normal circumstances, was grounds for hanging.

But clap by clap, row by row, Fenway Park began to erupt in sound. The sound of applause. They all could see the Yankees' Golden Boy was old and hobbled and failing. Finally, Mickey Mantle was harmless.

Hell, he was hitting—what was it now, .237? When Mantle saw it in the Sunday paper, the day they list all the averages, he wondered if he was hung over or just some bad dream.

Once, not so long ago, Mantle had hit .353. Another year, he hit .365. With his speed—his speed was magical when he was young—they predicted some year he'd hit .400. That year never came. Over time, injuries took his speed away. Finally, he was done.

As their cheers, the rousing, heartfelt cheers from the Fenway faithful washed down around him as he walked to the plate, Mantle smiled to himself.

"I get a better hand here than I did in The Stadium."

It was true. It was one of the mysteries of the fickle New York crowd. Nobody could quite understand why New Yorkers would cheer for Billy Martin and Whitey Ford and Yogi Berra as if they were their own children. But Mantle, for the longest time, drew little but boos.

Ty Cobb, who knew a thing or two about being booed, once dropped by the Yankee dugout in the middle of all the noise and was asked about it. He was remarkably prescient.

"They've got to cheer when he's as good as he can be," Cobb said.

The implication, of course, was that he wasn't. And never would be.

That was the problem with Mantle. Forget the 500-plus home runs, the Triple Crown, the MVP awards, all the great plays. Forget all of it, he could have done more. At least, that's how it seemed to everyone who watched him play. Mantle himself sensed it.

"Me and the fans really had a go-round the first couple of years," he said once. "I didn't like them and they didn't like me."

And Mantle's failed potential was evident to everyone. The *New York Times*'s Arthur Daley would say as much just a few months after his final season ended.

"Did he really accomplish all that his extraordinary physical gifts had once indicated he would? He did not. His legs bothered him throughout his stay with the Yankees, hobbling him so cruelly that he never really reached the heights that had been ordained for him."

*"Fenway fans warm to Mantle"*

The fans knew it wasn't all physical. There was a stubbornness about Mantle that frustrated some in the game.

Ted Williams said as much.

"Mantle had the power, and he wouldn't concede with two strikes," Williams said. "He didn't know what the heck you were talking about. He would swing the same way with no strikes as he was with two strikes.

"If he had ever got it in his mind, 'All I want to do is make contact with two strikes—swing as hard but choke up an inch or two'—if he had not struck out 2,000 times and got 400 more balls to hit, I guarantee he'd have had another 150 hits (raising his career average to .317). Well, he was the great Mantle, but he just ticked .300."

Actually, the great Mantle, careerwise, was just below .300 now. He had been since late August. There was no way to get it headed back in the other direction. Not now.

For this final season, Mantle had been around the .240s until that damn Cleveland Indians' staff came to The Stadium to close out the Yankees' home schedule in late September. This was not a staff to be facing when you were losing your ability to hit a fastball.

Mantle's plummet began. A switch-hitter, he went 0-for-4 batting righty against the Tribe's fearsome "Sudden" Sam McDowell, one of the game's hardest throwers. Except on this night, Sam had struck out a career-low: one.

That was the first game of a twi-nighter. Mantle pinch hit in the second game and popped out.

The next day, he got the Yankees' only hit against the Indians' sensational Luis Tiant in his final game at Yankee Stadium, but his batting average kept sinking. While Tiant fanned 11, winning his twenty-first game of the season in the Year of the Pitcher, lowering his American League-leading ERA to 1.60, Mantle was headed in the other direction.

The Yankee great drew a ninth-inning walk in his final plate appearance in the Bronx that night before a grand crowd of 5,723. Some farewell.

For the year, the Yanks drew just 1,10025,124, the fewest since the war years. The fans didn't miss much. Mantle wound up his final three games in New York 1-for-8. It was on to Boston to wrap things up.

And that first night in Boston, what a surprise. There was no announcement or anything, no Mickey Mantle Farewell Tour where everybody could trot out rocking chairs and motorcycles and parting gifts and make a big show, a staged production out of saying goodbye. Mantle came out of the dugout and the place started clapping. That was respect. That was genuine.

On that night, Mantle went 0-3. Yankee Manager Ralph Houk, wanting to acknowledge the Boston crowd, had Mantle in the lineup Saturday afternoon against the American League's defending Cy Young Award winner, Boston's Jim Lonborg.

Lonborg had injured his knee in a skiing accident over the winter and was trying to round back into form. There was reason for optimism in the Mantle camp when they found out who Boston was starting.

Turns out the Mick had had some success against him 10 days earlier in New York, hitting his 536th and final career homer off him batting left-handed.

So when his name announced to the Fenway crowd one last time, a cheer went up, as it had the night before. He was going to miss all this.

Mantle looked down. Here he was, in the same place Ted Williams stood eight years earlier, almost to the day, when Williams had swatted one into the bullpen, trotting around the bases hurriedly, head down, running off into the sunset with a dramatic home run.

It was a nice thought. Mantle looked out to Lonborg and waved the bat back and forth. Hard thrower. Gotta be quick. Like last time.

He thought about that last home run. The great thing about it was nobody made anything out of it, like they did with No. 535.

Mantle had hit that home run left-handed, too, off the 1968 Pitcher of the Year, the Tigers' Denny McLain, Mr. 31 wins himself. It had happened in Detroit 10 days ago.

Here it was, mid-September and McLain was pitching a shutout when Mantle hobbled to the plate in the eighth inning. Denny was up, 6-0 and felt something for the aging Yankee star.

McLain gestured in to his catcher, Jim Price, trying to get Mantle's attention. He was going to groove a fastball for him.

"Where do you want it?" McLain asked.

Mantle gestured with his bat, about shoulder high, then laughed. Not quite believing his good fortune, Mantle was a bit late and fouled the pitch off. McLain had delivered it just where Mantle had asked.

McLain laughed and gestured he'd do it again. Mantle, laughing, nodded.

Sure enough, the pitch came and Mantle got this one. He hit it into the seats in right field. That was No. 535.

When Joe Pepitone, up next, did the same thing to McLain, gesturing where he wanted the ball, McLain knocked him flat on the seat of his pinstripes.

Back in Fenway, they were still clapping. Maybe he wasn't through. He hadn't made up his mind about retirement yet. His leg hurt like hell and he'd been at this for so long. Yet it all went by so fast. Just because all his pals were done didn't mean he had to be, did it?

His old partner in off-the-field hijinx, Whitey Ford, had retired after a painful—and ugly—inning in Detroit in May. Roger Maris, now playing out the string with the St. Louis Cardinals, was going to quit, too. At least he'd get to go out in a World Series like DiMaggio did.

Like Mick, Roger wasn't hitting much either, around .255 in his final campaign. His last career home run was a couple days before Mantle's 535th off McLain. It was Roger's fifth of the season.

He got me in average, Mantle thought, but I got him in home runs (Mantle finished with 18).

He was looking for one more. Lonborg wound and threw and as the fastball tailed in, Mantle swung from his heels and lifted a high pop up toward short.

Boston's Rico Petrocelli drifted under it and Mantle peeled off from his trot down the first-base line and headed back to the dugout, his 8,102nd and final at-bat completed.

He walked to the end of the dugout and put his helmet and bat back. Then he saw Houk go over and tell Andy Kosco that he was in at first base for him. His season was over.

With his right knee hurting and his 36-year-old body worn down from the year, Houk put him on a plane back to Dallas Saturday night. On Sunday, the Yankees won their regular-season finale at Fenway, 4-3. The Mick would never be back.

About two weeks later, his old outfield mate Roger Maris, playing in Game Seven of the World Series against Detroit's Mickey Lolich, got to take his final swings.

At 34, two years younger than Mantle, Maris was all through, too. He'd broken a bone in his hand during the season and never let it heal properly. Like Mantle, he had to play his final season in the big leagues unable to hit the fastball.

Mantle was watching when Maris's final at-bat came in the seventh inning of Game Seven vs. Detroit in the World Series. The Cardinals trailed, 3-0 against Mickey Lolich. Like his ol' pal Mantle, Maris popped out to shortstop, too. Mickey Stanley made the catch.

A little later, Maris got around to discussing his final season. Maris could have been talking for the both of them.

"It got so this year, I couldn't hit a home run, even in batting practice," Maris said. "That was the toughest part to swallow—to watch those fastballs go by or foul them off. It's tough to realize that you're not able to do what you hope to be capable of doing. . . . Now you know you don't have the good whip to the bat. . . . You hate to continue on in the same circumstances because you're just pressing your luck. Keep it up and you go out the way you don't want to be remembered."

*"Boston says goodbye to Mantle"*

After all that mess, Maris decided then and there he was all done. Over the winter, Mantle considered retirement and didn't report to Spring Training until March 2, three days after the regulars. When he did, his mind was made up.

He had a long talk over breakfast with Yankees' president Mike Burke, then on a Saturday afternoon, called a press conference at the Yankee Clipper Motel in Fort Lauderdale.

"I can't hit any more," Mantle said flatly, announcing his retirement as an active player. "I feel bad that I didn't hit .300 (for his career, finishing at .298) but there's no way I could go back and get it over .300 again. I can't hit when I need to. I can't go from first to third when I need to. There's no use trying."

Though some thought he might hang around to try to get 3,000 hits—he finished with 2,415—or 550 home runs—he was 14 away, Mantle was never big on numbers.

"They said Mickey was a great team man," Mantle said proudly years later. "If I could have one thing on my tombstone, I wouldn't want 536 home runs. I'd rather have 'He was a great friend and teammate.'"

All the same, Mantle knew what opportunities he missed. In the late 1980s, there was a story going around about Mantle meeting then-A's power-and-speed sensation Jose Canseco in a bar. Mantle offered him to toast him on his big season.

"Nice goin' Jose," Mantle said. "Forty homers. Forty stolen bases. If I'd have known it was going to be such a goddamned big deal, I'd have done it three or four times."

# Mick's Quiet Goodbye

| NEW YORK | ab. | r. | h. | bi. |
|---|---|---|---|---|
| Clarke, 2b | 3 | 0 | 0 | 0 |
| Gibbs, c | 4 | 0 | 0 | 0 |
| Mantle, 1b | 1 | 0 | 0 | 0 |
| Kosko, 1b | 3 | 1 | 1 | 1 |
| White, lf | 3 | 1 | 0 | 0 |
| Pepitone, cf | 2 | 2 | 1 | 1 |
| Tresh, ss | 4 | 0 | 0 | 0 |
| Robinson, rf | 3 | 0 | 2 | 1 |
| Cox, 3b | 4 | 0 | 1 | 1 |
| Stottlemyre, p | 2 | 0 | 0 | 0 |
| Colavito, ph | 1 | 0 | 0 | 0 |
| McDaniel, p | 1 | 0 | 0 | 0 |
| **TOTALS:** | **31** | **4** | **5** | **4** |

| BOSTON | ab. | r. | h. | bi. |
|---|---|---|---|---|
| Andrews, 2b | 2 | 2 | 0 | 0 |
| Jones, 1b | 4 | 0 | 1 | 1 |
| Yastrzemski, lf | 1 | 1 | 0 | 0 |
| Harrelson, rf | 3 | 0 | 1 | 0 |
| Thomas, rf | 1 | 0 | 0 | 0 |
| Smith, cf | 4 | 0 | 0 | 1 |
| Foy, 3b | 4 | 0 | 0 | 0 |
| Petrocelli, ss | 4 | 0 | 0 | 0 |
| Gibson, c | 3 | 0 | 1 | 0 |
| Lonborg, p | 3 | 0 | 0 | 0 |
| **TOTALS:** | **29** | **3** | **3** | **2** |

```
New York ......  000  000  2 1 1—4
Boston ........  000  1 2 0  000—3
```

|  | IP | H | R | ER | BB | SO |
|---|---|---|---|---|---|---|
| Stottlemyre | 6 | 3 | 3 | 2 | 5 | 1 |
| McDaniel (W, 4-1) | 2 | 0 | 0 | 0 | 0 | 2 |
| Lonborg (L, 6-10) | 9 | 5 | 4 | 4 | 4 | 9 |

E: Tresh. LOB: New York 5, Boston 4. 2B: Cox. HR: Kosko (15), Pepitone (15). SB: Clarke, Smith. SF: Robinson. T: 2:27. A: 25,534.

# MICKEY CHARLES MANTLE

Born October 20, 1931, at Spavinaw, Okla.
Died August 13, 1995, at Dallas, Tex.
Height 6-0  Weight 201
Threw right- and batted left- and right handed.
Named to Hall of Fame, 1974.

| YEAR | CLUB | LEAGUE | POS. | G. | AB. | R. | H. | 2B. | 3B. | HR. | RBI. | B.A. | PO. | A. | E. | F.A. |
|------|------|--------|------|-----|------|------|------|-----|-----|-----|------|------|------|-----|-----|-------|
| 1949 | Independence | K-O-M | SS | 89 | 323 | 54 | 101 | 15 | 7 | 7 | 63 | .313 | 121 | 245 | 47 | .886 |
| 1950 | Joplin | W.A. | SS | 137 | 519 | 141 | 199 | 30 | 12 | 26 | 136 | .383 | 202 | 340 | 55 | .908 |
| 1951 | New York | Amer. | OF | 96 | 341 | 61 | 91 | 11 | 5 | 13 | 65 | .267 | 135 | 4 | 6 | .959 |
| 1951 | Kansas City | A.A. | OF | 40 | 166 | 32 | 60 | 9 | 3 | 11 | 50 | .361 | 110 | 4 | 4 | .966 |
| 1952 | New York | Amer. | OF-3B | 142 | 549 | 94 | 171 | 37 | 7 | 23 | 87 | .311 | 348 | 16 | 14 | .963 |
| 1953 | New York | Amer. | OF-SS | 127 | 461 | 105 | 136 | 24 | 3 | 21 | 92 | .295 | 322 | 10 | 6 | .982 |
| 1954 | New York | Amer. | OF-1 | 146 | 543 | 129 | 163 | 17 | 12 | 27 | 102 | .300 | 334 | 25 | 9 | .976 |
| 1955 | New York | Amer. | OF-SS | 147 | 517 | 121 | 158 | 25 | 11 | 37 | 99 | .306 | 376 | 11 | 2 | .995 |
| 1956 | New York | Amer. | OF | 150 | 533 | 132 | 188 | 22 | 5 | 52 | 130 | .353 | 370 | 10 | 4 | .990 |
| 1957 | New York | Amer. | OF | 144 | 474 | 121 | 173 | 28 | 6 | 34 | 94 | .365 | 324 | 6 | 7 | .979 |
| 1958 | New York | Amer. | OF | 150 | 519 | 127 | 158 | 21 | 1 | 42 | 97 | .304 | 331 | 5 | 8 | .977 |
| 1959 | New York | Amer. | OF | 144 | 541 | 104 | 154 | 23 | 4 | 31 | 75 | .285 | 366 | 7 | 2 | .995 |
| 1960 | New York | Amer. | OF | 153 | 527 | 119 | 145 | 17 | 6 | 40 | 94 | .275 | 326 | 9 | 3 | .991 |
| 1961 | New York | Amer. | OF | 153 | 514 | 132 | 163 | 16 | 6 | 54 | 128 | .317 | 351 | 6 | 6 | .983 |
| 1962 | New York | Amer. | OF | 123 | 377 | 96 | 121 | 15 | 1 | 30 | 89 | .321 | 214 | 4 | 5 | .978 |
| 1963 | New York | Amer. | OF | 65 | 172 | 40 | 54 | 8 | 0 | 15 | 35 | .314 | 99 | 2 | 1 | .990 |
| 1964 | New York | Amer. | OF | 143 | 465 | 92 | 141 | 25 | 2 | 35 | 111 | .303 | 217 | 3 | 5 | .978 |
| 1965 | New York | Amer. | OF | 122 | 361 | 44 | 92 | 12 | 1 | 19 | 46 | .255 | 165 | 3 | 6 | .966 |
| 1966 | New York | Amer. | OF | 108 | 333 | 40 | 96 | 12 | 1 | 23 | 56 | .200 | 172 | 2 | 0 | 1.000 |
| 1967 | New York | Amer. | 1B | 144 | 440 | 63 | 108 | 17 | 0 | 22 | 55 | .245 | 1089 | 91 | 8 | .993 |
| 1968 | New York | Amer. | 1B | 144 | 435 | 57 | 103 | 14 | 1 | 18 | 54 | .237 | 1195 | 76 | 15 | .988 |
| Major League Totals | | | | 2401 | 8102 | 1677 | 2415 | 344 | 72 | 536 | 1509 | .298 | 6734 | 290 | 107 | .985 |

## WORLD SERIES RECORD

| YEAR | CLUB | LEAGUE | POS. | G. | AB. | R. | H. | 2B. | 3B. | HR. | RBI. | B.A. | PO. | A. | E. | F.A. |
|------|------|--------|------|-----|------|------|------|-----|-----|-----|------|------|------|-----|-----|-------|
| 1951 | New York† | Amer. | OF | 2 | 5 | 1 | 1 | 0 | 0 | 0 | 0 | .200 | 4 | 0 | 0 | 1.000 |
| 1952 | New York | Amer. | OF | 7 | 29 | 5 | 10 | 1 | 1 | 2 | 3 | .345 | 16 | 0 | 0 | 1.000 |
| 1953 | New York | Amer. | OF | 6 | 24 | 3 | 5 | 0 | 0 | 2 | 7 | .208 | 14 | 0 | 0 | 1.000 |
| 1955 | New York | Amer. | OF-PH | 3 | 10 | 1 | 2 | 0 | 0 | 1 | 1 | .200 | 4 | 0 | 0 | 1.000 |
| 1956 | New York | Amer. | OF | 7 | 24 | 6 | 6 | 1 | 0 | 3 | 4 | .250 | 18 | 1 | 0 | 1.000 |
| 1957 | New York | Amer. | OF-PH | 6 | 19 | 3 | 5 | 0 | 0 | 1 | 2 | .263 | 8 | 0 | 1 | .889 |
| 1958 | New York | Amer. | OF | 7 | 24 | 4 | 6 | 0 | 1 | 2 | 3 | .250 | 16 | 0 | 0 | 1.000 |
| 1960 | New York | Amer. | OF | 7 | 25 | 8 | 10 | 1 | 0 | 3 | 11 | .400 | 15 | 0 | 0 | 1.000 |
| 1961 | New York | Amer. | OF | 2 | 6 | 0 | 1 | 0 | 0 | 0 | 0 | .167 | 2 | 0 | 0 | 1.000 |
| 1962 | New York | Amer. | OF | 7 | 25 | 2 | 3 | 1 | 0 | 0 | 0 | .120 | 11 | 0 | 0 | 1.000 |
| 1963 | New York | Amer. | OF | 4 | 15 | 1 | 2 | 0 | 0 | 1 | 1 | .133 | 6 | 0 | 0 | 1.000 |
| 1964 | New York | Amer. | OF | 7 | 24 | 8 | 8 | 2 | 0 | 3 | 8 | .333 | 12 | 0 | 2 | .857 |
| World Series Totals | | | | 65 | 230 | 42 | 59 | 6 | 2 | 18 | 40 | .257 | 126 | 1 | 3 | .977 |

† Injured right knee in fifth inning of second game: did not play for rest of Series.

Willie Mays's final big-league stop was a forgettable one with the New York Mets.

# WILLIE MAYS

## Say It Ain't So, Willie

**DATE:** October 15, 1973 (Game Four of the 1973 World Series)

**SITE:** Shea Stadium, New York, New York

**PITCHER:** Paul Lindblad of the Oakland A's

**RESULT:** Ground out to shortstop Bert Campaneris

**October 15, 1973, New York City**—The very last time Willie Howard Mays walked up to home plate with a bat in his hands was in Game Four of the 1973 World Series.

It was a cursory at-bat. Manager Yogi Berra had sent him up to pinch hit for pitcher Tug McGraw in the 10th inning of a tie game. He was hoping for one more shot of Mays's Magic.

Maybe he wasn't hitting much over .200 but the Old Man had come through the day before in a similar spot. He was still Willie Mays, wasn't he?

But here, Mays, batting against left-hander Paul Lindblad, rapped a routine ground ball to Oakland shortstop Bert Campaneris, who easily threw him out.

Though the series went the full seven games, Mays never played again. The reason was Game Three.

At 42, everybody knew Mays's best days were long behind him. The San Francisco Giants tried to ease him into retirement two years earlier but Willie found it hard to let go. San Francisco never seemed to warm to him anyhow. Funny how New York was unduly hard on center-fielder Mickey Mantle and San Francisco was never quite satisfied with their star.

Through a trade in May a year before, Mays found a way to come back to the city where he'd started with such flair and drama two decades earlier. And who thought he'd find himself in the middle of one more pennant race?

A year before, he'd won the first game he played against his Giants with a solo home run. But now his reflexes were gone. He was hitting just .211 and pitchers just threw it past him with regularity. For those who had watched him in previous seasons, it was a tough thing to see.

In September, he cracked a rib chasing a fly ball in Montreal and had to sit out and watch the Mets contend for a pennant through the final three weeks of the season.

The rest gave him time to think. On September 19, Mays told the New York press that he'd decided to retire.

"It's been a wonderful 22 years and I'm not just getting out of baseball because I'm hurt," Mays said. "I just feel the people of America shouldn't have to see a guy play who can't produce.

"I have three cracked ribs and at 42, you can't play the way you could at 20 anyway. If the Mets get in the World Series, I'm playing—I don't know how but I'm playing.

"But I got to face facts. I've been in a lot of slumps and come out of them but now I'm running out of time.

"It was my decision alone," Mays continued. "The way the ball club is going now, I don't have to say you have to play me. I'm not ashamed the way things have gone the last couple of months. They didn't run me out. In San Francisco, I don't think I would have played this year; the people would have run me out of the city. In New York, they let me hit .211."

Mays was quiet for a moment. Then he smiled.

"I thought I'd be crying right now," he said, "but so many people love me that I don't hurt too bad. Maybe I'll cry tomorrow."

The next night, he did. Facing a full house at Shea Stadium, Mays said goodbye.

"I didn't ever feel that I would quit baseball," he said, standing at the microphone next to the pitcher's mound in a dark blue Mets jacket with NY in gold letters over his heart.

"But as you know, it always comes a time for someone to get out. These kids over here, the way they are playing, tells me one thing. 'Willie, say goodbye to America.' Thank you very much."

He stepped back from the microphone and tears welled up in his eyes, just like everybody else in Shea Stadium.

There were signs all over the place. "A Giant among Mets" and "Say Hey Belongs to Shea" and "The Hour Has Come for No. 24." On the scoreboard, it read: "So long, yes. Good-bye, never."

Two weeks later, when the Mets won the pennant and reached the World Series against the Oakland Athletics, Mays pronounced his cracked ribs healed enough for him to play. But the "Say Hey Kid" had grown into an old man. We saw it for ourselves.

After Oakland won the Series opener, Mays found his way into Game Two as a pinch-runner and actually fell down rounding second base. For the most spectacular base runner of his era, it was only a hint of what was to come.

At the time, the Mets held a 6-4 lead heading to the ninth, hoping to even the Series. Mays trotted out to his domain—center field—in the ninth to try to wrap it up.

What baseball fan didn't remember the first time he or she likely heard of Willie Mays, the Giants' *wunderkind*? It had to be in the 1954 World Series, when Willie's Giants came up with a startling four-game sweep of the mighty Cleveland Indians, a team that had won more games in a single season than anyone in baseball history.

America was watching when Mays improbably found himself at the descending part of a long, majestic drive off the bat of Vic Wertz, way, way out in the deepest center field in all of baseball at New York's Polo Grounds.

With his back to home plate, the No. 24 stretched across his back in white flannel, he made the catch, losing his cap, and gaining a nation of breathless fans, all in one sweeping grab. Then he spun and made a wonderful throw back to the infield and suddenly, everybody was talking about it as if it were the greatest catch in World Series history.

"Oldest Met struggles in Game Three"

Years later, Mays would shrug off the catch and talk about the throw as if that were the real feat. But America thought differently.

Even though he was 42 now, nobody worried about him trotting out to center field to start the inning. Even if he were too old to get around on a fastball, Willie Mays would always be able to catch a fly ball, wouldn't he?

Suddenly, there was a line drive off the bat of Deron Johnson, a twisting, sinking shot to left center that Mays started slowly after. Everything seemed to be in slow motion.

The ball kept drifting and Mays looked as if he was stuck on flypaper. He couldn't move the sleek, silky way he used to; instead, his hands lowered, Mays scuttled across the outfield grass, then lunged for the ball with both hands in front of him and missed it by two feet.

The ball skittered past him and rolled to the wall.

This was not the way America wanted to remember Willie Mays. Not the player that seemed to be able to do anything on a baseball field. Except look mortal.

"Mays's woes in center field sadden fans"

Cleon Jones retrieved the ball and fired it in and the stadium was nearly silent, even as the Athletics mounted a stirring comeback that tied the game. Willie Mays, falling down chasing a fly ball? In the World Series? Who would believe it?

"I didn't see the ball," Mays said later, describing the blinding sun field at Oakland-Alameda County Stadium. "I tried to dive for it at the last second. We had a two-run lead and I shoulda played it safe."

Safe? Mays? Nobody ever went after a fly ball with more vengeance than Willie Mays. A ball sailing into his domain? It was his, always his, landing easily into that wonderful Mays basket catch. An out? From the time it left the bat.

Happily for Mays's fans—and what baseball fan wasn't in that category?—he had a chance to redeem himself a few innings later. The game had stretched into the 12th inning and with two runners on and two outs, the Old Man came up against the A's ace reliever Rollie Fingers.

He dug in with that odd, open stance, his huge hands still twitching on the knob of the bat as Fingers wound and threw. Mays threw the head of his bat at the ball and caught it on the end of the barrel.

The ball hopped once midway to the mound, then bounded high over Fingers's head into center field. Bud Harrelson trotted in to give New York a lead it was able to hold onto.

"I think it was a fastball, up," Mays said later. "I'd seen Fingers a lot on television and he likes to work inside and outside, up and down. Yesterday was the test. He threw me a fastball, then gave me a breaking pitch and came back with a fastball so I knew he'd feed me 80 percent fastballs."

Give the Old Man the hard stuff. He can't get around any more. Willie showed 'em.

By the end of the inning, New York had scored three more times on Oakland errors. With a 10-6 lead in the 12th, Mays trotted out to center field to see if he could help his Mets win the longest World Series game ever.

There was one more embarrassing moment. Reggie Jackson was up first and he swung mightily, blasting a shot right at Mays, watching carefully from deep center field.

Mays retreated on the sound of the hit, right to the fence, then ran along brushing up against the wall, almost like a blind man, making sure he was going in the right direction. He raised up his glove and the ball dropped in front of him on the warning track, two feet away.

"I saw it," Mays said later, trying to brush it off. "In a close game, I might have had a chance on it, but we had a four-run lead then and I didn't want to kill myself because we got a lot more games to play."

He didn't, as it turned out. Just that one pinch-hitting appearance. A week later, the Series ended with Mays watching from the bench. Who'd believe that Willie Mays would ever be benched for a Game Seven? The Mets lost 5-2, losing the Series to the A's, four games to three.

America suddenly felt very old. Was it that long ago that Mays scooted across that endless outfield at the Polo Grounds to flag down that long drive off the bat of Vic Wertz? After 660 home runs, all those marvelous, gravity-defying catches, was the thrilling ride over?

Willie Mays, whose visible exuberance for the game of baseball was always contagious, was finally worn out. He had to sit and watch a Game Seven. Say Hey, it was time to go.

*"Willie's errors mar Mets' Series win"*

"I didn't think about (retiring) during the game or anything," Mays said after, sitting before his locker as the A's celebrated their world title.

"I didn't play but just because it was my last game, it didn't make any difference to me if I played or not. If it was to help the ballclub, fine, but not because it was my last game.

"I didn't come in that way," Mays said quietly. "I don't want to go out having people feel sorry for me. I don't need that."

# Say Hey, Willie

## Game Three

### OAKLAND ( A.)

| | ab. | r. | h. | bi. |
|---|---|---|---|---|
| Campaneris, ss ......... | 6 | 1 | 3 | 1 |
| Rudi, lf .................... | 5 | 0 | 2 | 1 |
| Bando, 3b ................ | 4 | 1 | 2 | 0 |
| Jackson, rf .............. | 5 | 0 | 0 | 0 |
| Tenace, 1b .............. | 3 | 0 | 1 | 1 |
| Davalillo, cf ............ | 5 | 0 | 1 | 0 |
| Fosse, c .................. | 2 | 0 | 0 | 0 |
| Bourque, 1b ............ | 2 | 0 | 1 | 0 |
| Lewis, pr.................. | 0 | 0 | 0 | 0 |
| Lindblad, p ............. | 1 | 0 | 0 | 0 |
| Fingers, p ............... | 0 | 0 | 0 | 0 |
| Green, 2b ................ | 2 | 0 | 0 | 0 |
| Alou, ph ................. | 1 | 0 | 0 | 0 |
| Kubiak, 2b ............. | 1 | 1 | 0 | 0 |
| Hunter, p ................ | 2 | 0 | 0 | 0 |
| Johnson, ph ............ | 1 | 0 | 0 | 0 |
| Knowles, p ............. | 0 | 0 | 0 | 0 |
| Mangual, cf ............. | 2 | 0 | 0 | 0 |
| **TOTALS:** | **42** | **3** | **10** | **3** |

### NEW YORK (N.)

| | ab. | r. | h. | bi. |
|---|---|---|---|---|
| Garrett, 3b ............... | 4 | 1 | 2 | 1 |
| Millan, 2b ............... | 5 | 1 | 2 | 0 |
| Staub, rf .................. | 6 | 0 | 2 | 0 |
| Jones, lf ................... | 5 | 0 | 0 | 0 |
| Milner, 1b ............... | 3 | 0 | 1 | 0 |
| Grote, c ................... | 5 | 0 | 0 | 0 |
| Hahn, cf .................. | 5 | 0 | 1 | 0 |
| Harrelson, ss ........... | 5 | 0 | 2 | 0 |
| Seaver, p.................. | 3 | 0 | 0 | 0 |
| Beauchamp, ph ........ | 1 | 0 | 0 | 0 |
| Sadecki, p ............... | 0 | 0 | 0 | 0 |
| McGraw, p .............. | 0 | 0 | 0 | 0 |
| Mays, ph ................. | 1 | 0 | 0 | 0 |
| Parker, p ................. | 0 | 0 | 0 | 0 |
| **TOTALS:** | **43** | **2** | **10** | **1** |

| | | | | |
|---|---|---|---|---|
| Oakland.................... | 000 | 001 | 010 | 013 |
| New York ................ | 200 | 000 | 000 | 002 |

E: Hunter 4, Millan 2. LOB: Oakland 10, New York 14. 2B: Rudi, Hahn, Bando, Tenace, Staub. HR: Garrett. SB: Campaneris. SAC: Bando, Millan.

| | IP | H | R | ER | BB | SO | WP | Balks |
|---|---|---|---|---|---|---|---|---|
| Hunter ..................... | 6 | 7 | 2 | 2 | 3 | 5 | 1 | 0 |
| Knowles .................. | 2 | 0 | 0 | 0 | 1 | 0 | 0 | 0 |
| Lindblad (W 1-0)...... | 2 | 3 | 0 | 0 | 1 | 0 | 0 | 0 |
| Fingers .................... | 1 | 0 | 0 | 0 | 0 | 0 | 0 | 0 |
| Seaver .................... | 8 | 7 | 2 | 2 | 1 | 12 | 0 | 0 |
| Sadecki ................... | 0 | 1 | 0 | 0 | 0 | 0 | 0 | 0 |
| McGraw ................... | 2 | 1 | 0 | 0 | 1 | 1 | 0 | 0 |
| H. Parker (L, 0-1) .... | 1 | 1 | 1 | 0 | 1 | 1 | 0 | 0 |

S: Fingers. PB: Grote. T: 3:15. A: 54,817

## WILLIE HOWARD (SAY HEY) MAYS JR.
Born May 6, 1931, at Westfield, Ala.
Height 5-11  Weight 187
Threw and batted right-handed.
Named to Hall of Fame, 1979.

| YEAR | CLUB | LEAGUE | POS. | G. | AB. | R. | H. | 2B. | 3B. | HR. | RBI. | B.A. | PO. | A. | E. | F.A. |
|------|------|--------|------|----|-----|----|----|-----|-----|-----|------|------|-----|----|----|------|
| 1950 | Trenton | Int. St. | OF | 81 | 306 | 50 | 108 | 20 | 8 | 4 | 55 | .353 | 216 | 17 | 5 | .979 |
| 1951 | Minneapolis | A.A. | OF | 35 | 149 | 38 | 71 | 18 | 3 | 8 | 30 | .477 | 94 | 5 | 1 | .990 |
| 1951 | New York | Nat. | OF | 121 | 464 | 59 | 127 | 22 | 5 | 20 | 68 | .274 | 353 | 12 | 9 | .976 |
| 1952 | New York (a) | Nat. | OF | 34 | 127 | 17 | 30 | 2 | 4 | 4 | 23 | .236 | 109 | 6 | 1 | .991 |
| 1953 | New York | Nat. | | | | | (In Military Service) | | | | | | | | | |
| 1954 | New York | Nat. | OF | 151 | 565 | 119 | 195 | 33 | 13 | 41 | 110 | .345 | 448 | 13 | 7 | .985 |
| 1955 | New York | Nat. | OF | 152 | 580 | 123 | 185 | 18 | 13 | 51 | 127 | .319 | 407 | 23 | 8 | .982 |
| 1956 | New York | Nat. | OF | 152 | 578 | 101 | 171 | 27 | 8 | 36 | 84 | .296 | 415 | 14 | 9 | .979 |
| 1957 | New York | Nat. | OF | 152 | 585 | 112 | 195 | 26 | 20 | 35 | 97 | .333 | 422 | 14 | 9 | .980 |
| 1958 | San Francisco | Nat. | OF | 152 | 600 | 121 | 208 | 33 | 11 | 29 | 96 | .347 | 429 | 17 | 9 | .980 |
| 1959 | San Francisco | Nat. | OF | 151 | 575 | 125 | 180 | 43 | 5 | 34 | 104 | .313 | 353 | 6 | 6 | .984 |
| 1960 | San Francisco | Nat. | OF | 153 | 595 | 107 | 190 | 29 | 12 | 29 | 103 | .319 | 392 | 12 | 8 | .981 |
| 1961 | San Francisco | Nat. | OF | 154 | 572 | 129 | 176 | 32 | 3 | 40 | 123 | .308 | 385 | 7 | 8 | .980 |
| 1962 | San Francisco | Nat. | OF | 162 | 621 | 130 | 189 | 36 | 5 | 49 | 141 | .304 | 429 | 6 | 4 | .991 |
| 1963 | San Francisco | Nat. | OF-SS | 157 | 596 | 115 | 187 | 32 | 7 | 38 | 103 | .314 | 397 | 7 | 8 | .981 |
| 1964 | San Francisco | Nat. | OF-1-2-3-S | 157 | 578 | 121 | 171 | 21 | 9 | 47 | 111 | .296 | 376 | 12 | 6 | .985 |
| 1965 | San Fransico | Nat. | OF | 157 | 558 | 118 | 177 | 21 | 3 | 52 | 112 | .317 | 337 | 13 | 6 | .983 |
| 1966 | San Francisco | Nat. | OF | 152 | 552 | 99 | 159 | 29 | 4 | 37 | 103 | .288 | 370 | 8 | 7 | .982 |
| 1967 | San Francisco | Nat. | OF | 141 | 486 | 83 | 128 | 22 | 2 | 22 | 70 | .263 | 277 | 3 | 7 | .976 |
| 1968 | San Francisco | Nat. | OF-1B | 148 | 498 | 84 | 144 | 20 | 5 | 23 | 79 | .289 | 310 | 7 | 7 | .978 |
| 1969 | San Francisco | Nat. | OF-1B | 117 | 403 | 64 | 114 | 17 | 3 | 13 | 58 | .283 | 205 | 4 | 5 | .976 |
| 1970 | San Francisco | Nat. | OF-1B | 139 | 478 | 94 | 139 | 15 | 2 | 28 | 83 | .291 | 303 | 9 | 7 | .978 |
| 1971 | San Francisco | Nat. | OF-1B | 136 | 417 | 82 | 113 | 24 | 5 | 18 | 61 | .271 | 676 | 29 | 17 | .973 |
| 1972 | S.F.(h)-N.Y. | Nat. | OF-1B | 88 | 244 | 35 | 61 | 11 | 1 | 8 | 22 | .250 | 213 | 5 | 4 | .982 |
| 1973 | New York | Nat. | OF-1B | 66 | 209 | 24 | 44 | 10 | 0 | 6 | 25 | .211 | 246 | 6 | 4 | .984 |
| Major League Totals | | | | 2992 | 10881 | 2062 | 3283 | 523 | 140 | 660 | 1903 | .302 | 7752 | 233 | 156 | .981 |

a Entered military service May 29.
b Traded to New York Mets for cash and Pitcher Charlie Williams, May 11, 1972.

## CHAMPIONSHIP SERIES RECORD

| YEAR | CLUB | LEAGUE | POS. | G. | AB. | R. | H. | 2B. | 3B. | HR. | RBI. | B.A. | PO. | A. | E. | F.A. |
|------|------|--------|------|----|-----|----|----|-----|-----|-----|------|------|-----|----|----|------|
| 1971 | San Francisco | Nat. | OF | 4 | 15 | 2 | 4 | 2 | 0 | 1 | 3 | .267 | 5 | 0 | 0 | 1.000 |
| 1973 | New York | Nat. | PH-OF | 1 | 3 | 1 | 1 | 0 | 0 | 0 | 1 | .333 | 1 | 0 | 0 | 1.000 |
| Championship Series Totals—2 Years | | | | 5 | 18 | 3 | 5 | 2 | 0 | 1 | 4 | .278 | 6 | 0 | 0 | 1.000 |

## WORLD SERIES RECORD

| YEAR | CLUB | LEAGUE | POS. | G. | AB. | R. | H. | 2B. | 3B. | HR. | RBI. | B.A. | PO. | A. | E. | F.A. |
|------|------|--------|------|----|-----|----|----|-----|-----|-----|------|------|-----|----|----|------|
| 1951 | New York | Nat. | OF | 6 | 22 | 1 | 4 | 0 | 0 | 0 | 1 | .182 | 16 | 1 | 0 | 1.000 |
| 1954 | New York | Nat. | OF | 4 | 14 | 4 | 4 | 1 | 0 | 0 | 3 | .286 | 10 | 0 | 0 | 1.000 |
| 1962 | San Francisco | Nat. | OF | 7 | 28 | 3 | 7 | 2 | 0 | 0 | 1 | .250 | 19 | 0 | 0 | 1.000 |
| 1973 | New York | Nat. | O-PH-PR | 3 | 7 | 1 | 2 | 0 | 0 | 0 | 1 | .286 | 1 | 0 | 1 | .500 |
| World Series Totals—4 Years | | | | 20 | 71 | 9 | 17 | 3 | 0 | 0 | 6 | .239 | 46 | 1 | 1 | .979 |

The once lean-and-hungry Hank Aaron certainly looked a lot wider around the middle in his final seasons in a Milwaukee Brewers uniform.
©Ron Kuntz/DIAMOND IMAGES®

# HANK AARON

## One Last Swing for Hank

| | |
|---|---|
| **DATE:** | October 3, 1976 |
| **SITE:** | County Stadium, Milwaukee, Wisconsin |
| **PITCHER:** | Dave Roberts of the Detroit Tigers |
| **RESULT:** | Infield single to shortstop |

**October 3, 1976, Milwaukee**—There was barely a ripple from the paltry County Stadium crowd when Hank Aaron came out of the Brewers' dugout one last time.

Only 6,858 fans had showed up to watch these last-place Brewers, some 32 games out, face the next-to-last place Detroit Tigers, who were 24 games out on this final Sunday of the regular season.

Since the Green Bay Packers were on TV that Sunday afternoon playing the Seattle Seahawks, apparently many Milwaukeeans stayed home to watch that instead. The drama had been drained out of the Brewers' season long ago.

It was the sixth inning of a 5-1 game the Brewers were losing. There hadn't been much to cheer about all season long. Though it was well-known all around town that this would be the final major-league game—No. 3,298—of Aaron's 23-year career, Milwaukee fans knew there wasn't going to be much to see.

Not now. Not from this team. Not from the 42-year-old Aaron.

Like the other two peerless players from his era—Willie Mays and Mickey Mantle—Aaron hung on longer than he should have. He was in his second season as a designated hitter for the American League's Milwaukee Brewers and he was awful.

He played—that is, batted—in just 85 games, about half the season. Worse, he batted just .229, five points lower than he'd batted in 1975, his first year as an American Leaguer. He hadn't been able to hit a home run since hitting one off California Angels' reliever Dick Drago back on July 20. That was No. 755. He was staying on that number.

*"Hank beats one out for old time's sake"*

Yeah, he was back in the town he'd asked to be traded to, the town he began his big-league career in, just like Mays did in 1973. And like Mays, he was pretty lousy at the finish, too. Had Aaron known he'd fade like this, though, he wouldn't have played. He'd managed just 10 home runs, only 35 RBI—a rookie's numbers.

Unlike Mantle, though, Aaron's sad decline in batting average in his final two seasons didn't lower his career average below the prestigious .300 mark. He began the day at .305 and almost regardless of what happened today, he'd finish at .305.

The Tigers' starter on this final afternoon of the season was Detroit left-hander Dave Roberts, midway through a mediocre career (103-125), but winding up what would be his winningest season (16-17) ever in the majors.

Robert had already gotten Aaron out twice and had allowed just one run, walking no one. Even with a runner on third, he wasn't worried watching old No. 44 walk to the plate in his slow, deliberate way. He quietly watched Aaron pause, as he always did when he stepped into the batter's box, to fit the batting helmet over his head.

Aaron's once-whippet-like body had thickened with age. His pronounced backside was even more noticeable as he turned his head to the mound and wiggled the bat back and forth, those great wrists guiding it with confidence and ease.

He'd done a lot of great things in this town for the first 11 years of his career. The home run he hit in 1957 to give the Braves the pennant—that was the hit he'd always talk about.

Even after hitting No. 715, a clout that gave him one more home run than Babe Ruth. That home run in 1957, now that was exciting.

The chase of Ruth, all those letters, the publicity, the hate mail, none of it was much fun. Though Aaron hung around long enough to play two more seasons after swatting that historic home run, he hit just 40 more home runs over that span, giving him a career total of 755.

The Brewers hyped up Aaron's return when the 1975 season started—the same sort of thing San Francisco did a couple years earlier, unloading a fading Willie Mays on the Giants—but there was even less left of Aaron's game. At least Mays got to jump into a pennant race.

Many American League fans welcomed a chance to see the guy who passed Babe Ruth the first time around the league. But his game was long gone. So was whatever mystique Aaron had.

As Aaron stepped in this last time, he wondered about what he could do with these final swings. He would have loved to go out like Ted Williams did, with a long, majestic home run. Or maybe even like Stan Musial, with a pair of sharp singles.

Or maybe like Joe DiMaggio, he could slam a quiet double in the late innings of a World Series game, never saying a word to anyone that this was going to be it. Not until the game was all over.

But then all of a sudden, Roberts's pitch was on him, tailing inside and Aaron flipped those magnificent wrists one last time.

He caught the ball on the handle and drove it in the gap between short and third. It bounced once, twice, three times as George Scott lumbered in toward home from third base.

Shortstop Jerry Manuel chased it deep in the hole and saw it skip off his glove. Aaron was safe at first. The run scored. The ball hadn't left the infield.

Brewers' manager Alex Grammas sent out infielder Jim Gantner to pinch run for Aaron. A cheer went up from the crowd as Aaron walked back to the dugout, his career now officially over. The game's biggest home run hitter had checked out with an infield hit.

In the locker room afterwards, Aaron seemed relieved the long run had ended.

"I guess this is the last press conference, boys," he smiled. "But at least I'm going out a little better than Nixon did. I've had enough. It's sad in a way that it's over. But in another way, I'm glad it's over."

All the nights of the one-on-one struggles with that pitcher had finally worn him down. And he wasn't afraid to admit it, now.

"Since I came over from the National League two years ago and acted as a DH here, I've sort of been preparing for this day," Aaron said. "I've lost my desire to compete and I could feel it at the start of this season. It just wasn't there anymore.

"Wasn't hungry anymore. The routine, the traveling, it finally got to me. And when you don't have the hunger anymore. . . ."

*"Hank says goodbye with base hit"*

His honesty was disarming. How many other players, great ones, would step down with such frank analysis? Aaron, the guy who always seemed aloof, sort of removed from everyone, well, he wondered about how he'd fit into the outside world. Now.

"You know, this is one of the things I'll really miss, the clubhouse. It was always one place I could find peace, get away from the outside world.

"In Atlanta, when the Babe Ruth thing was going on, I came to the park at two in the afternoon to sleep for a couple hours. Only place it was quiet."

Now, the quiet beckoned.

"I'm not going to the World Series—not unless they play it in my backyard," he said, laughing. "I may not even watch it on TV. I don't know whether I'll ever be able to go in a restaurant and eat in peace, but I hope I'll have a little more privacy."

Finally, Hank Aaron was famous. Just when the spotlight hit him, he was ready to go back to being anonymous.

"I didn't get much recognition at the beginning," he said, finally, "but when it did come, man, it came in waves. I'm totally fulfilled."

Though later on in the locker room after the Brewers' 5-2 loss, the team's 95th defeat of the season, Hank did grouse a little at being pulled for a pinch-runner, preventing him from having a chance to score a run and break the flat-footed tie between he and Ruth for second place in all-time runs scored (2,174) the truth was, the slow-footed Aaron wasn't likely to score from first on anything but a home run. And if he had to settle for one tie with Ruth, that wasn't so bad, was it?

Interestingly, though Aaron's pursuit of Ruth brought him his first real headlines, when it came time for Cooperstown to make a place for him, Aaron never mentioned The Babe in his induction speech. He did mention Jackie Robinson, though.

"I feel especially proud to be standing here where some years ago Jackie Robinson, Roy Campanella paved the way and made it possible for Frank (Robinson) and me and for other blacks, to be hopeful in baseball. They proved to the world that man's ability is limited only by his lack of opportunity.

"Twenty-three years ago, I never dreamed this high honor would come to me. For it was not fame I sought, but rather the best baseball player I could possibly be."

For almost all of his long, productive major-league career, Aaron was exactly that. You could look at those last few years with Milwaukee and say Henry stayed too long.

Maybe so, but it seemed exactly long enough for all of us—even Hank—to appreciate all that he had done.

He played too long, sure. But how nice it would be if every retiring big leaguer could say what Aaron did: I'm totally fulfilled. Nobody deserved it more.

# Hank's Last Hit

| DETROIT | ab. | r. | h. | bi. |
|---|---|---|---|---|
| Scrivener, 3b ............ | 4 | 0 | 0 | 0 |
| J. Thomson, lf ......... | 5 | 0 | 1 | 0 |
| Staub, rf ................... | 5 | 0 | 0 | 0 |
| Horton, dh ............... | 4 | 2 | 2 | 0 |
| Meyer, 1b ................ | 4 | 1 | 2 | 0 |
| M. Stanley, cf .......... | 4 | 2 | 2 | 1 |
| Freehan, c ................ | 3 | 0 | 1 | 1 |
| P. Garcia, 2b .......... | 3 | 0 | 2 | 3 |
| Manuel, ss ................ | 4 | 0 | 0 | 0 |
| **TOTALS:** | **36** | **5** | **10** | **5** |

| MILWAUKEE | ab. | r. | h. | bi. |
|---|---|---|---|---|
| Yount, ss ................... | 4 | 0 | 0 | 0 |
| C. Moore, c ............... | 4 | 1 | 1 | 0 |
| G. Scott, 1b ............... | 4 | 1 | 2 | 0 |
| Aaron, dh ................. | 3 | 0 | 1 | 1 |
| Gantner, dh ............. | 1 | 0 | 0 | 0 |
| Lezcano, rf ............... | 4 | 0 | 0 | 0 |
| D. Thomas, lf .......... | 4 | 0 | 1 | 0 |
| Sutherland, 2b .......... | 4 | 0 | 1 | 0 |
| Bowling, cf ............. | 3 | 0 | 0 | 0 |
| Heidemn, 3b ............ | 3 | 0 | 2 | 0 |
| **TOTALS:** | **34** | **2** | **8** | **1** |

```
Detroit ..................... 0 1 0   1 0 3   0 0 0  5
Milwaukee .............. 0 0 0   1 0 1   0 0 0  2
```

E: J. Thompson, C. Moore, D. Roberts, Sutherland. DP: Detroit 1, Milwaukee 2.
LOB: Detroit 8, Milwaukee 5. 2B: Horton, G. Scott. SB: M. Stanley. SF: P. Garcia.

| | IP | H | R | ER | BB | SO |
|---|---|---|---|---|---|---|
| D. Roberts (W, 16-17) . | 9 | 8 | 2 | 1 | 0 | 2 |
| Beare (L, 2-3) ............. | 6 | 9 | 5 | 5 | 2 | 7 |
| Haas ........................... | 3 | 1 | 0 | 0 | 1 | 2 |

T: 2:09.   A: 6,858.

## HENRY LOUIS (HANK) AARON
Born February 5, 1934, at Mobile Ala.
Height 6-0  Weight 190
Threw and batted right-handed.
Named to Hall of Fame, 1982.

| YEAR | CLUB | LEAGUE | POS. | G. | AB. | R. | H. | 2B. | 3B. | HR. | RBI. | B.A. | PO. | A. | E. | F.A. |
|---|---|---|---|---|---|---|---|---|---|---|---|---|---|---|---|---|
| 1952 | Eau Claire | North. | SS | 87 | 345 | 79 | 116 | 19 | 4 | 9 | 61 | .336 | 137 | 265 | 35 | .920 |
| 1953 | Jacksonville | Sally | 2B | 137 | 574 | 115 | 208 | 36 | 14 | 22 | 125 | .362 | 330 | 310 | 36 | .947 |
| 1954 | Milwaukee | Nat. | OF | 122 | 468 | 58 | 131 | 27 | 6 | 13 | 69 | .280 | 223 | 5 | 7 | .970 |
| 1955 | Milwaukee | Nat. | OF-2B | 153 | 602 | 105 | 189 | 37 | 9 | 27 | 106 | .314 | 340 | 93 | 15 | .967 |
| 1956 | Milwaukee | Nat. | OF | 153 | 609 | 106 | 200 | 34 | 14 | 26 | 92 | .328 | 316 | 17 | 13 | .962 |
| 1957 | Milwaukee | Nat. | OF | 151 | 615 | 118 | 198 | 27 | 6 | 44 | 132 | .322 | 346 | 9 | 6 | .983 |
| 1958 | Milwaukee | Nat. | OF | 153 | 601 | 109 | 196 | 34 | 4 | 30 | 95 | .326 | 305 | 12 | 5 | .984 |
| 1959 | Milwaukee | Nat. | OF-3B | 154 | 629 | 116 | 223 | 46 | 7 | 39 | 123 | .355 | 263 | 22 | 5 | .983 |
| 1960 | Milwaukee | Nat. | OF-2B | 153 | 590 | 102 | 172 | 20 | 11 | 40 | 126 | .292 | 321 | 13 | 6 | .982 |
| 1961 | Milwaukee | Nat. | OF-3B | 155 | 603 | 115 | 197 | 39 | 10 | 34 | 120 | .327 | 379 | 15 | 7 | .983 |
| 1962 | Milwaukee | Nat. | OF-1B | 156 | 592 | 127 | 191 | 28 | 6 | 45 | 128 | .323 | 341 | 11 | 7 | .981 |
| 1963 | Milwaukee | Nat. | OF | 161 | 631 | 121 | 201 | 29 | 4 | 44 | 130 | .319 | 267 | 10 | 6 | .979 |
| 1964 | Milwaukee | Nat. | OF-2B | 145 | 570 | 103 | 187 | 30 | 2 | 24 | 95 | .328 | 284 | 28 | 6 | .981 |
| 1965 | Milwaukee | Nat. | OF | 150 | 570 | 109 | 181 | 40 | 1 | 32 | 89 | .318 | 298 | 9 | 4 | .987 |
| 1966 | Atlanta | Nat. | OF-2B | 158 | 603 | 117 | 168 | 23 | 1 | 44 | 127 | .279 | 315 | 12 | 4 | .988 |
| 1967 | Atlanta | Nat. | OF-2B | 155 | 600 | 113 | 184 | 37 | 3 | 39 | 109 | .307 | 322 | 12 | 7 | .979 |
| 1968 | Atlanta | Nat. | OF-1B | 160 | 606 | 84 | 174 | 33 | 4 | 29 | 86 | .287 | 418 | 20 | 5 | .989 |
| 1969 | Atlanta | Nat. | OF-1B | 147 | 547 | 100 | 164 | 30 | 3 | 44 | 97 | .300 | 299 | 13 | 5 | .984 |
| 1970 | Atlanta | Nat. | OF-1B | 150 | 516 | 103 | 154 | 26 | 1 | 38 | 118 | .298 | 319 | 10 | 7 | .979 |
| 1971 | Atlanta | Nat. | 1B OF | 139 | 495 | 95 | 162 | 22 | 3 | 47 | 118 | .327 | 733 | 40 | 5 | .994 |
| 1972 | Atlanta | Nat. | 1B-OF | 129 | 449 | 75 | 119 | 10 | 0 | 34 | 77 | .265 | 996 | 70 | 17 | .984 |
| 1973 | Atlanta | Nat. | OF | 120 | 392 | 84 | 118 | 12 | 1 | 40 | 96 | .301 | 206 | 5 | 5 | .977 |
| 1974 | Atlanta (a) | Nat. | OF | 112 | 340 | 47 | 91 | 16 | 0 | 20 | 69 | .268 | 142 | 3 | 2 | .986 |
| 1975 | Milwaukee | Amer. | DH-OF | 137 | 465 | 45 | 109 | 16 | 2 | 12 | 60 | .234 | 2 | 0 | 0 | 1.000 |
| 1976 | Milwaukee | Amer. | DH-OF | 85 | 271 | 22 | 62 | 8 | 0 | 10 | 35 | .229 | 1 | 0 | 0 | 1.000 |
| American League Totals—2 Years | | | | 222 | 736 | 67 | 171 | 24 | 2 | 22 | 95 | .232 | 3 | 0 | 0 | 1.000 |
| National League Totals—21 Years | | | | 3076 | 11628 | 2107 | 3600 | 600 | 96 | 733 | 2202 | .310 | 7433 | 429 | 144 | .982 |
| Major League Totals—23 Years | | | | 3298 | 12364 | 2174 | 3771 | 624 | 98 | 755 | 2297 | .305 | 7436 | 429 | 144 | .982 |

**a** Traded to Milwaukee Brewers for outfielder Dave May and minor league pitcher Roger Alexander, November 2, 1974.

### CHAMPIONSHIP SERIES RECORD

| YEAR | CLUB | LEAGUE | POS. | G. | AB. | R. | H. | 2B. | 3B. | HR. | RBI. | B.A. | PO. | A. | E. | F.A. |
|---|---|---|---|---|---|---|---|---|---|---|---|---|---|---|---|---|
| 1969 | Atlanta | Nat. | OF | 3 | 14 | 3 | 5 | 2 | 0 | 3 | 7 | .357 | 4 | 1 | 1 | .833 |

### WORLD SERIES RECORD

| YEAR | CLUB | LEAGUE | POS. | G. | AB. | R. | H. | 2B. | 3B. | HR. | RBI. | B.A. | PO. | A. | E. | F.A. |
|---|---|---|---|---|---|---|---|---|---|---|---|---|---|---|---|---|
| 1957 | Milwaukee | Nat. | OF | 7 | 28 | 5 | 11 | 0 | 1 | 3 | 7 | .393 | 11 | 0 | 0 | 1.000 |
| 1958 | Milwaukee | Nat. | OF | 7 | 27 | 3 | 9 | 2 | 0 | 0 | 2 | .333 | 14 | 0 | 0 | 1.000 |
| World Series Totals—2 Years | | | | 14 | 55 | 8 | 20 | 2 | 1 | 3 | 9 | .364 | 25 | 0 | 0 | 1.000 |

Standing in front of a photo of himself in his heyday, Cleveland ace Bob Feller hangs up his famous No. 19. Feller, the greatest strikeout artist of his day, didn't strike out a single batter in his final game.

©Ron Kuntz/DIAMOND IMAGES®

# BOB FELLER

## *Slow Finish for Rapid Robert*

| | |
|---|---|
| **DATE:** September 30, 1956 | |
| **SITE:** Municipal Stadium, Cleveland, Ohio | |
| **OPPONENT:** Detroit Tigers | |
| **RESULT:** Complete game 8-4 loss | |

**September 30, 1956, Cleveland**—The season was gone, the game was gone and so, Bob Feller figured, was his arm.

After 20 big-league campaigns in a Cleveland uniform, the 37-year-old right-hander stood on the mound on the final Sunday in September and readied his final pitch to Detroit center fielder Bill Tuttle.

He needed just one more out to get the Indians into the ninth. Then, with the Tribe trailing 8-4, three more outs would put them into the offseason and Feller, probably, into retirement.

He looked over at the scoreboard again. Detroit 8, Cleveland 4. It wasn't quite riding off into the sunset. They had announced the final day's attendance at 5,910 and many of them had left already. So much for saying a sweet good-bye.

To tell you the truth, it was an odd day. All season long, Feller was the forgotten man in the bullpen, the guy that hung on long enough to make everyone uncomfortable when he came around and started throwing.

For a player of his magnitude to be relegated to mop-up duty or worse, batting practice, something was unseemly about it.

As columnist Red Smith was quick to note the week before his finale, quoting Hank Greenberg: "'There's something wrong with the picture of him warming up in the bullpen.'"

"Of course the picture is wrong," Smith wrote. "So are those figures: no victories, three defeats. It always seems wrong when this happens, though there never could have been a moment's doubt that the year would come when Feller wouldn't win a game. When Cy Slapnicka led him off the Iowa sandlots, he started the boy toward this year."

After noting that Feller's record would leave him shy of the coveted 300-win club, Smith went on.

"To be sure, there is meat enough in Feller's record to feed any man's pride. In 1938 he struck out eighteen Tigers in nine innings. In 1946 he fanned 348 batsmen, smacking a record that Rube Waddell had held for 42 years. He pitched three no-hit games. In one four-year span, he struck out 1,007 batters in 1,238 innings. He was, simply, the greatest pitcher of his time."

But his time was long past. And considering he wasn't the easiest fella in the world to get along with, Feller took the whole thing pretty well. Since everybody knew he was about to be out of a job as was Indians' manager Al Lopez, who, after six years as the Tribe's manager had announced his resignation the day before.

*Cleveland Plain Dealer* photographer Marvin Greene got Feller to pose with Lopez and also retiring Western Union press box chief Al Brandeis for a front-page photo that they ran on the front of the paper's sports section.

Here were the three of them thumbing through the help wanted ads. There was something a little strange about the greatest pitcher in Cleveland history going out as comic relief.

Considering he came into the game with a won-loss record of 0-3 with an earned-run average of 4.41, it's a wonder he could laugh at all. Well, correct that. Feller's 4.41 ERA was before the Detroit Tigers had pounded him for eight runs in these eight innings. (It would wind up at 4.78.)

He'd only had one other start the whole year and sure wasn't fooling anybody. Why, he came into this game having worked just 50 innings all season long—about nine innings per month—and the former strikeout king had fanned just 18 batters or one more than he'd fanned in a single game against Philadelphia back when he was 17 years old.

With Lopez leaving and the Indians locked into second place, there really wasn't anything to play for. Except trying to help Feller leave with a win. Lopez gave him the ball even though he knew, Detroit knew, and probably even Feller himself knew it wasn't going to happen.

From his opening inning, Feller had a pretty good idea how it was going to go. After he'd gotten leadoff hitter Harvey Kuenn out, Feller gave up a home run to somebody named Wayne Belardi, the sixth of his season and 28th and final home run of Belardi's career. Belardi retired, a .242 career hitter, over the winter.

But his home run let Detroit go ahead to begin with. Cleveland never could catch up.

There was plenty of chatter in the Detroit dugout, though. Kuenn and the Tigers' Boy Wonder, Al Kaline, were battling for the American League lead in hits and Feller settled it for 'em.

Kuenn got three hits; Kaline managed just a triple. Kuenn's three hits got his average up to .332 but that still left him a distant third in the AL batting race behind Triple Crown winner Mickey Mantle (.356) and runner-up Ted Williams (.345.)

In the fourth, the Tigers kept after Feller, bunching three hits in the fourth to make it 4-1, then added four more runs off the old-timer in the sixth.

Though Feller had allowed 14 hits, walking three, Lopez never moved off the bench. He was going to let him finish his final game. He'd done that much for the Cleveland Indians. He'd earned that.

Why, Feller couldn't ever have imagined he'd complete a game where he'd allowed 14 hits.

Wasn't he the guy who'd thrown 12 career one-hitters and three no-hitters?

Wasn't he the guy who, in his most magnificent season, returned from World War II to pitch a whopping 371 innings for Lou Boudreau's Indians, fanning a record 348 (a record later broken by Sandy Koufax, then Nolan Ryan), pitching 36 complete games, posting a 26-15 record with an amazing 2.18 ERA for a sixth-place Indians' team.

But that amazing workload took its toll. Though Feller was only 27 years old at the time and would go on to pitch for 10 more years, he never again fanned more than 200 batters in a season. Still, he won.

At 36, he went 13-3 for the 1954 Indians, the winningest team in baseball history with four 20-game winners (Bob Lemon, Herb Score, Mike Garcia, Early Wynn).

Oddly, he never got to pitch in that World Series. The Tribe was swept in four games by the New York Giants.

There was talk that Feller was going to retire because his 1955 season was a big dropoff. He appeared in just 25 games, only 83 innings, 11 starts, with just 25 strikeouts.

Since the Indians were well stocked with pitchers, retirement seemed to make sense. But Feller, always keen with a dollar, was involved in trying to set up baseball's pension plan. And the players didn't want him to go.

"I probably should have retired in 1955," Feller said many years later. "But we were working on the pension plan. In those days, you had to have continuity.

"If I'd have retired, someone else would have taken over as the player representative with no continuity and no background in working on the pension plan. The owners did have continuity. So the players asked me to stay another year."

He did. It sure wasn't much fun. The Tribe seemed to continue to skid after that World Series sweep two years earlier. They won just 88 games, the fewest they'd won since 1947 and had only hit .244 as a team, their worst since the war years.

And their failures were clear to everyone. Cleveland was a combined 51-15 against the league's three worst teams—Baltimore, Washington, and Philadelphia—a pretty impressive won-lost record. But against the AL champion Yankees, they were 10-12.

"*Cleveland ace toes rubber for last time*"

So now, this was it. He was down to his last out and that'd be it.

Feller wound and delivered and just from the sound of the swing, Feller knew it'd be a ground ball. He started walking with that familiar ploughboy walk toward the Cleveland dugout. His day, his career, was over.

Lopez sent Gene Woodling up to pinch hit for Feller leading off the ninth. When the game ended a moment later and the Indians' season closed with a defeat, Feller felt a sense of relief.

So, you can bet, did Cleveland management.

"I know they don't want me on the team another year," Feller said, candidly, after his 162nd career loss. "And I doubt that there's any job in the front office that will interest me."

And managing? Somebody asked Feller that on Saturday, after hearing of Lopez's resignation.

"No thanks," he said.

Though he surely knew the truth, he still tried to sound brave at the finish when the sportswriters came around one last time.

"I'm not yet convinced I'm all through," he said. "I want to talk to (Indians' players) Jim (Hegan) and (Mel) Harder in the next few weeks and see what they say. Maybe I'll be pitching somewhere else next year."

How did it feel to go out like that?

"I've had better stuff," Feller said in possibly the understatement of the century. "But my arm felt good and I didn't tire. That's the important thing."

Yet in his final appearance in a big-league game, one of the game's greatest strikeout artists had left his sport in most unusual fashion.

Bob Feller faced 41 hitters that final afternoon at Municipal Stadium. He didn't strike out a single one.

# Not a Single K

|  | DETROIT | | | |  | CLEVELAND | | | |
|---|---|---|---|---|---|---|---|---|---|
|  | ab. | h. | e. | a. |  | ab. | h. | e. | a. |
| Kuenn, ss ...... | 5 | 3 | 2 | 1 | Caffie, lf ...... | 5 | 2 | 3 | 0 |
| Belardi, 1b .... | 5 | 3 | 6 | 1 | Pope, cf ....... | 5 | 0 | 1 | 0 |
| Maxwell, lf ... | 5 | 1 | 1 | 0 | Ward, 1b ...... | 4 | 0 | 12 | 0 |
| Kaline, rf ..... | 3 | 1 | 2 | 0 | Rosen, 3b ...... | 2 | 0 | 1 | 2 |
| Bertola, 3b .... | 5 | 1 | 2 | 1 | Smith, 3b ...... | 2 | 2 | 0 | 2 |
| Tuttle, cf ..... | 5 | 2 | 1 | 0 | Colavito, rf .... | 4 | 1 | 2 | 0 |
| Bolling, 2b .... | 4 | 1 | 3 | 2 | Kuhn, ss ....... | 4 | 1 | 4 | 5 |
| House, c ...... | 3 | 1 | 9 | 1 | Averill, c ...... | 4 | 3 | 0 | 0 |
| Garver, p ..... | 1 | 0 | 0 | 1 | Stickland, 2b ... | 4 | 1 | 4 | 5 |
| **a** Torgeson .... | 1 | 1 | 0 | 0 | Feller, p ....... | 3 | 0 | 0 | 2 |
| Hoeft, p ...... | 0 | 0 | 1 | 2 | **c** Woodling .... | 1 | 0 | 0 | 0 |
| **b** Small ...... | 1 | 0 | 0 | 0 |  |  |  |  |  |
| Foytack, p .... | 0 | 0 | 0 | 0 |  |  |  |  |  |
| **TOTALS:** | **38** | **14** | **27** | **9** | **TOTALS:** | **36** | **10** | **27** | **16** |

**a** Doubled for Garver in fourth.　**b** Grounded out for Hoeft in seventh.　**c** Flied out for Feller in ninth.

```
Detroit  ......  1 0 0   3 0 4   0 0 0—8
Cleveland ....   0 0 0   0 2 2   0 0 0—4
```

R: Kuenn, Belardi 2; Tuttle, Bolling, House 2; Torgeson, Smith, Kuhn, Averill 2. E: Kuenn, Bolling, House. RBI: Belardi, Torgeson 2, Kuenn 3, Kaline 2, Caffie, Smith, Strickland. 2B: Torgeson, Averill. 3B: Kaline. HR: Belardi, Smith. SB: Kaline. S: Hoeft. DP: Kuhn, Strickland, Ward; Strickland, Kuhn, Ward; Bertola, Bolling, Bellardi. LOB: Detroit 7, Cleveland, 7. BB: Feller 3. SO: Garver 3, Hoeft 4, Foytack 3. HO: Garver 2 in 3, Hoeft 5 in 4, Foytack 3 in 2. R-ER: Garver 0-0, Hoeft 4-2, Feller 8-8, Foytack 0-0. W: Hoeft (20-14). L:  Feller (0-4). U: Umont, Berry, Honochick, Napp. T: 2:00. A: 5,910.

# ROBERT WILLIAM ANDREW FELLER
Born November 3, 1918, at Van Meter, Iowa
Height 6-0  Weight 185
Threw and batted right-handed.
Named to Hall of Fame, 1962.

| YEAR | CLUB | LEAGUE | G. | IP. | W. | L. | Pct. | H. | R. | ER. | SO. | BB. | ERA. |
|------|------|--------|-----|------|-----|-----|------|------|------|------|------|------|------|
| 1936 | Cleveland | Amer. | 14 | 62 | 5 | 3 | .625 | 52 | 29 | 23 | 76 | 47 | 3.34 |
| 1937 | Cleveland | Amer. | 26 | 149 | 9 | 7 | .563 | 116 | 68 | 56 | 150 | 106 | 3.38 |
| 1938 | Cleveland | Amer. | 39 | 278 | 17 | 11 | .607 | 225 | 136 | 126 | 240 | 208 | 4.08 |
| 1939 | Cleveland | Amer. | 39 | 297 | 24 | 9 | .727 | 227 | 105 | 94 | 246 | 142 | 2.85 |
| 1940 | Cleveland | Amer. | 43 | 320 | 27 | 11 | .711 | 245 | 102 | 93 | 261 | 118 | 2.62 |
| 1941 | Cleveland | Amer. | 44 | 343 | 25 | 13 | .658 | 284 | 129 | 120 | 260 | 194 | 3.15 |
| 1942-43-44 | Cleveland | Amer. | | | | | (In Military Service) | | | | | | |
| 1945 | Cleveland | Amer. | 9 | 72 | 5 | 3 | .625 | 50 | 21 | 20 | 59 | 35 | 2.50 |
| 1946 | Cleveland | Amer. | 48 | 371 | 26 | 15 | .634 | 277 | 101 | 90 | 348 | 153 | 2.18 |
| 1947 | Cleveland | Amer. | 42 | 299 | 20 | 11 | .645 | 230 | 97 | 89 | 196 | 127 | 2.68 |
| 1948 | Cleveland | Amer. | 44 | 280 | 19 | 15 | .559 | 255 | 123 | 111 | 164 | 116 | 3.57 |
| 1949 | Cleveland | Amer. | 36 | 211 | 15 | 14 | .517 | 198 | 104 | 88 | 108 | 84 | 3.75 |
| 1950 | Cleveland | Amer. | 35 | 247 | 16 | 11 | .593 | 230 | 105 | 94 | 119 | 103 | 3.43 |
| 1951 | Cleveland | Amer. | 33 | 250 | 22 | 8 | .733 | 239 | 105 | 97 | 111 | 95 | 3.49 |
| 1952 | Cleveland | Amer. | 30 | 192 | 9 | 13 | .409 | 219 | 124 | 101 | 81 | 83 | 4.73 |
| 1953 | Cleveland | Amer. | 25 | 176 | 10 | 7 | .588 | 168 | 78 | 70 | 60 | 60 | 3.58 |
| 1954 | Cleveland | Amer. | 19 | 140 | 13 | 3 | .813 | 127 | 53 | 48 | 59 | 39 | 3.09 |
| 1955 | Cleveland | Amer. | 25 | 83 | 4 | 4 | .500 | 71 | 43 | 32 | 25 | 31 | 3.47 |
| 1956 | Cleveland | Amer. | 19 | 58 | 0 | 4 | .000 | 63 | 34 | 32 | 18 | 23 | 4.97 |
| Major League Totals | | | 570 | 3828 | 266 | 162 | .621 | 3271 | 1557 | 1384 | 2581 | 1764 | 3.25 |

## WORLD SERIES RECORD

| YEAR | CLUB | LEAGUE | G. | IP. | W. | L. | Pct. | H. | R. | ER. | SO. | BB. | Ave. |
|------|------|--------|-----|------|-----|-----|------|------|------|------|------|------|------|
| 1948 | Cleveland | Amer. | 2 | 14 1/3 | 0 | 2 | .000 | 10 | 8 | 8 | 7 | 5 | 5.02 |

St. Louis Cardinals ace Bob Gibson's final major-league pitch was hit for a grand slam.
©DIAMOND IMAGES®

# BOB GIBSON

*Bad Time for a Slam*

**DATE:** September 3, 1975

**SITE:** Busch Stadium, St. Louis, Missouri

**OPPONENT:** Pete LaCock of the Chicago Cubs

**RESULT:** Allowed grand slam to LaCock in seventh, which helped Cubs go on to win. Gibson left the game and took the loss.

**September 3, 1975, St. Louis**—The count ran full.

Bob Gibson took a deep breath and fingered the white baseball in his long, calloused fingers as he stood on the hill and took the sign from St. Louis Cardinals' catcher Ted Simmons.

So many pitches. So many innings.

He looked around and saw the bases were full of Chicago Cubs. Gibson stared in at the Cubs' left-handed hitter, who waved the bat at him eagerly. Who was this kid? What was his name again? LaCock. Quite a name.

That's it. Standing at the plate with a three-ball, two-strike count on him was Ralph Pierre LaCock Jr., the so-so hit, no-field son of *Hollywood Squares* host Peter Marshall and actress Joanna Dru.

A 23-year-old rookie, itching, as he would put it to an adoring news media a little bit later, to break into the Cubs' lineup, Cubs' manager Jim Marshall had sent LaCock to the plate against the 39-year-old Gibson, hoping to break open a close game.

"Gibson gopher ball ruins night"

Here was a classic baseball matchup, an eager rookie against a wily old pro, a fading veteran, still trying to hang on.

Except the fierce Gibson didn't see himself as fading. Not really. He should have been starting, that's the way he figured it. Manager Red Schoendienst saw it another way.

When the right-hander began the 1975 season, he was still penciled in as a starter. Coming off an 11-13 season where he posted a career-high 3.83 ERA in 33 starts, the famous Gibson fastball was slowing. He fanned just 129 in 240 innings, the lowest per-game strikeout ratio (4.8) of his career.

He struggled in three of his first five starts and was 1-5 on May 31 when he was demoted to the Cardinal bullpen. He won just twice more the rest of the season, making only four more starts.

But to Gibson, standing on the same mound where he'd been so dominating for so many years, it was impossible for him to see things had changed that much. No matter what his numbers said.

Five years later, on the eve of his induction to Cooperstown, he told writer Roger Angell that he never let age back him down.

"I always threw hard," he said then. "They didn't use me much my final season, after I'd announced I was going to retire—I never did understand that.

"But once, when I hadn't pitched in three weeks, they brought me into a game against Houston in extra innings—I was the last pitcher we had—and I struck out the side on nine pitches that were nothing but fastballs.

"So I still had something left, even at the end. . . ."

It didn't feel like that right now, though. The score had been tied at 6 when Gibson came on in relief of Cardinals' starter Ron Reed, who had been pinch hit for in the Cards' five-run sixth. It was the eighth relief appearance of Gibson's final season.

Gibson retired the Cubs' Bill Madlock, that season's batting champion (.354) with his first pitch. But the game's momentum quickly swung back to the Cubs when Gibson walked Jose Cardenal and an infield error let Champ Summers get on. A walk to Andre Thornton loaded the bases.

Though Gibson retired Manny Trillo on a sharp grounder right back at him, forcing Cardenal at the plate, the veteran righty then fired a wild pitch past Simmons to let the Cubs score the tie-breaking run score from third. Relievers aren't supposed to do that.

So, fearing further trouble, with first base open, pinch-hitter Jose Morales was intentionally walked, bringing up the nine-spot in the order and pinch-hitter LaCock.

If you weren't really paying attention, it was easy to see the big red "45" underneath "Gibson" on the back of the bright white Cardinal jersey and imagine that it was 1968 all over again.

That was Gibson's extraordinary season, perhaps the finest single season by a pitcher in the long history of baseball. Gibson recorded a 1.12 earned-run average that year, throwing 13 shutouts, completing 28 of 34 starts, posting a 22-9 record for the NL champs.

His was the most dominant season of all in the Year of the Pitcher, a pitching-dominated year that prompted Major League Baseball to uniformly lower the mounds across both leagues the following spring.

And Gibson's dominance wasn't just limited to National League performances. When he worked the opening game of the 1968 World Series against the Detroit Tigers, all of America got to see what National League hitters had been flailing at all season long.

Facing a Tiger team that led the American League in runs (671) and home runs (185), Gibson scorched them with a brilliant, World Series record 17-strikeout performance in the opener on this very mound seven years earlier. Had there ever been a more dominating Series performance? Well, maybe Don Larsen's perfect game. But Larsen didn't strike out 17 hitters, including the last three in the ninth, the way that Gibson did.

The Cardinal catcher in that Series was broadcaster Tim McCarver, who didn't need much encouragement to remember the specifics of that game.

Gibson fanned the side in the ninth inning, including retiring slugger Willie Horton on a called third strike to end the game on a sharp-breaking slider, his 144th pitch.

*"LaCock blast sinks Gibson, Cards"*

"I can still see that last pitch," McCarver told writer Roger Angell, "and I'll bet Willie Horton thinks to this day that the ball hit him—that's how much that ball broke. Talk about a batter shuddering!"

Gibson's third baseman in that game was Mike Shannon, who also marveled at what he saw in that ballgame. Gibson was so dominating that only two batters managed so much as a ground ball off his electric stuff. Neither came Shannon's way.

In the years since that game, Shannon has talked with Tiger batters who can't help but talk about what it was like, batting against Gibson at his absolute peak.

"Most of them had never seen Gibby before," Shannon told Angell, "and they had no idea what they were up against. It's as if they can't believe it to this day. I've never seen major-league hitters overmatched that way. It was like watching a big-league pitcher against Little League batters. It was frightening."

But by the end of that season, the strain on Gibson was showing. You could get a sense of where he was in a bylined piece that ran in the *St. Louis Post-Dispatch* during an off-day near the end of the 1968 World Series with Detroit.

"All day yesterday reporters kept coming up to me, asking if it was true that I was thinking about retiring and if it is true that my arm hurt so much I would not be able to pitch a seventh game.

"Apparently, somebody wrote a story to that effect, adding that I need an operation and that arthritis in my elbow would shorten my career. If I need an operation, I wish somebody would tell me. Sure, my arm hurts. It hurts every time I pitch. I don't think there's a pitcher alive whose arm does not hurt, if he has pitched long enough.

"The way this probably got started is that I said I hoped I didn't have to pitch again and I do . . . I don't want to pitch again. I want this thing to finish up today. But if I have to, I will pitch. If I had to, I would have pitched yesterday."

It turned out Gibson did pitch in Game Seven. He and eventual Series' MVP Mickey Lolich matched each other for six scoreless innings. But after Gibson got two outs in the seventh, he faltered and allowed four hits, turning the Series. Gibson, possibly the greatest of all postseason pitchers, lost his final World Series game.

A lot can change in seven years. Gibson was now 39. His Cardinal team was in the middle of the pack in the National League. With 119 hits allowed in 109 innings, he wasn't overmatching anybody anymore.

But still, he was Bob Gibson, as arrogant, as confident, as bold a pitcher who ever stood on a mound. He had reason to be, didn't he?

"He was the most intimidating player in the league," Ted Simmons, Gibson's former catcher, recalled in Daniel Okrent's *Nine Innings*. "He'd stare in at the batter, and I could feel his eyes burn. Every pitch was a war for him, every hitter a threat. He never gave in and he never gave up. He won by force of his personality and by his concentration."

Gibson stared in at LaCock. Who was this guy? Was he ready to hit against Bob Gibson? *The* Bob Gibson? Didn't he win 11 straight postseason games, including seven straight in a World Series? Didn't he win two Game Sevens, vs. the New York Yankees in 1964—in Yankee Stadium!—and vs. the Boston Red Sox in 1967 at Fenway Park! And had the usually reliable Curt Flood made the kind of catch that he normally did in Game Seven in 1968, he might have won that one, too. Wasn't he the greatest big-game pitcher in modern times?

He wound and fired. LaCock saw the ball come out of Gibson's hand, saw the tall, athletic form lunge to the right, to the first base side as the white baseball flew plateward. He swung and the crack was unmistakable.

The ball soared toward right field, over right fielder Willie Davis's head into the seats. Grand slam. The first of LaCock's career as a professional or an amateur.

Gibson swallowed hard, then walked around the base of the mound, hollering at LaCock in that high, squeaky voice that always seemed surprising, coming from such an imposing man. The St. Louis fans, booing loudly as LaCock ran around the bases, couldn't hear. Fortunately.

When Gibson got to the other side of the mound, Schoendienst was waiting for him. Reliever Mike Wallace, a lefty, was on his way in to take over. Gibson, who'd been honored by the St. Louis fans with Bob Gibson Night two days earlier, stalked off silently. It was not exactly walking off into the sunset.

Reading the *St. Louis Post-Dispatch* the next day, Cardinal fans had to bite their lip.

"Cubs' Lucky Seventh Slams Door on Gibby" read the headline on the day's top story.

"Gibby, Cards take a pounding"

Down below, though, in Dick Kaegel's story, was a quote from Madlock, one that was even more troubling than the grand slam.

"A few guys on the bench said he looked like he was just going through the motions," Madlock said, adding (figuring he might have to still face him sometime) "now I didn't say that—that's just what I heard."

Bob Gibson? Going through the motions? Maybe it was, indeed, time to go.

Though he never pitched again, Gibson hung with the Cardinals for two more weeks. On Wednesday night, as the Cardinals were getting ready to face the Montreal Expos, Gibson cleared out his lockers and left the team.

He did take time to talk to the *Post-Dispatch*.

"I was a little disappointed at the way they used me," Gibson said. "I think I could have pitched better if it hadn't been for the way they did. The biggest disappointment I've ever had in baseball was being taken out of the starting rotation this year."

"I really didn't pitch any differently than I had, but they just didn't want me any more."

# A Last Pitch to Forget

### CHICAGO

| | ab. | r. | h. | bi. |
|---|---|---|---|---|
| Kessinger, ss . . . . | 4 | 0 | 1 | 1 |
| Wallis, cf . . . . . . . | 5 | 0 | 0 | 0 |
| Madlock, 3b . . . . | 5 | 0 | 3 | 0 |
| Cardenal, rf . . . . . | 4 | 0 | 1 | 0 |
| Summers, lf . . . . . | 4 | 1 | 2 | 0 |
| Hiser, pr . . . . . . . | 0 | 1 | 0 | 0 |
| Mittrwald, c . . . . . | 1 | 0 | 0 | 0 |
| Thornton, 1b . . . . | 2 | 4 | 2 | 0 |
| Trillo, 2b . . . . . . . | 4 | 1 | 1 | 1 |
| Swisher, c . . . . . . | 3 | 1 | 2 | 2 |
| J. Mrales, rf . . . . . | 0 | 1 | 0 | 0 |
| Prall, p . . . . . . . . . | 2 | 1 | 0 | 0 |
| Detore, p . . . . . . . | 0 | 0 | 0 | 0 |
| Schultz, p . . . . . . | 0 | 0 | 0 | 0 |
| LaCock, ph . . . . | 1 | 1 | 1 | 4 |
| P. Rusci, p . . . . . . | 1 | 0 | 0 | 0 |
| **TOTALS:** | **36** | **11** | **13** | **8** |

### ST. LOUIS

| | ab. | r. | h. | bi. |
|---|---|---|---|---|
| Brock, lf . . . . . . . | 4 | 0 | 2 | 3 |
| McBride, cf . . . . . | 5 | 0 | 1 | 0 |
| W. Davis, rf . . . . . | 4 | 1 | 1 | 0 |
| T. Simmns, c . . . . | 5 | 2 | 2 | 0 |
| R. Smith, 1b . . . . | 3 | 1 | 1 | 1 |
| Sizemore, 2b . . . . | 4 | 0 | 0 | 0 |
| Reitz, 3b . . . . . . . | 3 | 0 | 0 | 1 |
| Tyson, ss . . . . . . . | 3 | 1 | 0 | 0 |
| Reed, p . . . . . . . . | 2 | 0 | 1 | 0 |
| Bradford, ph . . . . | 0 | 0 | 0 | 0 |
| Fairly, ph . . . . . . . | 0 | 0 | 0 | 0 |
| Lintz, pr . . . . . . . . | 0 | 1 | 0 | 0 |
| Gibson, p . . . . . . . | 0 | 0 | 0 | 0 |
| Wallace, p . . . . . . | 0 | 0 | 0 | 0 |
| K. Hernandez, ph | 1 | 0 | 1 | 0 |
| **TOTALS:** | **34** | **6** | **9** | **5** |

```
Chicago . . . . . . . . . .   0 2 0   1 0 3   5 0 0—11
St. Louis . . . . . . . .   0 1 0   0 0 5   0 0 0—6
```

| | IP | H | R | ER | BB | SO |
|---|---|---|---|---|---|---|
| Prall . . . . . . . . . . . . | 5 2-3 | 6 | 5 | 4 | 4 | 2 |
| Dettore . . . . . . . . . | 0 | 1 | 1 | 1 | 0 | 0 |
| Schultz (W, 1-0) . . . | 1-3 | 0 | 0 | 0 | 0 | 0 |
| P. Reuschel . . . . . . . | 3 | 2 | 0 | 0 | 0 | 2 |
| Reed . . . . . . . . . . . | 6 | 9 | 6 | 4 | 2 | 4 |
| Gibson (L, 3-10) . . . | 1 | 2 | 5 | 5 | 3 | 0 |
| Wallace . . . . . . . . . | 2 | 2 | 0 | 0 | 1 | 3 |

E: Swisher, T. Simmons, Reitz, Madlock, Tyson. DP: Chicago 1, St. Louis 1. LOB: Chicago 7, St. Louis 7. 2B: Madlock 2, Summers, Thornton, Brock. HR: LaCock (6). S: Trillo, Prall. SF: Kessinger, Reitz. Save: P. Reuschel (3). HBP: By Dettore (Fairly). T: 2:46. A: 14,119.

## ROBERT (BOB) GIBSON

Born November 9, 1935, at Omaha, Neb.
Height 6-1  Weight 193
Threw and batted right-handed.
Named to Hall of Fame, 1981.

| YEAR | CLUB | LEAGUE | G. | IP. | W. | L. | Pct. | H. | R. | ER. | SO. | BB. | ERA. |
|------|------|--------|----|-----|----|----|------|----|----|-----|-----|-----|------|
| 1957 | Omaha | Amer. Assoc. | 10 | 42 | 2 | 1 | .667 | 46 | 26 | 20 | 25 | 27 | 4.29 |
| 1957 | Columbus | Sally | 8 | 43 | 4 | 3 | .571 | 36 | 26 | 18 | 24 | 34 | 3.77 |
| 1958 | Omaha | Amer. Assoc. | 13 | 87 | 3 | 4 | .429 | 79 | 45 | 32 | 47 | 39 | 3.31 |
| 1958 | Rochester | International | 20 | 103 | 5 | 5 | .500 | 88 | 35 | 28 | 75 | 54 | 2.45 |
| 1959 | Omaha | Amer. Assoc. | 24 | 135 | 9 | 9 | .500 | 128 | 59 | 46 | 98 | 70 | 3.07 |
| 1959 | St. Louis | Nat. | 13 | 76 | 3 | 5 | .375 | 77 | 35 | 28 | 48 | 39 | 3.32 |
| 1960 | St. Louis | Nat. | 27 | 87 | 3 | 6 | .333 | 97 | 61 | 54 | 69 | 48 | 5.59 |
| 1960 | Rochester | International | 6 | 41 | 2 | 3 | .400 | 33 | 15 | 13 | 36 | 17 | 2.85 |
| 1961 | St. Louis | Nat. | 35 | 211 | 13 | 12 | .520 | 186 | 91 | 76 | 166 | 119 | 3.24 |
| 1962 | St. Louis | Nat. | 32 | 234 | 15 | 13 | .536 | 174 | 84 | 74 | 208 | 95 | 2.85 |
| 1963 | St. Louis | Nat. | 36 | 255 | 18 | 9 | .667 | 224 | 110 | 96 | 204 | 96 | 3.39 |
| 1964 | St. Louis | Nat. | 40 | 287 | 19 | 12 | .613 | 250 | 106 | 96 | 245 | 86 | 3.01 |
| 1965 | St. Louis | Nat. | 38 | 299 | 20 | 12 | .625 | 243 | 110 | 102 | 270 | 103 | 3.07 |
| 1966 | St. Louis | Nat. | 35 | 280 | 21 | 12 | .636 | 210 | 90 | 76 | 225 | 78 | 2.44 |
| 1967 | St. Louis | Nat. | 24 | 175 | 13 | 7 | .650 | 151 | 62 | 58 | 147 | 40 | 2.98 |
| 1968 | St. Louis | Nat. | 34 | 305 | 22 | 9 | .710 | 198 | 49 | 38 | 268 | 62 | 1.12 |
| 1969 | St. Louis | Nat. | 35 | 314 | 20 | 13 | .606 | 251 | 84 | 76 | 269 | 95 | 2.18 |
| 1970 | St. Louis | Nat. | 34 | 294 | 23 | 7 | .767 | 262 | 111 | 102 | 274 | 88 | 3.12 |
| 1971 | St. Louis | Nat. | 31 | 246 | 16 | 13 | .552 | 215 | 96 | 83 | 185 | 76 | 3.04 |
| 1972 | St. Louis | Nat. | 34 | 278 | 19 | 11 | .633 | 226 | 83 | 76 | 208 | 88 | 2.46 |
| 1973 | St. Louis | Nat. | 25 | 195 | 12 | 10 | .545 | 159 | 71 | 60 | 142 | 57 | 2.77 |
| 1974 | St. Louis | Nat. | 33 | 240 | 11 | 13 | .458 | 236 | 111 | 102 | 129 | 104 | 3.83 |
| 1975 | St. Louis | Nat. | 22 | 109 | 3 | 10 | .231 | 120 | 66 | 61 | 60 | 62 | 5.04 |
| Major League Totals—17 Years | | | 528 | 3885 | 251 | 174 | .591 | 3279 | 1420 | 1258 | 3117 | 1336 | 2.91 |

## WORLD SERIES RECORD

Holds records for most consecutive games won, lifetime (7); most strikeouts, game (17), October 2, 1968; most strikeouts, series (35), 1968.
Shares record for most games won, series (3), 1967.

| YEAR | CLUB | LEAGUE | G. | IP. | W. | L. | Pct. | H. | R. | ER. | SO. | BB. | ERA. |
|------|------|--------|----|-----|----|----|------|----|----|-----|-----|-----|------|
| 1964 | St. Louis | Nat. | 3 | 27 | 2 | 1 | .667 | 23 | 11 | 9 | 31 | 8 | 3.00 |
| 1967 | St. Louis | Nat. | 3 | 27 | 3 | 0 | 1.000 | 14 | 3 | 3 | 26 | 5 | 1.00 |
| 1968 | St. Louis | Nat. | 3 | 27 | 2 | 1 | .667 | 18 | 5 | 5 | 35 | 4 | 1.67 |
| World Series Totals | | | 9 | 81 | 7 | 2 | .778 | 55 | 19 | 17 | 92 | 17 | 1.89 |

Sandy Koufax didn't have much help from his teammates in his final game of the 1966 World Series.
©DIAMOND IMAGES®

# SANDY KOUFAX

## *Short and Oh So Sweet*

**DATE:** October 6, 1966

**SITE:** Dodger Stadium, Los Angeles, California

**OPPONENT:** Andy Etchebarren of Baltimore Orioles

**RESULT:** Koufax got Etchebarren to hit into an inning-ending double play in the sixth. But he already trailed 4-0 thanks to three errors in a single inning by center-fielder Willie Davis. Koufax ended up taking the loss in Game Two of the 1966 World Series.

**October 6, 1966, Los Angeles**—He needed an out. Just one out. Since when could the dominant pitcher of his time, heck, maybe ANY time, be humbled into praying for a little out?

Sandy Koufax stood on the mound at Dodger Stadium in Chavez Ravine on a sunny Thursday afternoon, staring in at the Baltimore Orioles' beetle-browed catcher Andy Etchebarren. Koufax had to wonder what he had done to deserve this.

Here it was, Game Two of the 1966 World Series and his Dodgers were looking like a bunch of rookies on the first day of Spring Training. What was it, five errors? Six? He'd lost count.

This was the World Series, what they'd been fighting for all season long, chasing a second-straight title. Koufax, pitching for the third time in eight days with an aching arm, was now into his 329th inning of the season. What more did he have to do?

Etchebarren waved his bat. This was the guy who started it all last time up, Koufax thought. How unlikely was that.

A career .235 hitter in his first full big-league season with the Orioles, Koufax had whistled three faster-than-fast fastballs past a stunned Etchebarren in his first at-bat. His battery mate that day, Baltimore's 20-year-old future Hall of Famer Jim Palmer, kneeling in the on-deck circle at the time, called Koufax's pitches to Etchebarren "radio fastballs."

"You could hear them," Palmer said, "but you couldn't see them."

But when Etchebarren batted again in the fifth, Koufax needed some help. He needed a routine play that suddenly wasn't so routine after all. All Hell broke loose and the game—and maybe the World Series—turned.

One of the beauties of the game of baseball is even all-time greats still need routine plays made behind them. It's never a one-man show, no matter how dominating a pitcher can be.

It's a game that looks easy enough. We've all played it, imitated big-league stars by making those great catches in our front yards and Little League parks, taking those mighty swings and hitting dramatic home runs.

But under the indiscriminate magnifying glass of history, the game's magic can turn on the most unsuspecting performer at the most shocking times. Fine players can become remembered more for their gaffes than the achievements of a long and distinguished career.

From Fred Merkle's boner to the time Johnny Pesky held the ball to Mickey Owen's dropped third strike to Bill Buckner's bobble, goats are a part of baseball lore, too.

*"Palmer outpitches Dodger ace"*

As Koufax toed the rubber for the first pitch to Etchebarren, he knew that all-time champion World Series goat—Dodgers' outfielder Willie Davis.

The inning before, the speedy Davis set a World Series record with three errors as Baltimore mounted a 2-0 lead off Koufax while Dodger hitters flailed haplessly at relentless Palmer fastballs. What were the odds of Cy Young winner Sandy Koufax, a 27-game winner at the peak of his powers, being outpitched by a 20-year-old rookie fireballer in his first World Series start?

It all seemed so shocking, like watching a classical pianist break into "I've Got a Lovely Bunch of Coconuts" in the middle of a Carnegie Hall recital. A virtuoso all season long—a 27-game winner, an ERA of 1.73—Koufax's pitching performances were like perfectly conducted baseball symphonies. But this sounded like Spike Jones.

A year earlier, Koufax had wrought one of the game's masterpieces, hurling a perfect game while retiring 27 batters in a row. It was only the second perfect game in major league baseball in the decade following Don Larsen's perfecto in the 1956 World Series. (This is not counting Harvey Haddix's 12 perfect innings; a game he lost in the 13th.)

Last October, Koufax had made national headlines by refusing to pitch the World Series opener because it fell on Yom Kippur. The headlines this year would be different.

Koufax went to the stretch and cast a glimpse over at Orioles second baseman Dave Johnson, leading off first. After his flare single, the last hit ever off Koufax, Sandy was tired. He'd worked a lot of innings the past two seasons, nearly 700 of them, counting the 30 World Series innings. And there was a mighty price to pay for such overwork: Pain.

Some experts concluded that Koufax's elbow problems stemmed from an incident in a game against the Braves where he jammed his elbow sliding back into the base on a pickoff attempt. Others maintain he simply threw too hard for his body to stand it for too long a time.

Whatever the cause, Koufax's arm problems were relentless. Sometimes, after games, his arm would swell to the size of a midget's leg and he wouldn't be able to bend it.

According to Jane Leavy's *Sandy Koufax, A Lefty's Legacy*, his arm was so often stiff before a game that Koufax would coat his arm with Capsolin, an old pitcher's salve that felt like a burn on his skin, distracting him from the arthritic ache in his elbow.

Through the years, most players had learned to cut the substance with Vaseline or cold cream. Koufax applied it straight to his skin and the odor from it was so strong, it could bring tears to the eyes of any nearby players.

After the game, Koufax would plunge the arm into a bucket of ice and hope the cold would help keep the swelling down. Sometimes, the elbow would swell up to the size of Koufax's knee joint and was impossible to bend. His coats had to be retailored. It was no way to live.

In between starts, Koufax would take Empirin for pain, sit for painful cortisone shots directly into the joint, even take his chances with an anti-inflammatory drug that some people insisted killed a few horses. The drug was called Butazolidin. It's now off the market.

In an era where fragile aces like Boston's Pedro Martinez and New York's Mariano Rivera are carefully monitored, their pitch counts carefully documented and consulted, it seems incredible that a pitcher with Koufax's extraordinary talent wasn't treated more cautiously by the team that owned his contract.

In *Legacy*, Leavy recounts a story of Koufax being allowed to pitch a complete game in Spring Training in 1965, an unheard of occurrence, especially with a player of Koufax's value to the franchise.

The next morning, Koufax showed his roommate, Dick Tracewski, what price he paid for pitching that game.

"The elbow was black," Leavy quotes Tracewski. "And it was swollen. There were muscles that were pulled and there was hemorrhaging. From the elbow to the armpit, it looked like a bruise. A black, angry hemorrhage. It was an angry arm, an angry elbow. And all he says is 'Roomie, look at this.'"

"*No support for Sandy K in Dodger defeat*"

As the 1965 season wore down, so did Koufax. After consulting with Dr. Robert Kerlan, Koufax made the decision to play one more season—1966—but told no one save his friend, writer Phil Collier, who wrote the story, then filed it away in his drawer cabinet until Sandy gave him the okay.

After pitching a pair of shutouts in the 1965 World Series to give the Dodgers the world title (Koufax worked two complete games on two days' rest) the arm continued to give him problems. In April 1966, Kerlan advised Koufax that it was time to retire.

Koufax nodded and pitched on. One more year.

So now, that year was about up. It was Game Two of the 1966 World Series, his elbow aching as though an alligator had a hold of it. Trailing 4-0, he just wanted to get out of the inning.

After 350 innings and who knows how much ice, how many shots, and how much suffering, Koufax looked at Etchebarren and thought about a double-play ball. That wasn't Sandy's style of pitching, but hey, at least it wouldn't be a fly ball.

Koufax looked out at center-fielder Willie Davis and thought about all the wonderful catches he'd made over the past few years, helping him save ballgames. It wasn't fair that the newspapers tomorrow would blister Davis just because he had trouble in a tough sun field. But baseball wasn't always fair—he knew that, too.

He looked over at the scoreboard and there were numbers for the Orioles in the fifth and in the sixth. It didn't say how they got them, but for anyone who was there or watched on TV, it would be hard to forget.

It happened so fast.

As the fifth inning began, Boog Powell, a lefty hitter, sliced a single to left to get things started. After Dave Johnson sacrificed him to second, Paul Blair lofted a high fly to center-fielder Willie Davis. But Davis, normally a solid outfielder, promptly lost the ball in the sun, allowing runners to go to second and third.

Next up was Etchebarren, the No. 8 hitter. Instead of walking him to load the bases and set up a force at any base—conventional baseball strategy with the pitcher batting next—Dodger manager Walt Alston was confident Koufax didn't need any force play to get out of any jam. He let him pitch to Etchebarren.

It was a bad call. Etchebarren lofted a high, very catchable fly ball to Davis in center again and once more, to the horror of Dodger fans everywhere, Davis lost the ball in the sun and it dropped. Then he panicked, picked up the bobbled ball, and promptly fired the ball past third.

It was 2-0 Orioles. When Luis Aparicio followed by ripping a double past third, Etchebarren rumbled in with the third unearned run of the inning.

In the sixth, Frank Robinson's long fly ball to the wall was again misplayed by Davis (this one wasn't ruled an error), allowing him to get to third. Powell singled him in to make it 4-0, Baltimore. Then, after an out, Dave Johnson flared one into right center. Which brought him to this spot. One more pitch. One more out.

With one pitch, if he threw it in the right place, Koufax might get the slow-footed Etchebarren to chase it, hit it on the ground, and start an inning-ending double play. He wound and fired the pitch, a low fastball and, sure enough, Etchebarren chased it, rapping a slow roller that was quickly turned into a double play to end the inning. The walk to the dugout seemed long and sad.

*"Error-prone Dodgers sink Sandy"*

When manager Walt Alston sent up a pinch hitter for Koufax in the bottom of the sixth, the great left-hander's career was over. Nobody knew it at the time. Remember, the Dodgers had trailed in the 1965 World Series vs. the Minnesota Twins and came back to win. Maybe if the Series went long enough, Koufax would be back.

But it wasn't to happen. The Dodgers, hitting abominably, faded quickly against the young and sassy Baltimore staff and, suddenly, the Series had ended. The Orioles had won.

And the Dodgers, well, they'd ridden Koufax to a pair of World Series berths and one title. But by working him over 700 innings in his final two years, perhaps they made him into a bright and brilliant comet that was about to burn out.

The last pitcher who had thrown more than 350 innings in a nonwartime season was Cleveland's Bob Feller, who returned from the service to throw a stunning 371 innings for the Tribe in 1946, fanning a then-record 348.

Apparently, the workload partially tamed him. Feller played another decade but never again struck out more than 200 batters in a single season. It was a long, slow, gradual fade.

Koufax's numbers, despite the between-start suffering, kept getting better, even though elbow and circulation problems in his finger, threatened to end his career at any time. Somehow, he battled through it all, never missed a start. On November 17, he officially announced his retirement.

With much of the Dodger brass on a trip to Japan and unrepresented at the noon press conference at the Beverly Wilshire, Koufax made it official. He was done.

"If there was a man who did not have the use of one of his arms," Koufax explained to the press that afternoon, "and you told him it would cost a lot of money if he could buy back that use, he'd give every dime he had, I believe."

There would be no more shots, no more pills, and no more potions. At the very tip-top of his game, he'd decided to say goodbye.

"I don't regret one minute of the last twelve years," he said softly, "but I think I would regret one year that was too many."

Five days after Christmas, three weeks into his retirement, Sandy Koufax turned 31.

# Sandy's Last Stand

## Game Two

| BALTIMORE | ab. | r. | h. | rbi. | po. | a. |
|---|---|---|---|---|---|---|
| Aparicio, ss ..... | 5 | 0 | 2 | 1 | 4 | 1 |
| Blefary, lf ....... | 5 | 0 | 0 | 0 | 1 | 0 |
| F. Robinson, rf ... | 3 | 2 | 1 | 0 | 1 | 0 |
| B. Robinson, 3b .. | 4 | 1 | 1 | 0 | 1 | 1 |
| Powell, 1b ...... | 3 | 1 | 2 | 1 | 8 | 0 |
| D. Johnson, 2b ... | 4 | 0 | 2 | 1 | 2 | 4 |
| Blair, cf ........ | 3 | 1 | 0 | 0 | 4 | 0 |
| Etchebarren, c ... | 3 | 1 | 0 | 0 | 6 | 0 |
| Palmer, p ....... | 4 | 0 | 0 | 0 | 0 | 2 |
| | | | | | | |
| **TOTALS:** | **34** | **6** | **8** | **3** | **27** | **8** |

| LOS ANGELES | ab. | r. | h. | rbi. | po. | a. |
|---|---|---|---|---|---|---|
| Wills, ss ...... | 4 | 0 | 0 | 0 | 3 | 1 |
| Gilliam, 3b .... | 4 | 0 | 0 | 0 | 2 | 3 |
| W. Davis, cf ... | 4 | 0 | 0 | 0 | 2 | 0 |
| Fairly, rf ...... | 3 | 0 | 0 | 0 | 3 | 0 |
| Lefebvre, 2b ... | 3 | 0 | 0 | 0 | 3 | 0 |
| L. Johnson, lf .. | 4 | 0 | 1 | 0 | 1 | 0 |
| Roseboro, c ... | 4 | 0 | 1 | 0 | 8 | 1 |
| Parker, 1b ..... | 2 | 0 | 1 | 0 | 5 | 1 |
| Koufax, p ..... | 2 | 0 | 0 | 0 | 0 | 1 |
| Perranoski, p .. | 0 | 0 | 0 | 0 | 0 | 1 |
| Regan, p ...... | 0 | 0 | 0 | 0 | 0 | 0 |
| **a** T. Davis ..... | 1 | 0 | 1 | 0 | 0 | 0 |
| Brewer, p ..... | 0 | 0 | 0 | 0 | 0 | 0 |
| **TOTALS:** | **31** | **0** | **4** | **0** | **27** | **8** |

**a** Singled for Regan in eighth.

```
Baltimore .........  000  031  020—6
Los Angeles .......  000  000  000—0
```

| | IP | H | R | ER | BB | SO | HBP | WP | Balks |
|---|---|---|---|---|---|---|---|---|---|
| Palmer (W) .... | 9 | 4 | 0 | 0 | 3 | 6 | 0 | 1 | 0 |
| Koufax (L) .... | 6 | 6 | 4 | 1 | 2 | 2 | 0 | 0 | 0 |
| Perranoski ..... | 1 1/3 | 2 | 2 | 2 | 1 | 1 | 0 | 0 | 0 |
| Regan ........ | 2/3 | 0 | 0 | 0 | 1 | 1 | 0 | 1 | 0 |
| Brewer ....... | 1 | 0 | 0 | 0 | 0 | 1 | 0 | 0 | 0 |

E: Gilliam, W. Davis 3, Fairly, Perranoski. DP: Gilliam, Roseboro, Parker. LOB: Baltimore 6, Los Angeles 7. 2B: L. Johnson, Aparicio. 3B: F. Robinson. SF: Powell. BB: Off Palmer 3 (Fairly, Parker, Lefebvre), Koufax 2 (F. Robinson, Blair), Perranoski 1 (F. Robinson), Regan 1 (Etchebarren). SO: By Palmer 6 (W. Davis 2, Lefebvre 2, Fairly 2), Koufax 2 (Etchebarren, Palmer), Perranoski 1 (Blefary), Regan 1 (Palmer), Brewer 1 (Blefary). WP: Regan, Palmer. U: Chylak, Perekoudas, Rice, Steiner, Drummond, Jackowski. T: 2:26. A: 55,947.

## SANFORD (SANDY) KOUFAX
Born December 30, 1935, at Brooklyn N.Y.
Height 6-2  Weight 198
Threw left-handed and batted right-handed.
Named to Hall of Fame, 1972.

| YEAR | CLUB | LEAGUE | G. | IP. | W. | L. | Pct. | H. | R. | ER. | SO. | BB. | ERA. |
|------|------|--------|-----|------|-----|----|------|------|-----|-----|------|-----|------|
| 1955 | Brooklyn | Nat. | 12 | 42 | 2 | 2 | .500 | 33 | 15 | 14 | 30 | 28 | 3.00 |
| 1956 | Brooklyn | Nat. | 16 | 59 | 2 | 4 | .338 | 66 | 37 | 32 | 30 | 29 | 4.88 |
| 1957 | Brooklyn | Nat. | 34 | 104 | 5 | 4 | .556 | 83 | 49 | 45 | 122 | 51 | 3.89 |
| 1958 | Los Angeles | Nat. | 40 | 159 | 11 | 11 | .500 | 132 | 89 | 79 | 131 | 105 | 4.47 |
| 1959 | Los Angeles | Nat. | 35 | 153 | 8 | 6 | .571 | 136 | 74 | 69 | 173 | 92 | 4.06 |
| 1960 | Los Angeles | Nat. | 37 | 175 | 8 | 13 | .381 | 133 | 83 | 76 | 197 | 100 | 3.91 |
| 1961 | Los Angeles | Nat. | 42 | 256 | 18 | 13 | .581 | 212 | 117 | 100 | 269 | 96 | 3.52 |
| 1962 | Los Angeles | Nat. | 28 | 184 | 14 | 7 | .667 | 134 | 61 | 52 | 216 | 57 | 2.54 |
| 1963 | Los Angeles | Nat. | 40 | 311 | 25 | 5 | .833 | 214 | 68 | 65 | 306 | 58 | 1.88 |
| 1964 | Los Angeles | Nat. | 29 | 223 | 19 | 5 | .792 | 154 | 49 | 43 | 223 | 53 | 1.74 |
| 1965 | Los Angeles | Nat. | 43 | 336 | 26 | 8 | .765 | 216 | 90 | 76 | 382 | 71 | 2.04 |
| 1966 | Los Angeles | Nat. | 41 | 323 | 27 | 9 | .750 | 241 | 74 | 62 | 317 | 77 | 1.73 |
| Major League Totals | | | 397 | 2325 | 165 | 87 | .655 | 1754 | 806 | 713 | 2396 | 817 | 2.76 |

## WORLD SERIES RECORD

| YEAR | CLUB | LEAGUE | G. | IP. | W. | L. | Pct. | H. | R. | ER. | SO. | BB. | ERA. |
|------|------|--------|-----|------|-----|----|------|------|-----|-----|------|-----|------|
| 1959 | Los Angeles | Nat. | 2 | 9 | 0 | 1 | .000 | 5 | 1 | 1 | 7 | 1 | 1.00 |
| 1963 | Los Angeles | Nat. | 2 | 18 | 2 | 0 | 1.000 | 12 | 3 | 3 | 23 | 3 | 1.50 |
| 1965 | Los Angeles | Nat. | 3 | 24 | 2 | 1 | .667 | 13 | 2 | 1 | 29 | 5 | 0.38 |
| 1966 | Los Angeles | Nat. | 1 | 6 | 0 | 1 | .000 | 6 | 4 | 1 | 2 | 2 | 1.50 |
| World Series Totals | | | 8 | 57 | 4 | 3 | .571 | 36 | 10 | 6 | 61 | 11 | 0.95 |

Handsome, intensely proud, Pittsburgh Pirate great Roberto Clemente collected his 3,000th hit in his final regular-season at-bat at Three Rivers Stadium. He died in a plane crash that winter.

Photo courtesy of National Baseball Hall of Fame Library, Cooperstown, New York.

# ROBERTO CLEMENTE

*Into History*

**DATE:** September 30, 1972 (final regular-season at-bat)

**SITE:** Three Rivers Stadium, Pittsburgh, Pennsylvania

**PITCHER:** Jon Matlack of the New York Mets

**RESULT:** Clemente doubled to left-center field in the fourth inning, his 3,000th career hit. He never played another regular-season game.

**September 30, 1972, Pittsburgh**—Empty seats.

Standing on the top step of the Pittsburgh Pirate dugout off the first-base side, Roberto Clemente took a long, slow look around the nearly empty Three Rivers Stadium.

There was nobody here. Maybe 10,000 people. What did he have to do? Was this all he meant to them?

It was a cool Saturday in September, the last Saturday of the month. The defending World Champion Pirates were once again headed for the postseason.

They'd already clinched the National League Eastern title against these same Mets about a week earlier at Shea Stadium. The suspense of the pennant race was over for now. The story on this day was Clemente.

Or at least it was supposed to be. Except it didn't look that way in Pittsburgh. Not this afternoon.

To think that only 10 men before him in the long history of the game had gotten this far. Babe Ruth didn't make it.

Neither did Ted Williams, Joe DiMaggio, Jimmy Foxx, Lou Gehrig, or former Pirate greats Ralph Kiner, Pie Traynor, Lloyd Waner, or Kiki Cuyler—all of whom would eventually reach the Hall of Fame.

Now, with the regular-season nearly over, the great Clemente was a single hit away from reaching 3,000. At home, yet. How excited was all of Pittsburgh about it?

Only 13,117 were in the stands that afternoon, one of the smallest crowds of the season. A proud man, someone who seemed to seek out slights, unintentional or otherwise, Clemente felt hurt. As he so often did.

It wasn't like they didn't know about Clemente's quest for 3,000, either. The night before, a crowd of 24,193 showed up on a chilly Friday night to watch Pirate starter Nelson Briles battle New York's Tom Seaver. Since the race was over, you had to think they were there to see if Clemente could reach his milestone against the Mets great, who was going for his 20th win.

They went home with something to talk about, almost from the first pitch. After Pittsburgh's little lefty Vic Davalillo opened with a walk and Dave Cash grounded out, a roar rippled through the stands as Clemente walked to the plate.

He waited for the cheers to subside, then stepped in and Seaver wound and fired and Clemente rapped a Seaver breaking pitch hard into the turf, bouncing it high over the mound.

The ball skittered past Seaver's reach, out to second baseman Ken Boswell, who made a belated attempt to stop the ball, then kicked it. The Forbes Field fans roared, figuring that Clemente had his milestone hit.

*"Buc belter gets biggest hit"*

But up in the press box, official scorer Luke Quay of the *McKeesport Daily News* quickly ruled it an error. Problem was, it took longer than usual to register that on the Forbes Field scoreboard.

Mets' first baseman Ed Kranepool, who had just caught Boswell's late throw, assumed it was a hit, as did the Forbes Field crowd. He handed the ball to Pirates first-base coach Don Leppert, figuring Clemente would want the keepsake and the fans went wild for the Latin star.

It was then that the scoreboard flashed the "1" in the error column after the Mets' totals on the scoreboard. The Forbes Field fans cut loose with a chorus of boos.

On first base, Clemente seethed, as usual. The pressure of the 3,000-hit chase was starting to get to him. A player who was a career .300 hitter, he had at least a .400 average as a complainer and this gave him more ammunition.

The rest of the night wasn't productive. He took a called third strike, grounded out to Seaver, and lined out hard to right fielder Rusty Staub in the ninth.

He wondered if he'd have enough games left in the season to make it to 3,000. In baseball, only regular-season records count toward those immense lifetime totals—500 home runs, 3,000 hits, 300 wins. Time was running out. Clemente felt it as far back as Spring Training.

"I've got to get those 3,000 hits," he said then. "I might get sick or die and no other Latin will do it."

Immediately, Clemente thought about coming out of the game early in Philadelphia the night before. On Thursday, Clemente had collected hit No. 2,999 in his second at-bat, a single off the Phillies' great Steve Carlton in what turned out to be Carlton's 26th win of the season.

Since Clemente really wanted to collect hit No. 3,000 at home, he got manager Bill Virdon to let him take himself out of the game, though Pittsburgh trailed 2-1 at the time. That 2-1 score held up for Carlton and the lowly Phillies.

That's how much he wanted to achieve that milestone before the fans of Pittsburgh. If he'd only have known how they were to repay him Saturday afternoon.

After Friday night's controversial call, Clemente was bitter.

"This is nothing new," Clemente sneered. "Official scorers have been robbing me of hits like this for 18 years. . . ."

This was the Clemente the writers often heard. Instead of swallowing hard and muttering some typical baseball cliché about going out and getting 'em next time, the emotional Pirate star would lash out at the fans or the media or those who didn't understand what sort of physical price he was paying each and every time he pulled on a uniform.

Though he could see for himself that on the field he was every bit the equal of Willie Mays or Hank Aaron or Mickey Mantle, he was nowhere near the national figure they were. Well, at least not until the 1971 World Series against Baltimore, which Clemente made his personal showcase.

Yet here it was, only a year later, and only 13,117 showed up to see him try for his 3,000th hit. What did he have to do?

Clemente never did find out. And years earlier, he'd made it clear that being overlooked truly bothered him.

You could read that in a long feature story that appeared in *Sports Illustrated* in 1966, a season in which Clemente won the NL's MVP award for his .317 average and 119 RBI.

Veteran writer Myron Cope wrote a long profile on Clemente titled "Aches and Pains and Three Batting Titles" in which Cope introduced Clemente to a national audience by mostly mocking the always-complaining Clemente.

"Relatively small at 5-feet 10-inches and 180 pounds when able to take nourishment, the chronic invalid has smooth skin, glistening muscles, and perfect facial contours that suggest the sturdy mahogany sculpture peddled in the souvenir shops of his native Puerto Rico.

"Many Pittsburghers have concluded that the only thing that can keep Clemente from making them forget Paul Waner is a sudden attack of good health."

Cope's piece made several good points. In it, a Clemente friend explains, "You have to understand that the Latin is touchy."

And later on, talking with Cope about his image, Clemente was certainly that: "If a Latin player or even an American negro is sick," Clemente said, "they say it is all in the head. Felipe Alou once went to his team doctor and the doctor said 'You don't have anything.' So he went to a private doctor and the doctor said, 'You have a broken foot.'"

Consequently, Clemente concluded, his reputation as a malingerer clouded his on-field excellence.

"With my eyes blind, I can throw to the base," he said. "I know that. If [Mickey] Mantle has the arm I have you will put it in headlines because he is an American. You never give me credit. How many players in history win three batting titles? The sportswriters don't mention that. They ask me, what you think about dis, what you think about dat?"

Remembering that Pittsburgh was a steel town, hearing a Latin player complain about how he hurt all the time—when his spectacular play on the field never showed any evidence of ill health—put Clemente in an awkward situation.

In 14 of his 18 seasons, he'd played in at least 124 games and for nine years in a row, played more than 144 (out of 162). That's a pretty impressive track record for a guy who said he was hurting all the time.

Everybody could see what an extraordinary player he was. His 1971 World Series was one of the greatest sustained performances of any great player in baseball history.

But there would never be the outpouring of love for him that there was for Papa Bear Willie Stargell, no matter what he did. There was a distance there. Roberto Clemente was just always out of reach.

The language barrier didn't help such a sensitive soul, either. For much of his career, the Pittsburgh press made him sound like a savage. Once, a female Pirate fan asked him if he wore loincloths at home.

"I know I don't speak as bad as they say I speak," Clemente told Cope. "I know that I don't have the good English pronunciation because my tongue belongs to Spanish, but I know where the verb, the article, the pronoun, whatever it is, go. I never in my life start a sentence with 'me.' 'Me Tarzan, you Jane.'"

So when Clemente heard his name announced to lead off the fourth inning of Saturday's game, he walked quietly to the plate, never once looking around at the nearly empty stands, refusing to let himself measure the volume of their cheers or feel the excitement of those who were there.

New York Mets starter Jon Matlack, a left-hander with a good curveball, had gotten him in his first at-bat, striking him out with a sharp curve.

Clemente thought about that as he carefully set up in the far corner of the batter's box, waving that unusually white bat back and fourth as he trained his sights on Matlack.

He took a pitch, then on Matlack's second offering, a low curveball, Clemente reached out with the fat part of the bat and drove the ball hard into the gap in left-center field.

Just from the sound alone, he knew it would be a hit and Clemente took off quickly, easing into second base standing up as the relay throw from Mets outfielder Dave Schneck came in to shortstop Jim Fregosi. Fregosi gave the ball to umpire Doug Harvey, who then handed it to Clemente and shook his hand.

"*A fine finish for Roberto Clemente*"

The Forbes Field scoreboard flashed the news that Clemente was one of 11 players in major-league history who had reached 3,000 hits. The noise was considerable, despite the tiny crowd, and Clemente, standing on second base, raised his cap to all the fans.

He stayed in the game for one more inning, then retired to the dugout. Mets' outfielder Willie Mays, who with Hank Aaron was the only other active player with over 3,000 hits, walked over from the other dugout to give Clemente a hug.

Afterwards, Clemente was his usual self: complaining. He said that he'd had a sleepless night after his near-miss on Friday thanks to telephone calls from home.

"Then my wife (Vera) had to be at the airport at six o'clock to meet some friends so we didn't even bother to go to bed," Clemente told the *New York Times*. "When I arrived at the ballpark, I had no sleep at all."

Clemente credited teammate Willie Stargell for helping him get hit No. 3,000.

"I haven't been swinging good lately so Willie picked out one of my bats . . . a heavier one that I have been using. He handed it to me and told me to 'go get it.'"

After the game, Clemente also told the writers that he'd take the next three regular-season games off so that he'd get a week of rest to be ready for the Pirates' postseason series with Cincinnati.

"I play better when I am rested," he said.

As it turned out, Clemente didn't quite get the complete rest he wanted. After collecting his 3,000th hit, the Pirates' public relations staff noticed that Clemente had just tied Honus Wagner for the most games in a Pirate uniform, 2,432.

With three games left in the regular season, Pirate staffer Bill Guilfoile urged Manager Bill Virdon to get Clemente into a game, to break Wagner's record. Though at 38, Clemente had another fine season and there was no talk of retirement, Virdon didn't want to wait until next season.

Sure enough, he let Clemente play the ninth inning of the team's next-to-last game with the St. Louis Cardinals, breaking Wagner's record.

It turned out that the Pirates' season went a little bit longer. Pittsburgh was knocked out of postseason, losing a five-game series to the Cincinnati Reds in heartbreaking fashion.

After the Pirates won two of the first three games (Clemente went hitless in the first two), Pittsburgh fell apart in Game Four, committing three errors and playing generally lousy baseball, falling 7-1 to lefty Ross Grimsley.

Only Clemente did anything of note for Pittsburgh, collecting both of their hits, including a seventh-inning home run.

In Game Five in Cincinnati, Pittsburgh carried a 3-2 lead into the bottom of the ninth but reliever Dave Giusti gave up a solo home run to Johnny Bench, then a single to Tony Perez and a single to pinch-hitter Denis Menke.

Pirates' manager Bill Virdon went to the bullpen, bringing in starter Bob Moose, hoping that he might work out of the jam. He nearly did.

Moose got Cesar Geronimo to fly out to Clemente in right for one out (pinch-runner George Foster advanced to third), then got Darrel Chaney to pop out to shortstop Gene Alley for the second out.

But with the count 1-1, Moose's third pitch sailed past catcher Manny Sanguillen and Foster scampered home from third to win it for Cincinnati. They were on to the World Series. The Pirates were done.

By October 10, Clemente's season was over. He went back home to Puerto Rico where, in December, he got involved with relief efforts to aid earthquake victims in Managua.

On New Year's Eve, he boarded a plane leaving San Juan International Airport, fearing that profiteers were stealing the relief supplies that were intended for the earthquake victims. The DC-7 crashed shortly after takeoff. Clemente's body was never found.

Six years earlier, Clemente had talked about helping people, how important it was. "Anybody who have the opportunity to serve their country or their island and don't, God should punish them. If you can be good, why should you be bad?

"Today, life is moving too fast for these kids," he said. "You see 15-year-old boys and girls holding hands. They hang out on street corners. Maybe if I can keep them interested in sports, they will not always be talking about stealing and about gangster movies. I'm proud to do good for my island.

"I like to work with kids," Clemente told Cope, concluding his 1966 interview. "I'd like to work with kids all the time, if I live long enough."

Thirty-two years later, Roberto Clemente remains the only Puerto Rican player to have collected 3,000 hits, the milestone hit coming in what turned out to be his final regular-season at-bat.

# Into History

| NEW YORK (Mets) | ab. | r. | h. | bi. |
|---|---|---|---|---|
| Garrett, 3b | 4 | 0 | 0 | 0 |
| Boswell, 2b | 4 | 0 | 1 | 0 |
| Milner, lf | 3 | 0 | 0 | 0 |
| Staub, rf | 3 | 0 | 0 | 0 |
| Rauch, p | 0 | 0 | 0 | 0 |
| Marshall, ph | 1 | 0 | 0 | 0 |
| Kranepool, 1b | 3 | 0 | 1 | 0 |
| Fregosi, ss | 3 | 0 | 0 | 0 |
| Schreck, cf | 3 | 0 | 0 | 0 |
| Dyer, c | 1 | 0 | 0 | 0 |
| Nolan, c | 2 | 0 | 0 | 0 |
| Matlack, p | 2 | 0 | 0 | 0 |
| Hahn, rf | 0 | 0 | 0 | 0 |
| TOTALS: | 29 | 0 | 2 | 0 |

| PITTSBURGH | ab. | r. | h. | bi. |
|---|---|---|---|---|
| Goggin, 2b | 4 | 0 | 2 | 0 |
| Stennett, cf | 4 | 0 | 0 | 0 |
| Clemente, rf | 2 | 1 | 1 | 0 |
| Mazeroski, ph | 1 | 0 | 0 | 0 |
| Davalillo, rf | 1 | 0 | 0 | 0 |
| Stargell, 1b | 3 | 1 | 1 | 0 |
| Zisk, lf | 1 | 2 | 0 | 0 |
| Sanguillen, c | 3 | 1 | 1 | 1 |
| Pagan, 3b | 3 | 0 | 0 | 0 |
| Hernandez, ss | 3 | 0 | 1 | 2 |
| J. Ellis, p | 2 | 0 | 0 | 0 |
| Clines, ph | 1 | 0 | 0 | 0 |
| Johnson, p | 0 | 0 | 0 | 0 |
| TOTALS: | 28 | 5 | 6 | 3 |

```
New York ....... 0 0 0   0 0 0   0 0 0—0
Pittsburgh ....... 0 0 0   3 0 2   0 0 x—5
```

| | IP | H | R | ER | BB | SO |
|---|---|---|---|---|---|---|
| Matlack (L, 14-10) | 6 | 5 | 5 | 3 | 5 | 5 |
| Rauch | 2 | 1 | 0 | 0 | 0 | 1 |
| Ellis (W, 15-7) | 6 | 1 | 0 | 0 | 2 | 4 |
| Johnson | 3 | 1 | 0 | 0 | 1 | 2 |

E: Garrett. DP: New York 3. LOB: New York 5, Pittsburgh 4. 2B: Clemente. 3B: J. Hernandez. Save: Johnson (3). PB: Dyer, Nolan. T: 2:10. A: 13,117.

## ROBERTO WALKER CLEMENTE
Born August 18, 1934, at Carolina, Puerto Rico.
Died December 31, 1972, at San Juan, Puerto Rico.
Height 5-11  Weight 185
Threw and batted right-handed.
Named to Hall of Fame, 1973.

| YEAR | CLUB | LEAGUE | POS. | G. | AB. | R. | H. | 2B. | 3B. | HR. | RBI. | B.A. | PO. | A. | E. | F.A. |
|---|---|---|---|---|---|---|---|---|---|---|---|---|---|---|---|---|
| 1954 | Montreal (a) | Int. | OF-3B | 87 | 148 | 27 | 38 | 5 | 3 | 2 | 12 | .257 | 81 | 1 | 1 | .988 |
| 1955 | Pittsburgh | National | OF | 124 | 474 | 48 | 121 | 23 | 11 | 5 | 47 | .255 | 253 | 18 | 6 | .978 |
| 1956 | Pittsburgh | Nat. | OF-2B-3B | 147 | 543 | 66 | 169 | 30 | 7 | 7 | 60 | .311 | 275 | 20 | 15 | .952 |
| 1957 | Pittsburgh | Nat. | OF | 111 | 451 | 42 | 114 | 17 | 7 | 4 | 30 | .253 | 272 | 9 | 6 | .979 |
| 1958 | Pittsburgh | Nat. | OF | 140 | 519 | 69 | 150 | 24 | 10 | 6 | 50 | .289 | 312 | 22 | 6 | .982 |
| 1959 | Pittsburgh | Nat. | OF | 105 | 432 | 60 | 128 | 17 | 7 | 4 | 50 | .296 | 229 | 10 | 13 | .948 |
| 1960 | Pittsburgh | Nat. | OF | 144 | 570 | 89 | 179 | 22 | 6 | 16 | 94 | .314 | 246 | 19 | 8 | .971 |
| 1961 | Pittsburgh | Nat. | OF | 146 | 572 | 100 | 201 | 30 | 10 | 23 | 89 | .351 | 256 | 27 | 9 | .969 |
| 1962 | Pittsburgh | Nat. | OF | 144 | 538 | 95 | 168 | 28 | 9 | 10 | 74 | .312 | 269 | 19 | 8 | .973 |
| 1963 | Pittsburgh | Nat. | OF | 152 | 600 | 77 | 192 | 23 | 8 | 17 | 76 | .320 | 239 | 11 | 11 | .958 |
| 1964 | Pittsburgh | Nat. | OF | 155 | 622 | 95 | 211 | 40 | 7 | 12 | 87 | .339 | 289 | 13 | 10 | .968 |
| 1965 | Pittsburgh | Nat. | OF | 152 | 589 | 91 | 194 | 21 | 14 | 10 | 65 | .329 | 288 | 16 | 10 | .968 |
| 1966 | Pittsburgh | Nat. | OF | 154 | 638 | 105 | 202 | 31 | 11 | 29 | 119 | .317 | 318 | 17 | 12 | .965 |
| 1967 | Pittsburgh | Nat. | OF | 147 | 585 | 103 | 209 | 26 | 10 | 23 | 110 | .357 | 273 | 17 | 9 | .970 |
| 1968 | Pittsburgh | Nat. | OF | 132 | 502 | 74 | 146 | 18 | 12 | 18 | 57 | .291 | 297 | 9 | 5 | .984 |
| 1969 | Pittsburgh | Nat. | OF | 138 | 507 | 87 | 175 | 20 | 12 | 19 | 91 | .345 | 226 | 14 | 5 | .980 |
| 1970 | Pittsburgh | Nat. | OF | 108 | 412 | 65 | 145 | 22 | 10 | 14 | 60 | .352 | 189 | 12 | 7 | .966 |
| 1971 | Pittsburgh | Nat. | OF | 132 | 522 | 82 | 178 | 29 | 8 | 13 | 86 | .041 | 267 | 11 | 2 | .993 |
| 1972 | Pittsburgh | Nat. | OF | 102 | 378 | 68 | 118 | 19 | 7 | 10 | 60 | .312 | 199 | 5 | 0 | 1.000 |
| Major League Totals —18 Years | | | | 2433 | 9454 | 1416 | 3000 | 440 | 166 | 240 | 1305 | .317 | 4697 | 269 | 142 | .972 |

a Drafted by Pittsburgh Pirates from Brooklyn Dodgers' organization, November 22, 1954.

### CHAMPIONSHIP SERIES RECORD

| YEAR | CLUB | LEAGUE | POS. | G. | AB. | R. | H. | 2B. | 3B. | HR. | RBI. | B.A. | PO. | A. | E. | F.A. |
|---|---|---|---|---|---|---|---|---|---|---|---|---|---|---|---|---|
| 1970 | Pittsburgh | National | OF | 3 | 14 | 1 | 3 | 0 | 0 | 0 | 1 | .214 | 7 | 0 | 0 | 1.000 |
| 1971 | Pittsburgh | National | OF | 4 | 18 | 2 | 6 | 0 | 0 | 0 | 4 | .333 | 12 | 0 | 0 | 1.000 |
| 1972 | Pittsburgh | National | OF | 5 | 17 | 1 | 4 | 1 | 0 | 1 | 2 | .235 | 10 | 0 | 0 | 1.000 |
| Championship Series Totals—3 Years | | | | 12 | 49 | 4 | 13 | 1 | 0 | 1 | 7 | .265 | 29 | 0 | 0 | 1.000 |

### WORLD SERIES RECORD

| YEAR | CLUB | LEAGUE | POS. | G. | AB. | R. | H. | 2B. | 3B. | HR. | RBI. | B.A. | PO. | A. | E. | F.A. |
|---|---|---|---|---|---|---|---|---|---|---|---|---|---|---|---|---|
| 1960 | Pittsburgh | National | OF | 7 | 29 | 1 | 9 | 0 | 0 | 0 | 3 | .310 | 19 | 0 | 0 | 1.000 |
| 1971 | Pittsburgh | National | OF | 7 | 29 | 3 | 12 | 2 | 1 | 2 | 4 | .414 | 15 | 0 | 0 | 1.000 |
| World Series Totals—2 Years | | | | 14 | 58 | 4 | 21 | 2 | 1 | 2 | 7 | .362 | 34 | 0 | 0 | 1.000 |

Though the Cardinals tried to retire him a few times before, Stan "The Man" Musial finally said goodbye his way—with a pair of base hits—in the final game of the 1963 season.

Photo courtesy of National Baseball Hall of Fame Library, Cooperstown, New York.

# STAN MUSIAL

*Back from the Bench*

---

**DATE:** September 29, 1963

**SITE:** Sportsman's Park, St. Louis, Missouri

**PITCHER:** Jim Maloney of Cincinnati Reds in sixth inning

**RESULT:** RBI single in sixth, his second hit of the game, which gave Musial 1,815 hits at home, a number that exactly matched the number of hits he had on the road in his 22-year career.

---

**September 29, 1963, St. Louis**—"As long as I live," Stan Musial said softly, standing alone at the microphone in the middle of the diamond at Busch Stadium one sunny Sunday afternoon in late September, "this is a day I'll always remember. This is a day of both great joy and sorrow; the sorrow which always comes when we have to say farewell. My heart is filled with thanks for so many who made these 22 years possible."

He looked around at the 27,576 all around the stadium standing and cheering for him, a St. Louis monument to rival the great arch. He looked down. Stan "The Man" Musial thought quickly to himself, "Gee, if they all knew how close I was to becoming a Pirate a few years back. . . ."

Just four summers earlier, in 1960, the magnificent Musial, nearing 40, was riding the pine and thinking about retirement. It looked like it was going to turn into yet another sad story of a one-time great player hanging on until he was embarrassed into retirement.

Imagine the fiery Ty Cobb, wearing that Philadelphia A's uniform with the white elephant on it, sharing a corner spot in the dugout next to Tris Speaker as the final moments of his career trickled into late summer.

Or the great Rogers Hornsby, stuck in a St. Louis Browns' uniform, grumbling to himself on the bench, wondering if he should put himself back in the lineup, as he watched Browns' style mishap after mishap occur on the field before him.

Or Ruth, fat and slow in a Braves' uniform; Christy Mathewson, a startling sight in a Cincinnati uniform, throwing pitches that were pounded all over the yard. There didn't seem to be any kind, uplifting, considerate way to explain to these baseball giants that now it was time to go home.

Writer Roger Angell explained as much in *Late Innings* shortly after learning of Willie Mays's election to the Hall of Fame. It was hard, Angell noted, to forget how age had weakened the great one.

"His enshrinement allowed me to remember Mays as he had been in his wonderful youth," he wrote. "The brilliant boy gliding across the long meadows of the Polo Grounds . . . and to forget the old, uncertain, querulous Willie Mays who came to the Mets in his final few seasons and clearly stayed too long in the game.

"The shift in my feelings (upon his election) was like the change that sometimes comes after we remember a close relative who has died . . . suddenly one morning, our sad last view of that person fades away and we are left instead with an earlier and more vivid picture—the one that stays with us."

For Stan Musial to regain that, to go back to where he was, where he would always be—forever, in memory—why, who would have bet on that?

Musial's troubles had their start in a 1959 season where he came to Spring Training a bit out of shape and, at the suggestion of management, didn't play much, trying to rest up for the season.

Problem was, Musial never did get into the kind of consistent groove that marked his extraordinary career, and he wound up the 1959 season at a grim .255, only a point higher than Boston's Ted Williams, who himself had a miserable, injury-plagued season over in the American League.

By year's end, the Cardinals were in seventh and Musial was on the bench. His numbers were the worst of his career. He'd hit just 14 home runs and drove in only 44 runs.

Though Musial went through a rigorous offseason training regimen and reported to Spring Training in 1960 in better shape, he was still on the bench well into May.

That's when the talk of the Pirates started. St. Louis' manager Solly Hemus, a former Musial teammate, was convinced that Stan was washed up after what he'd seen in 1959 and wasn't playing him. The team was going nowhere and Hemus pushed for a trade to shake things up.

The Cards dealt lefty Wilmer Mizell and infielder Dick Gray to Pittsburgh for second baseman Julian Javier and pitcher Ed Bauta. The two teams weren't done talking.

As the trade deadline approached, the Cardinals were still struggling and Pittsburgh had designs on the National League pennant (which it went on to win.)

Noticing that Musial hadn't been in the lineup, Pirate manager Danny Murtaugh approached St. Louis writer Bob Broeg and asked about Musial's absence. He found out Musial was healthy but that Cards' manager Hemus wasn't going to put him back in the lineup. Maybe the Pirates would?

Murtaugh scoffed.

"Heck, Stan would never leave the Cardinals," Murtaugh said.

"Until now, you would have been right" explained Broeg, who recounted this story in Musial's ghostwritten autobiography.

"But Hemus is convinced Stan is through and the guy wants a chance to prove he isn't. He might be interested in going to his old hometown area and getting the chance at one more World Series." (A World Series that the Pirates went on to win.)

When Musial admitted to Broeg that he'd consider it, Murtaugh was stunned.

"Musial could mean the difference for us in the race," the Pirate manager said, trying to imagine Musial in gray and black.

When Pittsburgh general manager Joe L. Brown caught wind of it, his sense of what was right for baseball overrode his sense of competition.

"As much as we'd like to have Musial," he told Broeg, " I just can't do it to [Cardinals GM] Bing Devine . . . to offer too little [Pittsburgh would only grab him if Musial was unconditionally released] would be taking advantage of public sentiment. . . . Devine would be on a spot where I don't care to put him."

So Musial remained a Cardinal. And as the 1960 season continued, Musial finally worked his way back into the lineup and the team surged into second place, behind Pittsburgh.

Guess who beat the Pirates three separate times with clutch home runs?

"Musial gets two hits in extra-inning win"

By the end of the year, St. Louis had fallen back to third. But Musial had worked his average up to .275, hit 17 home runs, and drove in 63 runs in 116 games, one more than he'd played the year before. He was back.

In 1961, Musial hit .288 and was productive the entire year. Once the Cardinals changed managers, Stan got better news. New Cards' manager Johnny Keane wanted him to play more in 1962, not less.

Musial responded with his last great season. The whole year was like one long highlight reel.

After collecting his 3,000th hit as a pinch-hitter in a game in Chicago in May (Musial's success on the road was extraordinary—more on that later), he went on to break Honus Wagner's National League record for most hits, Ty Cobb's major-league record of total bases, and Mel Ott's National League RBI record.

Even better, Musial was having a golden year at the plate, leading the National League in hitting late into the summer. In the season's final weeks, the Dodgers' Tommy Davis and Cincinnati's Frank Robinson surged past Musial. But it was still a banner year for Stan, who finished third in the race with a .330 mark. He also hit 19 home runs and had 82 RBI in 116 games. Not bad for a 41-year-old.

Naturally, the Cardinals invited Musial back in 1963 for his 22nd big-league season. Finally, it appeared age had caught up with him. He played in only 86 games, batted just .255, a dip of 75 points from the year previous. Even so, he still had his moments.

In the final week of the season, the Dodgers remarkable left-hander Sandy Koufax carried a no-hitter into the seventh inning against Musial's Cardinals. Guess who lined a single to center field to break up the no-hitter?

A few weeks earlier, facing Braves great Warren Spahn for the final time, Musial whacked a double, lifting his career batting average against the Hall of Fame lefty to .314 with 14 home runs.

As Musial's career wound down to its final days, somebody noted how consistent Stan was at home and on the road. For most players, playing at home meant a big difference in batting prowess.

Ted Williams, Musial's contemporary, batted .361 for his career at Fenway Park and .327 on the road, collecting 1,406 hits in Boston and 1,248 in other parks. That's the way it was for most players. Roberto Clemente hit .329 at home, .306 on the road. Carl Yastrzemski hit .306 at Fenway, .264 on the road.

Musial did hit 10 points higher at home (.336 to .326) but as Stan ran out on the field in St. Louis that late September afternoon in 1963, the consistency of his career numbers was truly amazing. Of the 3,628 career hits he'd collected through his 22-year career, 1,315 of them came in other ballparks, 1,313 of them came in St. Louis.

So ol' Stan had something unusual to shoot for in this finale against Cincinnati fireballer Jim Maloney, one of the game's hardest throwers. Maloney, chasing his 24rd win, was matched with St. Louis ace Bob Gibson this sunny afternoon. Gibson had a target, too. He was chasing his nineteenth victory.

In Musial's first at-bat, with the St. Louis crowd bursting with noise on every pitch, Stan took a slow curveball on the outside corner and home plate umpire Al Barlick rang him up.

It was the 696th and final strikeout of Musial's career, a span that would cover 10,972 official at-bats and 3,026 games. For a power hitter (475 career home runs) Musial only fanned 40 or more times in a season three times—a good month for

Reggie Jackson. Two of those 40-plus strikeout campaigns were the final two years of his career.

When Musial came up again in the fourth inning, Maloney still hadn't allowed a hit. Would Stan again spoil the no-hitter, as he'd done to Koufax a few days ago?

Sure enough, he worked the count to 1-1, then got a belt-high Maloney fastball on the fat part of his bat and rifled it past Maloney and a diving Cincinnati second baseman for hit No. 3,239. The Cincy second baseman turned out to be the man who later supplanted Musial as the NL's hit king, Pete Rose.

As Musial got to first, all of St. Louis, it seemed, was roaring for him. Manager Johnny Keane smiled and many expected to see him get the hook right there. But Cardinals' manager Johnny Keane left him in. The game was still scoreless. And you could always expect a little more from Musial, couldn't you?

"The Man comes through in finale"

He came up again in the sixth with one out. Curt Flood, who'd opened the inning with a double, was at second and once again, all of St. Louis stood and roared for No. 6, who smiled and drank it all in—the applause, the warmth, the love. He had come back from the bench, defied age and skeptics and last summer, nearly won his eighth batting title.

Maloney pitched carefully to Musial. He wound and fired a high fastball and Musial fouled it straight back. 0-1.

Next, he tried the pitch that had fooled Musial in his first at-bat, the curve, and bounced it in the dirt. 1-1. He tried the heat and missed outside. 2-1. Trailing in the count, many fireballers would have gone to the fastball, trying to get the count back to even. Maloney had other ideas.

He broke off a sharp-breaking curve, low and inside, to the lefty Musial. Stan was ready. He picked up the spin, kept his hands back, and rifle-shot a ground ball past first base into right field to score Flood and break the tie. It was Musial's 1,956th RBI, then an NL record.

With the Cardinals fans teary-eyed and tender, Keane sent out pinch-runner Gary Kolb and the fans booed, seeing Musial leave. There was a game to finish.

Talk about professionalism. Talk about consistency. Talk about rising to the occasion. Stan Musial may have been 42 but he knew what it meant to leave on the right note, exactly the right note. How was he able to get a pair of hits off one of the game's hardest throwers at the end of a long and difficult season? Because he was Stan Musial, that's how.

He'd waited long enough, battled hard enough to turn the game back his way. He waited his turn, trusted his talent, that golden swing, knew it would return if he was patient enough. Here, in his final moments as a player, it was all happening for him—and for St. Louis—one last time.

Unlike many of his peers, Musial was keenly aware of his town, his fans and the bond between the two. Having seen what Ted Williams's dramatic exit had been like in cantankerous Boston, he knew what he wanted for the fans of St. Louis.

How wonderful and fortuitous that Manager Johnny Keane sensed that Stan had one more hit in that dime-store bat and kept him in the game after that fourth-inning single. Maybe he hated to imagine the Cardinal lineup without Musial in it.

Earlier in the afternoon, Commissioner Ford Frick described Musial this way: "Here stands baseball's perfect warrior. Here stands baseball's perfect knight." How could Stan not come through after a pronouncement like that.

As it turned out, there was more than two hours more of baseball ahead before a Dal Maxville single to right scored rookie Jerry Buchek with the winning run in a 14-inning, 3-2 Cardinal victory. Musial had to wait all that time in the clubhouse, talking with writers, sipping beer, listening to the game on the radio.

*"Cards, Stan bow out nicely"*

When it was all finally over and the media crush surrounded Musial, waiting to hear what the one and only "Man" St. Louis would ever have had to say, he kept it simple.

"I love to play this game of baseball," he said softly. "I love putting on the uniform."

He said he was headed to the World Series, where he'd throw out the first ball for the opener, then go down to Fort Riley to see his grandson.

"And then . . ." Musial said, with the satisfied air of man closing a book that he so loved to read, he dreaded coming to the final page, "I'll retire. Retire. And take things easy."

Now that's how to finish a career, isn't it? One thousand, eight hundred and fifteen hits on the road. One thousand, eight hundred and fifteen hits at home. Coming back off the bench out of that paralyzing limbo of age and self-doubt to say goodbye on his terms. Not one, not two, not three, but *four* seasons later when he was good and ready to go.

That's why they called Stan Musial "The Man."

# Forever the Man

| CINCINNATI | ab. | r. | h. | bi. |
|---|---|---|---|---|
| Rose, 2b, lf | 6 | 0 | 3 | 0 |
| Harper, rf | 6 | 0 | 0 | 0 |
| Pinson, cf | 5 | 0 | 1 | 0 |
| Neal, 2b | 0 | 0 | 0 | 0 |
| Robinson, cf, lf | 6 | 0 | 0 | 0 |
| Coleman, 1b | 5 | 1 | 2 | 0 |
| Edwards, c | 2 | 0 | 0 | 0 |
| b Keough | 1 | 0 | 0 | 0 |
| Pavletich, c | 3 | 1 | 1 | 0 |
| Cardenas, ss | 6 | 0 | 2 | 2 |
| Kasko, 3b | 5 | 0 | 0 | 0 |
| Maloney, p | 2 | 0 | 0 | 0 |
| c Skinner | 1 | 0 | 1 | 0 |
| O'Toole, p | 0 | 0 | 0 | 0 |
| d Green | 1 | 0 | 0 | 0 |
| Worthington, p | 0 | 0 | 0 | 0 |
| Henry, p | 0 | 0 | 0 | 0 |
| h Walters | 1 | 0 | 0 | 0 |
| Jay, p | 1 | 0 | 0 | 0 |
| **TOTALS:** | **51** | **2** | **10** | **2** |

| ST. LOUIS | ab. | r. | h. | bi. |
|---|---|---|---|---|
| Flood, cf | 7 | 1 | 2 | 0 |
| Groat, ss | 4 | 0 | 0 | 0 |
| Maxvill, ss | 3 | 0 | 1 | 1 |
| Musial, lf | 3 | 0 | 2 | 1 |
| a Kolb, rf | 1 | 1 | 0 | 0 |
| g Beauchamp | 1 | 0 | 0 | 0 |
| Shannon, rf | 1 | 0 | 0 | 0 |
| Boyer, 3b | 6 | 0 | 4 | 0 |
| White, 1b | 5 | 0 | 2 | 0 |
| James, rf, lf | 5 | 0 | 0 | 1 |
| McCarver, c | 5 | 0 | 0 | 0 |
| Javier, 2b | 3 | 0 | 0 | 0 |
| e Altman | 1 | 0 | 1 | 0 |
| Buchek, ss | 2 | 0 | 1 | 0 |
| Gibson, p | 2 | 0 | 0 | 0 |
| f Clemens | 0 | 0 | 0 | 0 |
| Taylor, p | 0 | 0 | 0 | 0 |
| j Sawatski | 1 | 0 | 0 | 0 |
| Broglio, p | 1 | 1 | 0 | 0 |
| **TOTALS:** | **51** | **3** | **13** | **3** |

**a** Ran for Musial in the sixth.  **b** Struck out for Edwards in seventh.  **c** Singled for Maloney in eighth.  **d** Popped out for O'Toole in ninth.  **e** Singled for Javier in ninth.  **f** Walked for Gibson in ninth.  **g** Struck out for Kolb in 10th.  **h** Popped out for Henry in 11th.  **j** Called out on strikes for Taylor in 11th.

```
Cincinnati ........  000  000  002  000  00—2
St. Louis ........  000  002  000  000  01—3
```

| | IP | H | R | ER | BB | SO |
|---|---|---|---|---|---|---|
| Maloney | 7 | 5 | 2 | 2 | 2 | 11 |
| O'Toole | 1 | 1 | 0 | 0 | 0 | 0 |
| Worthington | 1/3 | 1 | 0 | 0 | 2 | 1 |
| Henry | 1 2/3 | 1 | 0 | 0 | 0 | 1 |
| Jay (L, 7-18) | 3 1/3 | 5 | 1 | 1 | 0 | 3 |
| Gibson | 9 | 7 | 2 | 2 | 1 | 11 |
| Taylor | 2 | 1 | 0 | 0 | 2 | 1 |
| Broglio (W, 18-8) | 3 | 2 | 0 | 0 | 1 | 2 |

E: Boyer, Groat. 9: Cincinnati 13, St. Louis 14. DP: McCarver, Groat; McCarver, Buchek, Maxvill; Neal, Cardenas, Coleman. LOB: Cincinnati 12, St. Louis 13. 2B: Flood, Rose, Maxvill. S: Harper. SF: James. WP: Maloney, Gibson, Broglio 2. U: Barlick, Weyer, Vargo, Williams. T: 3:45. A: 27,576.

## STANLEY FRANK (THE MAN) MUSIAL
Born November 21, 1920, at Donora, Pa.
Height 6-0  Weight 180
Threw and batted left-handed.
Named to Hall of Fame, 1969.

| YEAR | CLUB | LEAGUE | POS. | G. | AB. | R. | H. | 2B. | 3B. | HR. | RBI. | B.A. | PO. | A. | E. | F.A. |
|------|------|--------|------|-----|------|------|------|-----|-----|-----|------|------|-------|-----|-----|------|
| 1938 | Williamson | Mt. St. | P | 26 | 62 | 5 | 16 | 3 | 0 | 1 | 6 | .258 | 7 | 22 | 6 | .829 |
| 1939 | Williamson | Mt. St. | PH-P | 23 | 71 | 10 | 25 | 3 | 3 | 1 | 9 | .352 | 5 | 19 | 3 | .889 |
| 1940 | Daytona Beach | Fla. St. | O-P | 113 | 405 | 55 | 126 | 17 | 10 | 1 | 70 | .311 | 183 | 69 | 11 | .958 |
| 1941 | Springfield | W.A. | OF | 87 | 348 | 100 | 132 | 27 | 10 | 26 | 94 | .379 | 185 | 7 | 3 | .985 |
| 1941 | Rochester | Int. | OF | 54 | 221 | 43 | 72 | 10 | 4 | 3 | 21 | .326 | 102 | 5 | 1 | .991 |
| 1941 | St. Louis | Nat. | OF | 12 | 47 | 8 | 20 | 4 | 0 | 1 | 7 | .426 | 20 | 1 | 0 | 1.000 |
| 1942 | St. Louis | Nat. | OF | 140 | 467 | 87 | 147 | 32 | 10 | 10 | 72 | .315 | 296 | 6 | 5 | .984 |
| 1943 | St. Louis | Nat. | OF | 157 | 617 | 108 | 220 | 48 | 20 | 13 | 81 | .357 | 376 | 15 | 7 | .982 |
| 1944 | St. Louis | Nat. | OF | 146 | 568 | 112 | 197 | 51 | 14 | 12 | 94 | .347 | 353 | 16 | 5 | .987 |
| 1945 | St. Louis | Nat. | | | | | | (In Military Service) | | | | | | | | |
| 1946 | St. Louis | Nat. | 1-OF | 156 | 624 | 124 | 228 | 50 | 20 | 16 | 103 | .365 | 1166 | 69 | 15 | .988 |
| 1947 | St. Louis | Nat. | 1B | 149 | 587 | 113 | 183 | 30 | 13 | 19 | 95 | .312 | 1360 | 77 | 8 | .994 |
| 1948 | St. Louis | Nat. | O-1B | 155 | 611 | 135 | 230 | 46 | 18 | 39 | 131 | .376 | 354 | 11 | 7 | .981 |
| 1949 | St. Louis | Nat. | O-1B | 157 | 612 | 128 | 207 | 41 | 13 | 36 | 123 | .338 | 337 | 11 | 3 | .991 |
| 1950 | St. Louis | Nat. | OF-1B | 146 | 555 | 105 | 192 | 41 | 7 | 28 | 109 | .346 | 760 | 39 | 8 | .990 |
| 1951 | St. Louis | Nat. | O-1B | 152 | 578 | 124 | 205 | 30 | 12 | 32 | 108 | .355 | 816 | 45 | 10 | .989 |
| 1952 | St. Louis | Nat. | O-1-P | 154 | 578 | 105 | 194 | 42 | 6 | 21 | 91 | .336 | 502 | 18 | 5 | .990 |
| 1953 | St. Louis | Nat. | OF | 157 | 593 | 127 | 200 | 53 | 9 | 30 | 113 | .337 | 294 | 9 | 5 | .984 |
| 1954 | St. Louis | Nat. | O-1B | 153 | 591 | 120 | 195 | 41 | 9 | 35 | 126 | .330 | 307 | 15 | 5 | .985 |
| 1955 | St. Louis | Nat. | 1-OF | 154 | 562 | 97 | 179 | 30 | 5 | 33 | 108 | .319 | 1000 | 94 | 9 | .992 |
| 1956 | St. Louis | Nat. | 1B-OF | 156 | 594 | 87 | 184 | 33 | 6 | 27 | 109 | .310 | 954 | 95 | 8 | .992 |
| 1957 | St. Louis | Nat. | 1B | 134 | 502 | 82 | 176 | 38 | 3 | 29 | 102 | .351 | 1167 | 99 | 10 | .992 |
| 1958 | St. Louis | Nat. | 1B | 135 | 472 | 64 | 159 | 35 | 2 | 17 | 62 | .337 | 1019 | 100 | 13 | .989 |
| 1959 | St. Louis | Nat. | 1B-OF | 115 | 341 | 37 | 87 | 13 | 2 | 14 | 44 | .255 | 624 | 63 | 7 | .990 |
| 1960 | St. Louis | Nat. | OF-1B | 116 | 331 | 49 | 91 | 17 | 1 | 17 | 63 | .275 | 300 | 19 | 3 | .991 |
| 1961 | St. Louis | Nat. | OF | 123 | 372 | 46 | 107 | 22 | 4 | 15 | 70 | .288 | 149 | 9 | 1 | .994 |
| 1962 | St. Louis | Nat. | OF | 135 | 433 | 57 | 143 | 18 | 1 | 19 | 82 | .330 | 164 | 6 | 4 | .977 |
| 1963 | St. Louis | Nat. | OF | 124 | 337 | 34 | 86 | 10 | 2 | 12 | 58 | .255 | 121 | 1 | 4 | .968 |
| Major League Totals | | | | 3026 | 10972 | 1949 | 3630 | 725 | 177 | 475 | 1951 | .331 | 12439 | 818 | 142 | .989 |

### WORLD SERIES RECORD

| YEAR | CLUB | LEAGUE | POS. | G. | AB. | R. | H. | 2B. | 3B. | HR. | RBI. | B.A. | PO. | A. | E. | F.A. |
|------|------|--------|------|-----|------|------|------|-----|-----|-----|------|------|-------|-----|-----|------|
| 1942 | St. Louis | Nat. | OF | 5 | 18 | 2 | 4 | 1 | 0 | 0 | 2 | .222 | 13 | 0 | 0 | 1.000 |
| 1943 | St. Louis | Nat. | OF | 5 | 18 | 2 | 5 | 0 | 0 | 0 | 0 | .278 | 7 | 2 | 0 | 1.000 |
| 1944 | St. Louis | Nat. | OF | 6 | 23 | 2 | 7 | 2 | 0 | 1 | 2 | .304 | 11 | 0 | 1 | .917 |
| 1946 | St. Louis | Nat. | 1B | 7 | 27 | 3 | 6 | 4 | 1 | 0 | 4 | .222 | 60 | 2 | 0 | 1.000 |
| World Series Totals | | | | 23 | 86 | 9 | 22 | 7 | 1 | 1 | 8 | .256 | 91 | 4 | 1 | .990 |

### PITCHING RECORD

| YEAR | CLUB | LEAGUE | G. | IP. | W. | L. | Pct. | H. | R. | ER. | SO. | BB. | ERA. |
|------|------|--------|-----|------|----|----|------|-----|-----|-----|-----|-----|------|
| 1938 | Williamson | Mt. State | 20 | 110 | 6 | 6 | .500 | 114 | 75 | 57 | 66 | 80 | 4.66 |
| 1939 | Williamson | Mt. State | 13 | 92 | 9 | 2 | .818 | 71 | 53 | 44 | 86 | 85 | 4.30 |
| 1940 | Daytona Beach | Fla. State | 28 | 223 | 18 | 5 | .783 | 179 | 108 | 65 | 176 | 145 | 2.62 |
| 1952 | St. Louis | Nat. | 1 | 0 | 0 | 0 | .000 | 0 | 0 | 0 | 0 | 0 | 0.00 |
| Major League Totals | | | 1 | 0 | 0 | 0 | 0 | .000 | 0 | 0 | 0 | 0 | 0.00 |

There wasn't a dry eye in the house on the Sunday afternoon Captain Carl
Yastrzemski said good-bye to Beantown.

# CARL YASTRZEMSKI

*To Yaz, with Love*

**DATE:** October 2, 1983

**SITE:** Fenway Park, Boston, Massachusetts

**PITCHER:** Dan Spillner of the Cleveland Indians

**RESULT:** Pop out to second baseman Jack Perconte

**October 2, 1983, Boston**—He looked down at his feet, planted in the same batter's box, maybe in the exact location where his predecessor had bowed out so memorably 23 years earlier.

Talk about following in Ted Williams's footsteps. Carl Yastrzemski literally did.

Now, it was all over. After 23 years, 3,308 games, 11,988 at bats—4,282 more than Ted Williams—3,419 hits and 1,845 walks, he was finally through.

With this last at-bat against Cleveland reliever Dan Spillner, a nondescript right-hander finishing a grand 2-9 season, Yaz would wrap it all up.

It was hard to focus the way he normally wanted to. The moment he stepped out of the Red Sox dugout, the crowd began to clap and wouldn't stop, even for the public address announcer.

Yastrzemski stood outside the batter's box, his bat by his side, his right arm waving his helmet to the overflow crowd that couldn't throw enough love his way.

They knew this was it; they'd never see No. 8 in that batter's box again. Then he had to step in and try to hit.

How different a finish it was for him compared to Williams. On Teddy Ballgame's final game—which wasn't announced in advance—there was a brief pregame ceremony on a September day 23 years ago. Williams then merely went through the motions of another drab ballgame. It only became electric when Williams came to bat for the final time, in the eighth.

Even after Ted's dramatic last at-bat home run, there was no nod to the fans, no final tip of the cap, nothing for them but the thrill of the moment, which, of course, has grown with the years.

Like the attendance, no doubt. But on this final day of reckoning, Yaz did beat Williams there. Ted drew just 10,454 to his Wednesday afternoon finale. There were 33,491 there for the Sunday afternoon farewell to Yaz.

In fact, Yaz's final weekend was a pure fan fest. Sure, there had been a time when Yaz had heard their boos, when he stuffed cotton in his ears when he ran out to left field. Boston's fans can be demanding and very hard to please. Some of them thought Yaz should have won the Triple Crown and been the American's League's MVP every season from 1967 to 1983.

Instead, after that Impossible Dream season of 1967, it took him eight years to get the Red Sox back into the World Series.

So if he'd heard more than his share of boos and took more than his share of blame in the newspapers and on the radio talk shows over that time, he understood, at last, how much they cared. So did he.

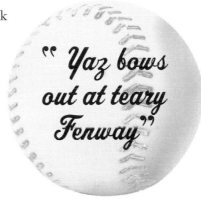

"Yaz bows out at teary Fenway"

Together, they came through the years, through all the stances and heartache and strains and bruises and disappointments. This hard-won audience finally loved him. He loved them, too.

You could see it as he stood there waving his helmet, turning as if to drink in all the sad and happy faces that showered him with such affection. They had noticed how long and how hard he'd kept at it. How much of himself—and his life, really—he gave to this team.

So the day of reckoning was healthy. No, he never quite matched Williams's standards of excellence at the plate. It wasn't for lack of trying. How he worked at it. All those hours and hours of extra hitting. At least a dozen different stances.

And worry. All those off-hours thinking about that next at-bat, that next game, that next pitch.

No, it was never easy for him. Never looked it, either. Maybe the great Ted Williams could study the enemy, declare that the dumbest guy in the ballpark was always the pitcher, come to the park and get his two hits every day. You'd never hear Yaz say something like that.

He could see the lines in his face when he got dressed before this last ballgame. Deep circles under his eyes. He could see the silver feathering in the sides of his thick brown hair. He looked like a man who worked hard for a living.

*"One last time around for Yaz"*

"The pervasive, unshakeable image of Carl Yastrzemski that I carry inside me," wrote Roger Angell in 1983, "is of his making an out in a game, in some demanding or critical situation—a pop-up instead of a base hit, or perhaps an easy grounder chopped toward a waiting infielder—with Yaz dropping his head in sudden disappointment and self-disgust as he flips the bat away and starts up the line, his chance gone again.

"No other great ballplayer I have seen was more burdened by the difficulties of this most unforgiving of all sports," Angell continued, "and by the ceaseless demands he made on his own skills, and by the expectations we had of him in every game and almost every at-bat. . . . Yaz wasn't glum, he was funereal."

Why? Why could someone who could play the game so well be so downhearted about it? Well, he never came right out and said it, but how *do* you step into the batter's box that Ted Williams had made his for 20 seasons?

So now, here it was. *His* final at-bat. Everybody remembered how Williams went out. What would Yaz do?

All New England knew his mannerisms as he stepped in. The hitch at the back of the pants, the jamming of the blue batting helmet down on his head with the palm of his hand, the twirl of the bat, the front foot poised. . . .

He laughed as he thought about that unmistakable voice he used to hear all the time every spring . . . Williams.

"That damn Yastrzemski; he's always got 15 million things to do before he gets into the batter's box."

No, he wasn't another Ted Williams. But who the hell was?

As you saw him standing at the plate on this sunny final Sunday, he was showing a little more of his back to the pitcher than he had before, the bat partially hidden by his body. Once he held the bat so high over his head, it looked as if he was trying to poke a cloud.

Now, it was as if age and gravity had finally brought his hands and tools down to a level more befitting a 44-year-old man. He didn't look threatening any more.

There was a time when he cocked those hands and ripped that bat through the strike zone with a dramatic, back-bending flourish that would sometimes move classically understated Red Sox announcer Ned Martin to blurt, "Mercy!" One writer said Yastrzemski had a chiropractor's dream of a swing. That was it, ferocious, at his best, almost untamed, out of control.

After his sudden surge of power in 1967—he hit 44 home runs—the stance seemed to change annually, a concession to age, to the way they happened to be pitching him that season, to a whim.

That was another element that further separated him from Williams, whose stance was defiant, his swing classical, elegant, unchanging through the seasons.

Unlike Williams who played left field except for his rookie season, Yastrzemski started in left but eventually moved to first base, then designated hitter, still hitting in the productive spots in the Red Sox lineup. Williams just about always hit third.

Like Williams, he wasn't able to bring home a World Series title, either. But, unlike Ted, in Yaz's two tries, 1967 and 1975, both were seven-game series and he hit like hell (.400 vs. the Cardinals, .310 vs. the Cincinnati Reds).

Like Williams, he was great in All-Star games, too. Always found a way to raise his game when it counted. That's what Boston fans just knew. They didn't need stats to tell them. The Boston writers dug them up anyway.

In the 22 most important games of his career—World Series, pennant races, playoffs—Yastrzemski batted .417, nearly 140 points higher than his lifetime average or about twice what Williams hit vs. St. Louis in his 1946 World Series against the St. Louis Cardinals.

Yaz was also the man at the plate when both those World Series ended. He flied out against Bob Gibson in Game Seven of the 1967 World Series and flied out against Will McEnaney in Game Seven of the 1975 World Series.

His most famous final out came in the Red Sox-Yankees 1978 playoff game, when Goose Gossage got him to pop out to Craig Nettles, ending the game in utter heartbreak for Boston fans, who'd had a huge lead that season, then squandered it, losing a playoff game at home.

For stunned Red Sox fans, it just didn't seem as if it really happened, as if it should have counted.

*Globe* columnist Ray Fitzgerald, writing moments after he saw the ball descend into Craig Nettles's glove, said "Somewhere there should be a film director wearing a beret and shouting through the megaphone: "Another take, gentlemen, and this time, let's get it right."

Angell, a Red Sox devotee, was wounded to the core. Writing about the moment in *Late Innings*, he brought the moment back vividly.

"Two out and the tying run on third. Yastrzemski up. A whole season, thousands of innings, had gone into this tableau. My hands were trembling. The faces around me looked haggard. Gossage, the enormous pitcher, reared and threw a fastball. Ball one. He flailed and fired again, and Yastrzemski swung and popped the ball into very short left field foul ground, where Graig Nettles, backing up, made the easy out. It was over.

"Afterward, Yaz wept in the training room, away from the reporters. In the biggest ballgame of his life, he had homered and singled and had driven in two runs, but almost no one would remember that. He is 39 years old, and he has never played on a world championship team; it is the one remaining goal of his career. He emerged after a while, dry-eyed, and sat by his locker and answered our questions quietly. He looked old. He looked fifty."

The scene so moved Angell, he even directed a criticism upward.

A Harvard professor had written: "The hero must go under at last, after prodigious deeds, to be remembered and immortal and to have poets sing his tale."

"I understand that," Angell wrote, "and I will sing the tale of Yaz always, but I still don't understand why it couldn't have been arranged for him to single to right center, or to double off the wall. I'd have sung *that*, too. I think God was shelling a peanut."

A couple years later, after Gossage had surrendered a game-winning home run to George Brett in the AL playoffs, writer Peter Gammons asked him about the pitch and Brett's final swing. What was it like, surrendering that game-winning home run? He was surprised at Gossage's answer.

"I think of Yaz," Gossage said. "I'd like to think of these moments as the best against the best, not winners and losers. The pitch to Yaz ran a little more than the pitch to Brett. Don't ask me why because I don't know. If time were called and we went back and I had to throw those pitches over again, George might pop up and Yaz might have hit the ball into the bleachers."

So this was it. No time for a pop-up. His last at-bat, competing with the ghost of Williams. Ol' Ted had gotten it right in his final turn at bat. Could Yaz follow him there, too?

That was on the mind of every soul inside Fenway Park. Every player on either team knew what was on Yaz's mind. So, of course, did Spillner, winding down a rotten season.

As reported in the *Boston Globe* the next day, Spillner already knew what the rules were for Yaz's last at-bat.

"We were in the bar with the umpires Friday night and Rich Garcia told us, 'Look, fellows, if he doesn't swing, it's a ball,' said Tribe pitcher Lary Sorensen.

With all that going on around him, the emotion of the moment got to Spillner, not exactly a precision pitcher on his best day. Once Yaz stepped in, he couldn't find the plate.

Ball one. Cheers. Ball two. More cheers, some boos. Ball three. Booooooos.

"I could see Spiller was trying to aim the ball," Yastrzemski said later. "It was coming in at 80 mph."

With a 3-0 count in his favor, 33,491 screaming for him to whack one, to go out like Ted did, Spillner wound and delivered.

The pitch, Yaz could see right off, was high. Up in his eyes. Williams would have taken it, no question. That was his way. If it was a fraction of an inch off the plate, he'd take it. Period. So he'd go out with a walk. Fine.

Yaz just couldn't. He and all those who came to cheer for him had too much riding on the pitch.

He swung from his heels and lifted a high pop-up to second baseman Jack Perconte. He laughed as he ran down to first base.

"I was trying to jerk it out," he admitted later.

He trotted back out to his old post, left field, in the eighth and Red Sox manager Ralph Houk, like Mike Higgins had done with Ted Williams years earlier, sent a substitute out to take his position.

Yastrzemski left to deafening roars and stopped on his way to the dugout to give his hat to a youngster seated along the rail.

In the locker room afterwards, Yastrzemski ordered champagne for all the writers and even toasted them for their fairness as they stood around his locker. He even remembered some of the writers who'd covered him early in his career who had since passed away. Ted Williams might not ever have talked to him again if he knew that.

There was something going on inside Yastrzemski. Never a forthcoming interview, he suddenly opened up, as if it were a great relief to him to have this career thing over with.

"I'm just a potato farmer from Long Island who had some ability," Yaz said then. "I'm not any different than a mechanic, an engineer, or the president of a bank."

The emotions, he was astonished to see them keep coming. Earlier in the day when he had his turn at the microphone before the game began, he spoke with such feeling, he had to halt a couple times to collect himself.

"I saw the sign that read 'Say it ain't so, Yaz' and I wish it weren't. This is the last day of my career as a player, and I want to thank all of you for being here with me today. It has been a great privilege to wear the Red Sox uniform the past 23 years, and to have played in Fenway in front of you great fans. I'll miss you, and I'll never forget you."

The great thing was, for those who saw that final weekend in person or on TV, they won't need any final home run in his last at-bat to keep it in their memory.

Yes, the signature Yastrzemski moment came the day before when, without any warning, Yaz broke away from a sweet pregame ceremony around the pitcher's mound and impulsively began to trot along the fence down the right-field line, reaching up to slap hands with a wildly excited Fenway crowd along the way.

Amazingly, he just kept going. All the way around the ballfield. No player had ever said good-bye like this.

Organist John Kiley, catching the moment perfectly, soared through "My Way" while Yaz kept waving, slapping hands down the line. He finally reached the 380 sign on the right-field bullpen wall where 23 years earlier, Williams had flied out in his next-to-last at-bat.

Then Kiley brilliantly swung into "The Impossible Dream," the unofficial theme song for Yaz and the Red Sox's improbable pennant drive 16 years earlier, his greatest year as a baseball player, and the joint melted.

By the time Yaz crossed through right center and center field, still waving, misty-eyed himself, Fenway was a sweet, soggy mess. No, it didn't seem 16 years ago. Yaz and all of Red Sox Nation were young again.

Finally, Yaz's trot got to his old workspace, left field. Seeing him jog across the worn grass, it had never occurred to Red Sox fans that someday he would leave that spot. It was if he would always be out there, like a lawn ornament.

Once he got to the left-field line, Yaz moved back along the edge of the wall, slapping hands with fan after fan while Kiley swung into his third number, an emotional "Auld Lange Syne."

Yaz stopped to shake hands with a few Indians' players, then stood at home plate, waving, his eyes wet, his lip trembling.

By the time he was back in the dugout, it didn't seem as if he'd be able to play. And that was only Saturday. Of course, Yaz did play and went 0-4, grounding out four times, including the game's final out.

There was one great surprise left. On that final Sunday, after that glorious last at-bat pop-up, Yaz stayed in the dugout until the game and season ended.

As fans were emptying Fenway feeling a little downhearted, he magically appeared again, in an undershirt, and trotted back out onto the field and gave them his own instant replay, starting down the right-field line and taking the whole park in one last time.

With a thunderous roar from the Red Sox fans still there, Carl Yastrzemski took one final, triumphant tour around the field.

Call it a victory lap.

# Say It Ain't So, Yaz

## CLEVELAND

| | ab. | r. | h. | bi. |
|---|---|---|---|---|
| Perconte, 2b | 2 | 0 | 1 | 0 |
| Harrah, 3b | 5 | 0 | 1 | 0 |
| Hargrv, 1b | 4 | 0 | 2 | 0 |
| Thrntn, dh | 4 | 0 | 0 | 0 |
| Vukvch, cf | 4 | 0 | 1 | 0 |
| A. Banstr, rf | 3 | 1 | 0 | 0 |
| C. Castill, rf | 1 | 0 | 0 | 0 |
| Rhmbrg, lf | 4 | 0 | 3 | 0 |
| Essian, c | 2 | 0 | 1 | 1 |
| Bando, c | 2 | 0 | 0 | 0 |
| Fischlin, ss | 2 | 0 | 0 | 0 |
| Perkins, ph | 1 | 0 | 0 | 0 |
| **TOTALS:** | **34** | **1** | **9** | **1** |

## BOSTON

| | ab. | r. | h. | bi. |
|---|---|---|---|---|
| Remy, 2b | 4 | 1 | 3 | 0 |
| Boggs, 3b | 1 | 1 | 0 | 0 |
| Rice, dh | 4 | 1 | 2 | 3 |
| Armas, cf | 2 | 0 | 0 | 0 |
| Graham, cf | 2 | 0 | 0 | 0 |
| Yastzmk, lf | 3 | 0 | 1 | 0 |
| C. Walker, lf | 0 | 0 | 0 | 0 |
| Nichols, rf | 2 | 0 | 0 | 0 |
| Stapltn, 1b | 3 | 0 | 0 | 0 |
| Allenson, c | 3 | 0 | 0 | 0 |
| Gutirrz, ss | 3 | 0 | 0 | 0 |
| **TOTALS:** | **27** | **3** | **6** | **3** |

```
Cleveland ................   0 1 0   0 0 0   0 0 0 1
Boston ......................   0 0 3   0 0 0   0 0 x 3
```

Game winning RBI: Rice (14). DP: Cleveland 2, Boston 2. LOB: Cleveland 10, Boston 6. 2B: Remy, HR: Rice(39). SB: Perconte (3), Nichols (7).

| | IP | H | R | ER | BB | SO |
|---|---|---|---|---|---|---|
| **CLEVELAND** | | | | | | |
| B. Andersn (L, 1-6) | 3 | 4 | 3 | 3 | 3 | 0 |
| Brennan | 1 | 0 | 0 | 0 | 1 | 1 |
| Jeffcoat | 1 1/3 | 2 | 0 | 0 | 3 | 1 |
| Spillner | 2 2/3 | 0 | 0 | 0 | 2 | 0 |
| **BOSTON** | | | | | | |
| Nipper (W, 1-1) | 9 | 9 | 1 | 1 | 4 | 2 |

HBP: Fischlin by Nipper. T: 2:38.

# CARL MICHAEL YASTRZEMSKI
Nickname: Yaz
Born August 22, 1939, in Southampton, N.Y.
Height: 5-11 Weight: 182
Threw right-handed and batted left-handed
Career total = 23 years
Named to Hall of Fame: 1989

| SEASON | TEAM | G | AB | R | H | 2B | 3B | HR | RBI | TB | BB | SO | SB | CS | BA |
|---|---|---|---|---|---|---|---|---|---|---|---|---|---|---|---|
| 1961 | Boston Red Sox | 148 | 583 | 71 | 155 | 31 | 6 | 11 | 80 | 231 | 50 | 96 | 6 | 5 | .266 |
| 1962 | Boston Red Sox | 160 | 646 | 99 | 191 | 43 | 6 | 19 | 94 | 303 | 66 | 82 | 7 | 4 | .296 |
| 1963 | Boston Red Sox | 151 | 570 | 91 | 183 | 40 | 3 | 14 | 68 | 271 | 95 | 72 | 8 | 5 | .321 |
| 1964 | Boston Red Sox | 151 | 567 | 77 | 164 | 29 | 9 | 15 | 67 | 256 | 75 | 90 | 6 | 5 | .289 |
| 1965 | Boston Red Sox | 133 | 494 | 78 | 154 | 45 | 3 | 20 | 72 | 265 | 70 | 58 | 7 | 6 | .312 |
| 1966 | Boston Red Sox | 160 | 594 | 81 | 165 | 39 | 2 | 16 | 80 | 256 | 84 | 60 | 8 | 9 | .278 |
| 1967 | Boston Red Sox | 161 | 579 | 112 | 189 | 31 | 4 | 44 | 121 | 360 | 91 | 69 | 10 | 8 | .326 |
| 1968 | Boston Red Sox | 157 | 539 | 90 | 162 | 32 | 2 | 23 | 74 | 267 | 119 | 90 | 13 | 6 | .301 |
| 1969 | Boston Red Sox | 162 | 603 | 96 | 154 | 28 | 2 | 40 | 111 | 306 | 101 | 91 | 15 | 7 | .255 |
| 1970 | Boston Red Sox | 161 | 566 | 125 | 186 | 29 | 0 | 40 | 102 | 335 | 128 | 66 | 23 | 13 | .329 |
| 1971 | Boston Red Sox | 148 | 508 | 75 | 129 | 21 | 2 | 15 | 70 | 199 | 106 | 60 | 8 | 7 | .254 |
| 1972 | Boston Red Sox | 125 | 455 | 70 | 120 | 18 | 2 | 12 | 68 | 178 | 67 | 44 | 5 | 4 | .264 |
| 1973 | Boston Red Sox | 152 | 540 | 82 | 160 | 25 | 4 | 19 | 95 | 250 | 105 | 58 | 9 | 7 | .296 |
| 1974 | Boston Red Sox | 148 | 515 | 93 | 155 | 25 | 2 | 15 | 79 | 229 | 104 | 48 | 12 | 7 | .301 |
| 1975 | Boston Red Sox | 149 | 543 | 91 | 146 | 30 | 1 | 14 | 60 | 220 | 87 | 67 | 8 | 4 | .269 |
| 1976 | Boston Red Sox | 155 | 546 | 71 | 146 | 23 | 2 | 21 | 102 | 236 | 80 | 67 | 5 | 6 | .267 |
| 1977 | Boston Red Sox | 150 | 558 | 99 | 165 | 27 | 3 | 28 | 102 | 282 | 73 | 40 | 11 | 1 | .296 |
| 1978 | Boston Red Sox | 144 | 523 | 70 | 145 | 21 | 2 | 17 | 81 | 221 | 76 | 44 | 4 | 5 | .277 |
| 1979 | Boston Red Sox | 147 | 518 | 69 | 140 | 28 | 1 | 21 | 87 | 233 | 62 | 46 | 3 | 3 | .270 |
| 1980 | Boston Red Sox | 105 | 364 | 49 | 100 | 21 | 1 | 15 | 50 | 168 | 44 | 38 | 0 | 2 | .275 |
| 1981 | Boston Red Sox | 91 | 338 | 36 | 83 | 14 | 1 | 7 | 53 | 120 | 49 | 28 | 0 | 1 | .246 |
| 1982 | Boston Red Sox | 131 | 459 | 53 | 126 | 22 | 1 | 16 | 72 | 198 | 59 | 50 | 0 | 1 | .275 |
| 1983 | Boston Red Sox | 119 | 380 | 38 | 101 | 24 | 0 | 10 | 56 | 155 | 54 | 29 | 0 | 0 | .266 |
| **Career Totals** | | 3308 | 11988 | 1816 | 3419 | 646 | 59 | 452 | 1844 | 5539 | 1845 | 1393 | 168 | 116 | .271 |

A life-size wooden sculpture of the elegant, electric Williams's swing—in exactly this pose—stands alongside one of Babe Ruth at the entrance to the Baseball Hall of Fame in Cooperstown.

# TED WILLIAMS

## *Perfect Swing, Perfect Finish*

| | |
|---|---|
| **DATE:** September 28, 1960 | |
| **SITE:** Fenway Park, Boston, Massachusetts | |
| **PITCHER:** Jack Fisher of the Baltimore Orioles | |
| **RESULT:** Home run into the right-field bullpen | |

**September 28, 1960, Boston**—Okay, so maybe he wouldn't go out with a home run.

That stubborn realization seemed to sink in slowly in the most stubborn of men as he walked out of the Boston Red Sox dugout and kneeled down in the on-deck circle. It was the eighth inning of a cool and overcast Wednesday afternoon in late September.

This was it.

The Baltimore Orioles were in town and, after a good run at the New York Yankees, they'd fallen a little short in their pennant run. Like Boston, they were just playing out the schedule.

After a walk and two long fly outs on this dank, damp day, it didn't look like Ted Williams, the Red Sox's famed slugger, was going to go out the way he wanted to, the way he'd been planning to, with a home run.

He knew this kid Fisher, Jack Fisher, a right-hander with a good fastball, was going to go right after him, just like he did in his two previous at-bats. Hard stuff against the old man.

He had thought he caught that last one in the fifth just right. The ball jumped off his bat and the fans rose to their feets. There was something about the sound of Ted Williams hitting one.

But the long, majestic fly ball backed Orioles center-fielder Al Pilarcik right to the 380 sign on the green wall of the bullpen in right center in Fenway Park. Then he caught it.

When Williams got back to the dugout, he saw Vic Wertz, who knew a little bit about being robbed by a center fielder—Wertz's everlasting moment of glory came when Willie Mays had robbed him in the World Series six years earlier—and shrugged.

"Damn, I hit the living hell out of that one," Williams said. "I really stung it. If that one didn't go out, nothing is going out today."

Yeah, all these young pitchers were going at ol' Ted now, like you'd expect young pitchers would against a tired 42-year-old. Chuck Stobbs did last week in Washington, striking him out twice with men in scoring position.

Ted had the last laugh there. The next night, Pedro Ramos tried the same thing and Ted got his revenge with a two-run shot over the right-field wall. It won the ballgame.

That was his 28th home run of the season, the 520th of his career, putting him third on the all-time list at that time behind Babe Ruth (714) and Jimmy Foxx (534.)

Here he was, down to his last at-bat and it looked like he was going out on 520.

This last week hadn't been much fun. Tuesday night in Baltimore, Williams fouled a ball off his ankle in the first inning and had to leave the game. He caught a plane back to Logan Wednesday afternoon where he was met by the local press. Williams shrugged it off.

"You might think this was a broken leg with all this fuss," Williams told the media. "I expect to finish the season playing. There is no reason why I shouldn't."

*"Williams's HR a signature blow"*

He didn't get back into the lineup until the Yankees came into Fenway on the weekend and swept the Sox to clinch the pennant.

Williams was still swinging the bat pretty well. On Friday night he had a double off Bob Turley. On Saturday, he had three hits against an assortment of Yankee pitchers. On Sunday, he had two hits off Ralph Terry.

But Williams went hitless in two trips in yesterday's embarrassing 17-3 loss to the Orioles. That was a reason to get out. Enough of those kinds of ballgames.

His average? Well, he was still over .300. About .316. Not bad for 42 years old.

The afternoon crowd was pretty sparse, considering Williams was New England's most notorious—if not necessarily loved—professional athlete. There wasn't a lot of fanfare over his final game in Boston.

Only a middling crowd of 10,454 showed up (even tiny Fenway can hold three times that) and there wasn't any big hullabaloo from the national media. It sounded like the Red Sox feared that might happen with a controversial star like Williams.

Williams broke the news that he was quitting on Sunday after the Yankees had clinched their 25th pennant by sweeping the Red Sox.

You can bet Ted laughed when he read the front-page story in Monday's *Boston Globe*, a story that was played above the bold headline "Strike vote threatens to idle all G.E. plants." It read simply: "Ted quits—as player."

"It is the hope of the Boston management that Fenway Park will be filled on Wednesday to bid farewell to Ted," *Globe* writer Hy Hurwitz wrote. Fat chance of that, Williams laughed. These Red Sox didn't draw.

There was no TV coverage, local or national, and none of the major papers had sent their columnists out to see Teddy's bye bye.

One reason was the Red Sox were a lousy team and they'd been out of the pennant race for some time. Another was the team was going on to New York to close out the regular season. Maybe some expected Williams would wrap it up there.

Or it could be they didn't see it as a big deal. Nobody saw it as an event. Athletes retire all the time, usually with a whimper. Who'd want to see Ted Williams go out with a whimper?

Williams had retired before—or so he had announced—five years earlier, taking $10,000 to write a magazine series for the *Saturday Evening Post*, "This Is My Last Year in Baseball."

He was heading into a divorce and ultimately didn't join the team until mid-May because of all the squabbling. But he could still hit. He hit .345 in 1956 and would have won the batting title if he'd had the necessary number of at-bats. The next year, 1957, he hit an amazing .388. So he played a little longer.

Now, though, this was the end of the line. The pennant race had already been decided—Williams had to sit in the dugout on Sunday afternoon and watch the Yankees run off nine straight wins—including this sweep at Fenway—to clinch one more pennant.

He watched Yankees reliever Luis Arroyo come in and get Boston's Pete Runnels, the AL batting champion, to foul out to third with the game-tying run right there. That was the Red Sox for you. Close but no cigar.

With the pennant race officially over, Williams had given Red Sox owner Tom Yawkey the okay in the clubhouse to announce to the newspapers that he'd be retiring at the end of the season. The Red Sox said Williams would go to spring training as a batting instructor. Some thought he'd be the Red Sox' new general manager.

During Wednesday's game, it had been announced in the press box during the game that Williams's No. 9 would be retired after the game. That drew a few cracks from the peanut gallery about Williams playing in his undershirt at Yankee Stadium. The official pronouncement that he wasn't going to New York hadn't been made yet, except to a few people in the Red Sox clubhouse.

Williams had already given the word to manager Mike Higgins that he wasn't going back to New York. This was going to be it. He could just imagine the chatter in the press box right above him.

Hell, Williams thought, those idiots ought to be happy. They'd been trying to retire me for years.

By now, Williams knew their ritual. Ted would come to spring training and see the "Is this it for Ted Williams?" stories, suffer through the "Williams's slow start may mean he's finished" stories that were sure to appear in the cold early months when Williams never hit his best, then expect the "Will Red Sox invite Williams back for one more year?" stories in the fall.

"Leaving with a bang, that's our Ted"

In a town with, at times, seven newspapers and a rabid—some might say unhealthy, baseball interest, Williams was always somebody worth writing about. Hell, at least one of them admitted it.

"The loss of Williams to a Boston sports columnist is like a bad case of athlete's fingers to Van Cliburn," wrote John Gillooly of the *Boston Daily Record*. "You just can't pound the keys any more. The song is ended.

"I am not going to crank through the microfilms of the *Daily Record* for the past year. . . . But I'll guess that if I wrote 280 columns in that 12-month [span] that 80 of them were about The Kid, the chromatic, bombastic, the quixotic—a demon one day and a delight the next. . . . Williams made columning easy."

Yeah, they were going to miss Ted Williams, all right. Even the bastards who hated him as much as he hated them. The thing was, nobody ever called them on any of the shit they wrote, even when they were dead wrong.

Ever.

Williams thought back to Bill Cunningham's analysis of his swing, back when he was a rookie. Williams could remember it word for word. He had that kind of recall if something ticked him off enough. And many things did.

"The Red Sox seem to think Williams is just cocky and gabby enough to make a colorful outfielder, possibly the Babe Herman type," Cunningham wrote. "Me? I don't like the way he stands at the plate. He bends his front knee inward, he moves his feet just before he takes a swing. That's exactly what I do just before I drive a golf ball and, knowing what happens to the golf balls I drive, I don't think this kid will ever hit half a Singer midget's weight in a bathing suit."

What a horse's ass. But who ever called them on it?

Once Williams learned the newspaper game, Ted fought back in his own way from time to time. Like giving an exclusive interview to the out of town guy, knowing full well that the Boston guys would catch wind of it and be pissed off that he gave someone else the scoop. That was a real "Kiss my ass" to the boys on the beat. Williams loved to do that.

Or after a disagreeable article, maybe he'd get in their face, tell 'em he smelled something awful in the locker room, then tell 'em it must have been the shit that they were writing.

And the stuff they wrote in the offseason, why, it was unbelievable. Williams feuding with his brother, Williams refusing to visit his mother in the offseason, Williams not being at the hospital for the birth of his daughter—there were so many more. Why was he the only player anywhere who had to deal with that crap?

More than once Williams wondered why the hell didn't they write that stuff about DiMaggio? Hell, DiMaggio was a great player but also out until all hours at New York nightclubs, banging showgirls left and right, a different one every night, drinking and smoking with the New York newspaper guys, calling them his pals.

They write about him like he's a god. Hell, DiMaggio had had his failed marriages, too. How come nobody ever wrote about that?

Even Red Smith, whom Williams liked, always fawned over DiMaggio. He remembered one time Smith wrote that DiMaggio was "excelled by Ted Williams in all offensive statistics and reputedly, Ted's inferior in crowd appeal and financial standing, (yet DiMaggio) still won the writers' accolade as the American League's most valuable in 1947. It wasn't the first time Williams earned this award with his bat and lost it with his disposition."

Well, that was true enough, Williams thought. But what does your personality have to do with what you do with a baseball uniform on? Can you play, can you hit or not? Was it a popularity contest or not? Writers, can kiss my. . . .

But his relations with the press cost him. In 1942, Williams won the Triple Crown and lost the MVP to one of the Yankees, Joe Gordon, who hit .322 to Williams's .356, drove in 103 runs to Ted's 137.

Even in 1941 when Williams hit .406 with six hits on the final day of the season, DiMaggio got the award for his 56-game hitting streak.

Williams always tried to be gracious about it. Joe was a great ballplayer. But he had to wonder what the New York media blitz did for Joe on a regular basis. Even Red Smith, for chrissakes.

"As a matter of fact," Smith continued in that same article, "if all other factors were equal save only the question of character, Joe would never lose out to any player. The guy who came out of San Francisco as a shy lone wolf, suspicious of Easterners and Eastern writers, today is the top guy in any sports gathering in any town. The real champ."

Were we supposed to *bow* when DiMaggio comes up? Williams laughed. Nobody ever puffed up Ted Williams that way. How much did DiMaggio do for charity, anyway? Anybody ever ask that question?

Ah, it didn't matter. The people at the Jimmy Fund knew who Ted Williams was and how much he cared and how much he helped kids. The hell with the New York press.

The more Williams thought about what happened to him in Boston, it wasn't fair. Not that he could ever say it. Then they'd really let him have it.

Sure, he was a hot head and ill tempered and childish and foul mouthed and ill behaved and you bet your life he'd go at those sons of bitches.

But how come we never found out what kind of dad, what kind of son, what kind of husband DiMaggio was? The Boston writers all had to know all that about Ted. Why didn't the New York writers want to know that about Joe? It was a fair question.

One year, a Boston writer called Williams's ex-wife to find out what he'd bought his kid for Christmas!

They didn't pull that crap with DiMaggio. If any one of them wrote a single word that DiMaggio didn't like, he'd cut them off. And they'd be out of a job. Don't think DiMaggio didn't know it.

Hey, if you've got that kind of clout, why not use it? No knock on Joe.

But you've got to wonder how would he have done with the Boston press? As nervous as he was? What would they have done with his legend? Especially near the end when he couldn't hit or play center field like he always had.

Many years later, the respected journalist David Halbertstam, a Williams fan, talked with famed sportswriter W. C. Heinz about DiMaggio and how the New York press handled him.

"I had been around DiMaggio a good deal," Heinz said, "I knew how most of the reporters played up to him, I knew how difficult he could be, and how coldly he could treat writers and how he would cut them off if he was displeased."

Contrast that with Williams's treatment by the voracious Boston press, as Halberstam would later note, not one of the shining moments in American journalism, and you have a much more complex picture.

And when, in 1959, an assortment of injuries knocked Williams down to just .254—hell, he was under .200 until the midsummer—the writers were just savage. It got so bad that even Red Sox owner Tom Yawkey told Ted he ought to retire.

Nobody, not even Yawkey was going to tell Ted Williams what to do. He was still eight home runs short of 500 and he wanted to get there, for sure. He decided he'd take a pay cut, a pretty good one—$35,000—from his $125,000 annual salary (wonder if DiMaggio would ever do that?) and worked himself into good shape when the year began. He'd show those sons a bitches who was washed up.

He blasted a home run in his first at-bat and hit all year long. And so, well, it was all over now.

It had been quite a day, Williams thought, taking one long last look around Fenway Park. He knew the writers were grousing about him right now up in the press box, those "knights of the keyboard," as he'd called them in that brief pregame ceremony. Screw 'em. There was no way he was going to let them off the hook at that pregame ceremony earlier today. They hurt too much. Too often. Somebody was going to call them on what they wrote. This was his last chance.

He knew it was supposed to be a happy, classy day but damn, he stood at the microphone by the pitcher's mound, sort of shifting his weight uneasily from one foot to the other and just let it go. He couldn't help it.

"Despite the fact of the disagreeable things that have been said of me—and I can't help thinking about it—by the knights of the keyboard up there, baseball has been the most wonderful thing in my life. . . .

"If I were starting all over and someone asked me where is the one place I would like to play, I would want it to be Boston, with the greatest owner in baseball and the greatest fans in America. Thank you."

That was his final shot in the war with the press. He was sure they'd fire back one last time. But Ted Williams just didn't know how to let anything go and he wasn't going to start now.

He heard his name announced for the last time and he started toward the plate. He could hear the crowd now, roaring, applauding, without a single boo in the house. He laughed. He always used to be able to pick out that boo.

He hefted the bat and thought to himself, "one more time, one more time." He'd started the season, this final season, with a home run in his very first at-bat, a 450-foot shot off Camilo Pascual. Wouldn't it be something if he could go out with one, too?

He stepped into the batter's box and Fisher deferentially waiting until the cheers died down, wound and threw. Ball one.

Williams, who rarely swung at the first pitch, was ready for a fastball and here it came. He uncoiled and swung mightily at it. Plop. He heard the ball land in Gus Triandos's glove. Strike one.

The crowd rumbled and buzzed around him. This was a challenge. Take that, you old bastard.

"The pitcher's always the dumbest guy in the ballpark," that was one of Williams's favorite lines.

He dug in. He knew what he was going to get next. Just knew it.

Fisher snapped his glove at Triandos's return throw as if he was eager to get another pitch headed homeward. He wound and threw—it was another hard fastball—and Williams let loose with the final swing of his glorious career and caught it flush.

The crack of the bat, an unmistakable sound when Williams hit one right, rang through the park and the 10,000 came to their feet as the ball soared deeper and deeper toward the right-field bullpen, toward Williamsburg, they used to call it.

Suddenly, it descended with a rush, clunking off the canopy over the bullpen. Home run. Goodbye.

Some time later, novelist John Updike, a Williams fan, wrote a piece about Williams's final game. He caught that moment perfectly: "He ran as he always ran out home runs—hurriedly, unsmiling, head down, as if our praise were a storm of rain to get out of. He didn't tip his cap. Though we thumped, wept, chanted, "We want Ted!" for minutes after he hid in the dugout, he did not come back. . . . The papers said that the other players, even the umpires on the field, begged him to come out and acknowledge us in some way. But he refused."

Immediately after the game, though, Williams was in no sentimental mood—at least not to share with the newspapers. Reporter Ed Linn noted that Williams was pleasant enough with the first wave of reporters. Those he liked came to his locker first. They got the good Ted.

"I was gunning for the big one. I let everything I had go. I really wanted that one," he said, smiling.

By the time those Williams wasn't as tolerant of arrived—including Linn—his mood had soured. What little goodwill he had toward the press had evaporated.

Linn asked Williams if he'd thought about tipping his cap when manager Mike Higgins had sent him back out to left field at the start of the ninth inning, only to have Carroll Hardy immediately replace him amid a roaring, foot-stomping ovation. Wasn't that heartwarming?

It was the writer's way of asking, didn't Williams really want that ending where everybody goes home happy?

Williams wasn't playing that game.

"I felt nothing," Williams said.

No sentimentality, the writer asked?

"I said *nothing*. Nothing, nothing, nothing."

And he knew what they'd say in the papers, too. That he was going to go to New York until he hit that home run, then decided to quit then and there.

The bastards. He told Higgins, he didn't pack for the trip to New York, he'd made up his goddamned mind before the game that this was it. Period. But they've got to have a little controversy.

And that Kaese, Harold Kaese from the *Globe*, he knew he'd find a way to go after him, too. He did too, in his column in Thursday's *Globe*.

Sure enough, here was Kaese making sure to mention Harry "The Cat" Brecheen, who'd stopped Williams in his only World Series appearance against the Cardinals in 1946, a guy who happened to be standing and watching Baltimore's Steve Barber warm up.

Gee, he was a key component of the final game story, wasn't he?

Then Kaese mentioned that more people had seen Williams play his first game at Fenway—his American League opener—or his first "farewell" in 1954 than this game. Then Kaese speculated on what some of his press box colleagues (including himself) might write for the next day's headlines, "Sox Pennant Hopes Soar, (Jackie) Jensen returns, Williams retires."

Then there was this. Low by even Kaese's standards. His description of Williams crossing the plate after his dramatic final home run.

"For Fisher, Gus Triandos, and Umpire Ed Hurley, Williams had a smiling curtsy as he touched the plate. Was Fisher "piping" the ball for Williams? Some wondered.

He threw nothing but fastballs his last two times up, but one had so much on it that Williams fanned it just before he homered."

Williams started to get angry when he read it. Then he laughed. Kaese had questioned the purity of the home run, the timing of Ted's retirement, slammed him about the Red Sox's failing attendance and his own rotten World Series 14 years earlier, all in a single column.

Kaese left Ted Williams with a home run, too.

What did Williams really feel about it all? That wasn't going in some friggin' newspaper. Not a *Boston* newspaper, that's for sure.

It wasn't until years later that he lowered his guard with TV's Bob Costas.

"I have to say that was certainly one of the more moving moments, the tingling in my body, that I ever had as a baseball player, that last home run," Williams said. "That it was all over and I did hit the home run."

Williams also explained that final at-bat in more detail. After he'd swung and missed that 1-0 fastball— the wire services ran a shot of Ted flailing at it, eyes closed, bat outstretched, his picture-perfect swing looking awkward and old—he saw something in Fisher's manner that flipped a switch.

*"Ted says good-bye, HIS way"*

"So here I am, the last time at bat," Williams told the Baseball Hall of Fame some years later, "I got the count one and nothing and Jack Fisher's pitching. He laid a ball right there. I don't think I ever missed in my life like I missed that one but I missed it. And for the first time in my life I said "Oh Jesus, what happened? Why didn't I hit *that* one?' I couldn't believe it. It was straight, not the fastest pitch I'd ever seen, good stuff. I didn't know what to think because I didn't know what I'd done on that swing. Was I ahead or was I behind? It wasn't a breaking ball and right in a spot that, boy, what a ball to hit. I swung, had a hell of a swing, and I missed it. I'm still there trying to figure out what the hell happened. Then I could see Fisher out there with his glove up to get the ball back quickly, as much as saying 'I threw that one by him, I'll throw another by him.' And I saw all that and I guess it woke me up, you know. Right away, I assumed 'He thinks he threw it by me.' The way he was asking for the ball back quick, right away, I said, "I know he's going to go right back with that pitch."

So Ted Williams, the greatest hitter who ever lived, sat back and waited for one more, one last, fastball. Then he hit it out of sight, ran around the bases and never tipped his cap, never looked back even when they screamed and clapped and stomped and hollered his name.

He heard them all right. But he sat in the dugout and pulled on his jacket.

"Gods," John Updike famously wrote a few months later, "don't answer letters."

Months later, when Williams saw Updike's story, you can bet he was laughing.

"Gee, I wonder if Joe D. saw that line about Gods and letters. . . ."

# Goodbye, Boston

|  | BALTIMORE | | | |
|---|---|---|---|---|
|  | ab. | r. | h. | rbi. |
| Brandt, cf ....... | 5 | 0 | 0 | 0 |
| Pilarcik, rf ...... | 4 | 0 | 1 | 0 |
| Robinson, 3b .... | 4 | 1 | 1 | 0 |
| Gentile, 1b ...... | 3 | 1 | 1 | 1 |
| Triandos, c ...... | 4 | 1 | 2 | 2 |
| Hansen, ss ...... | 4 | 1 | 2 | 0 |
| Stephens, lf ..... | 4 | 0 | 2 | 0 |
| Breeding, 2b ..... | 2 | 0 | 0 | 0 |
| **a** Woodling ...... | 1 | 0 | 0 | 1 |
| **b** Pearson ....... | 0 | 0 | 0 | 0 |
| Kraus, 2b ....... | 1 | 0 | 0 | 0 |
| Barber, p ........ | 0 | 0 | 0 | 0 |
| Fisher, p ........ | 4 | 0 | 0 | 0 |
|  |  |  |  |  |
| **TOTALS:** | 36 | 4 | 9 | 4 |

|  | BOSTON | | | |
|---|---|---|---|---|
|  | ab. | r. | h. | rbi. |
| Green, ss ....... | 3 | 0 | 0 | 0 |
| Tasby, cf ........ | 4 | 1 | 0 | 1 |
| Williams, 1b .... | 3 | 2 | 1 | 1 |
| Hardy, lf ........ | 0 | 0 | 0 | 0 |
| Pagliaroni, c ..... | 3 | 0 | 2 | 0 |
| Malzone, 3b ..... | 3 | 0 | 0 | 0 |
| Clinton, rf ...... | 3 | 0 | 0 | 1 |
| Gile, 1b ........ | 4 | 0 | 0 | 0 |
| Coughtry, 2b .... | 3 | 1 | 2 | 0 |
| Muffett, p ...... | 2 | 0 | 0 | 0 |
| **c** Nixon ........ | 1 | 0 | 0 | 0 |
| Fornieles, p ..... | 0 | 0 | 0 | 0 |
| **d** Wertz ........ | 1 | 0 | 1 | 0 |
| **e** Brewer ....... | 0 | 1 | 0 | 0 |
| **TOTALS:** | 30 | 5 | 6 | 3 |

Two out when winning run was scored. **a** Hit into force play for Breeding in sixth. **b** Ran for Woodling in sixth. **c** Grounded into double play for Muffett in seventh. **d** Doubled for Fornieles in ninth. **e** Ran for Wertz in ninth.

```
Baltimore ......  0 2 0   0 1 1   0 0 0—4
Boston .........  2 0 0   0 0 0   0 1 2—5
```

|  | IP | H | R | ER | BB | SO |
|---|---|---|---|---|---|---|
| Barber ............ | 1/3 | 0 | 2 | 2 | 3 | 0 |
| Fisher (L, 12-11) ..... | 8 1/3 | 6 | 3 | 2 | 3 | 5 |
| Muffett ............ | 7 | 9 | 4 | 4 | 0 | 4 |
| Fornieles (W, 10-5) ... | 2 | 0 | 0 | 0 | 0 | 2 |

E: Coughtry, Klaus. A: Baltimore 8, Boston 13. DP: Klaus, Hansen, Gentile. LOB: Baltimore 6, Boston 7. 2B: Stephens, Robinson, Wertz. HR: Triandos, Williams. SF: Clinton, Gentile. HBP: By Barber (Pagliaroni). WP: Barber, Muffett. U: Hurley, Rice, Stevens, Drummond. T: 2:18. A: 10,454.

## THEODORE SAMUEL (THE KID) WILLIAMS
Born August 30, 1918, at San Diego, Calif.
Died July 5, 2002, at Inverness, Flor.
Height 6-4  Weight 198
Threw right- and batted left-handed.
Named to Hall of Fame, 1966.

| YEAR | CLUB | LEAGUE | POS. | G. | AB. | R. | H. | 2B. | 3B. | HR. | RBI. | B.A. | PO. | A. | E. | F.A. |
|---|---|---|---|---|---|---|---|---|---|---|---|---|---|---|---|---|
| 1936 | San Diego | P.C. | OF | 42 | 107 | 18 | 29 | 8 | 2 | 0 | 11 | .271 | 64 | 5 | 2 | .972 |
| 1937 | San Diego | P.C. | OF | 138 | 454 | 66 | 132 | 24 | 2 | 23 | 98 | .291 | 213 | 10 | 7 | .970 |
| 1938 | Minneapolis | A.A. | OF | 148 | 528 | 130 | 193 | 30 | 9 | 43 | 142 | .366 | 269 | 17 | 11 | .963 |
| 1939 | Boston | Amer. | OF | 149 | 565 | 131 | 185 | 44 | 11 | 31 | 145 | .327 | 318 | 11 | 19 | .945 |
| 1940 | Boston | Amer. | OF | 144 | 561 | 134 | 193 | 43 | 14 | 23 | 113 | .344 | 302 | 15 | 13 | .961 |
| 1941 | Boston | Amer. | OF | 143 | 456 | 135 | 185 | 33 | 3 | 37 | 120 | .406 | 262 | 11 | 11 | .961 |
| 1942 | Boston | Amer. | OF | 150 | 522 | 141 | 186 | 34 | 5 | 36 | 137 | .356 | 313 | 15 | 4 | .988 |
| 1943-44-45 | Boston | Amer. | | | | | | | | (In Military Service) | | | | | | |
| 1946 | Boston | Amer. | OF | 150 | 514 | 142 | 176 | 37 | 8 | 38 | 123 | .342 | 325 | 7 | 10 | .971 |
| 1947 | Boston | Amer. | OF | 156 | 528 | 125 | 181 | 40 | 9 | 32 | 114 | .343 | 347 | 10 | 9 | .975 |
| 1948 | Boston | Amer. | OF | 137 | 509 | 124 | 188 | 44 | 3 | 25 | 127 | .369 | 289 | 9 | 5 | .983 |
| 1949 | Boston | Amer. | OF | 155 | 566 | 150 | 194 | 39 | 3 | 43 | 159 | .343 | 337 | 12 | 6 | .983 |
| 1950 | Boston (a) | Amer. | OF | 89 | 334 | 82 | 106 | 24 | 1 | 28 | 97 | .317 | 165 | 7 | 8 | .956 |
| 1951 | Boston | Amer. | OF | 148 | 531 | 109 | 169 | 28 | 4 | 30 | 126 | .318 | 315 | 12 | 4 | .988 |
| 1952 | Boston (b) | Amer. | OF | 6 | 10 | 2 | 4 | 0 | 1 | 1 | 3 | .400 | 4 | 0 | 0 | 1.000 |
| 1953 | Boston (b) | Amer. | OF | 37 | 91 | 17 | 37 | 6 | 0 | 13 | 34 | .407 | 31 | 1 | 1 | .970 |
| 1954 | Boston | Amer. | OF | 117 | 386 | 93 | 133 | 23 | 1 | 29 | 89 | .345 | 213 | 5 | 4 | .982 |
| 1955 | Boston | Amer. | OF | 98 | 320 | 77 | 114 | 21 | 3 | 28 | 83 | .356 | 170 | 5 | 2 | .989 |
| 1956 | Boston | Amer. | OF | 136 | 400 | 71 | 138 | 28 | 2 | 24 | 82 | .345 | 174 | 7 | 5 | .973 |
| 1957 | Boston | Amer. | OF | 132 | 420 | 96 | 163 | 28 | 1 | 38 | 87 | .388 | 215 | 2 | 1 | .995 |
| 1958 | Boston | Amer. | OF | 129 | 411 | 81 | 135 | 23 | 2 | 26 | 85 | .328 | 154 | 3 | 7 | .957 |
| 1959 | Boston | Amer. | OF | 103 | 272 | 32 | 69 | 15 | 0 | 10 | 43 | .254 | 94 | 4 | 3 | .970 |
| 1960 | Boston | Amer. | OF | 113 | 310 | 56 | 98 | 15 | 0 | 29 | 72 | .316 | 131 | 6 | 1 | .993 |
| Major League Totals | | | | 2292 | 7706 | 1798 | 2654 | 525 | 71 | 521 | 1839 | .344 | 4159 | 142 | 113 | .974 |

a Suffered fractured left elbow when he crashed into the left-field wall making catch in first inning of All-Star Game at Chicago, July 11, 1950; despite injury he stayed in game until ninth inning. Williams had played 70 American League games up to the All-Star affair—but appeared in only 19 more contests with the Red Sox for the rest of the season.
b In Military Service most of the season.

### PITCHING RECORD

| YEAR | CLUB | LEAGUE | G. | IP. | W. | L. | Pct. | H. | R. | ER. | SO. | BB. | ERA. |
|---|---|---|---|---|---|---|---|---|---|---|---|---|---|
| 1936 | San Diego | Pac. Coast | 1 | 1 1/3 | 0 | 0 | .000 | 2 | 2 | 2 | 0 | 1 | 13.50 |
| 1940 | Boston | Amer. | 1 | 2 | 0 | 0 | .000 | 3 | 1 | 1 | 1 | 0 | 4.50 |

### WORLD SERIES RECORD

| YEAR | CLUB | LEAGUE | POS. | G. | AB. | R. | H. | 2B. | 3B. | HR. | RBI. | B.A. | PO. | A. | E. | F.A. |
|---|---|---|---|---|---|---|---|---|---|---|---|---|---|---|---|---|
| 1946 | Boston | Amer. | OF | 7 | 25 | 2 | 5 | 0 | 0 | 0 | 1 | .200 | 16 | 2 | 0 | 1.000 |

# Resources

Since H. G. Wells's time machine wasn't available for this project, the author would like to express his deepest thanks to all those who assisted in covering the final appearances of these big-league giants. The following materials were invaluable in putting this book together.

## BOOKS

*Game Time*, Roger Angell. Published by Hartcourt Inc., Orlando, Fl., 2003.

*Once More around the Park*, Roger Angell. Published by Ballantine Books, New York, 1991.

*Five Seasons*, Roger Angell. Published by CBS Inc. by arrangement with Simon and Schuster Inc., New York, 1983.

*Season Ticket*, Roger Angell. Published by Popular Library, New York, 1978.

*Baseball Extra*, from the Eric. C. Caren Collection. Published by Castle Books, Edison, N.J., 2000

*Nine Innings*, Daniel Okrent. Published by Ticknor and Fields, 1985.

*Baseball's All-Time Greats: The Top 50 Players*, Mac Davis. Published by Bantam Books, New York, 1970.

*Total Baseball*, edited by John Thorn and Pete Palmer. Published by Warner Books, New York, 1989.

*Baseball*, Geoffrey C. Ward and Ken Burns. Published by Alfred A. Knopf, New York, 1994.

*The Autobiography of Baseball*, by Joseph Wallace. Published by Harry N. Abrams, New York, 1998.

*Real Grass, Real Heroes*, Dom DiMaggio with Bill Gilbert. Published by Zebra Books, New York, 1990.

*The Tumult and the Shouting*, Grantland Rice. Published by Dell Publishing Co., New York, 1954.

*Farewell to Sport*, Paul Gallico. Published by Pocket Books, New York, 1945.

*The Heart of the Order*, Thomas Boswell. Published by Doubleday, New York, 1989.

*Cracking the Show*, by Thomas Boswell. Published by Doubleday, New York 1995.

*Why Time Begins on Opening Day*, Thomas Boswell. Published by Doubleday, Garden City, N.Y., 1984.

*Game Day: Sports Writings by Thomas Boswell*. Published by Doubleday, New York, 1990.

*Voices from Cooperstown, Baseball's Hall of Famers Tell It Like It Was*, Anthony J. O'Connor. Published by Collier Books, MacMillan Co., New York, 1982.

*The Boys of Summer*, Roger Kahn. Published by Harper and Row, New York, 1972.

*Pete Rose: My Story*, Roger Kahn and Pete Rose. Published by MacMillan and Co., New York, 1989.

*The Fireside Book of Baseball, Volume 4*, edited by Charles Einstein. Published by Simon and Schuster, New York, 1987.

The Glory of Their Times, Lawrence Ritter. Published by First Vintage Books, New York, 1985.

*Cooperstown: Baseball Hall of Famers*. Published by Publications International, LTD, Lincolnwood, Il., 1999.

Men at Work, George Will. Published by MacMillan and Co., New York, 1990.

*Bunts*, George Will. Published by Scribner, New York, 1998.

*Babe: The Legend Comes to Life*, Robert Creamer. Published by Simon and Schuster, New York, 1974.

*Say It Ain't So, Joe! The True Story of Shoeless Joe Jackson and the 1919 World Series*, by Donald Gropman. Published by Little and Brown, New York, 1979.

My 66 Years in The Big Leagues, Connie Mack. Published by John C. Winston, Philadelphia, 1950.

*Ol' Diz, A Biography of Dizzy Dean*, Vince Staten. Published by Harper Collins, New York, 1992.

*Maybe I'll Pitch Forever*, Satchel Paige and David Lipman. Published by Doubleday, Garden City, N.Y., 1962.

*I Never Had It Made*, Jackie Robinson and Alfred Duckett. Published by A.E. Putnam, New York, 1972.

*Stan Musial: The Man's Own Story*, Stan Musial and Bob Broeg. Published by Bethany Press, St. Louis, 1977.

*Yaz*, by Carl Yastrzemski with Al Hirschberg. Published by Grosset and Dunlap, New York, 1968.

*Yaz: Baseball, the Wall and Me*, Carl Yastrzemski and Gerald Eskenaki. Published by Doubleday, New York, 1990.

*No Cheering in the Press Box*, Jerome Holtzman. Published by Holt, Reinhart and Winston, New York, 1975.

*Eight Men Out*, Eliot Asinof. Published by Holt, Reinhart and Winston, New York, 1963.

*My Life in Baseball: The True Record*, Ty Cobb and Al Stump. Published by Doubleday, New York, 1961.

*Ted Williams*, Edwin Pope. Published by Manor Books, New York, 1972.

*Ted Williams, A Baseball Life*, Michael Seidel. Published by Contemporary Books, Chicago, 1991.

*Ted Williams, A Portrait in Words and Pictures*. Published by Walker and Co., New York, 1991.

*The Ted Williams Reader*, edited by Lawrence Baldassaro. Published by Simon and Schuster, New York, 1991.

*Hitter: The Life and Turmoils of Ted Williams*, Ed Linn. Published by Harcourt and Brace, Orlando, Fl., 1993.

*My Turn at Bat*, by Ted Williams and John Underwood. Published by Simon and
Schuster, New York, 1988.

*Ted Williams's Hit List*, Ted Williams and Jim Prime. Published by Contemporary
Books, Toronto, 1995.

*Ted Williams, The Biography of an American Hero*, Leigh Montville. Published by
Doubleday, New York, 2004.

*Impossible Dreams: A Red Sox Collection*, edited by Glenn Stout. Published by Houghton
Mifflin Co., Boston, 2003.

*Games We Used to Play*, Roger Kahn. Published by Ticknor and Fields, New York,
1992.

*The New Bill James Historical Baseball Abstract*. Published by the Free Press, New York,
2001.

*The Bill James Historical Baseball Abstract*. Published by Villard Books, New York,
1988.

*The Ultimate Baseball Book*, edited by Daniel Okrent and Harris Lewine. Published by
Houghton Mifflin, Boston, 1981.

## NEWSPAPERS

Game stories, columns and beat coverage for the players collected in *Last Time Out* in
the following newspapers were viewed on microfilm at Florida State University's
Strozier Library: Grateful acknowledgement is given to these sportswriters.

*New York Times*

*New York Herald Tribune*

*St. Louis Post and Dispatch*

*Washington Post*

*Boston Globe*

*Boston Herald Traveler*

*Boston Record American*

*Los Angeles Times*

*Chicago Tribune*

*Philadelphia Daily News*

*Philadelphia Inquirer*

*Detroit Free Press*

*Miami Herald*